The History of
INDEPENDENT
CINEMA

by Phil Hall

Published in the USA by:
BearManor Media
P O Box 71426
Albany, Georgia 31708
www.bearmanormedia.com

ISBN 1-59393-335-5

Printed in the United States of America.

Book and cover design by Darlene Swanson of Van-garde Imagery, Inc.

Contents

AUTHOR'S NOTE

"If we shadows have offended, Think but this, and all is mended, That you have but slumber'd here, While these visions did appear."

– William Shakespeare

Writing a history of independent cinema produced in the United States has been tricky, to put it mildly. When tracing more than a century of output, coupled with a continuing evolution of the genre, it is obvious that something is going to get left out. Let's begin the book by noting what is *not* present.

In some cases, omissions are intentional. For starters, this book will not deal with the pornographic film industry's long and tumultuous history. Yes, skin flicks are technically considered to be independently produced films. However, that genre existed (and continues to exist) as a wholly separate entity with a long and convoluted history, deserving of its own study. Sorry, but everyone in this book is keeping their clothing on!

Furthermore, I've intentionally emphasized films that had a significant artistic, commercial or intellectual impact on motion-picture production and American culture. This book is not intended as a directory of every independent film ever made, but a celebration of the productions and individuals whose impact continues to resonate in both the film industry and the popular culture.

Also, the focus here will concentrate on U.S.-financed productions. After all, this is not a history of world cinema – that's another book! A major exception is made for the films of Orson Welles, who was unique as an American independent filmmaker who scared up financing from European sources for the creation of English-language productions. Needless to say, Welles was in a class by himself.

I am sure that many worthwhile films were either not cited or received less coverage than some may have anticipated. If there are any glaring omissions, I hope the reader will contact me via the book's publisher so I can make amends in future editions.

I would also like to use this opportunity to give thanks to those who supported this endeavor: Ben Ohmart at BearManor Media, my friends at *Film Threat* and the Online Film Critics Society, my family, Mike Watt (for his great foreword), Leslie Dallas (for her wonderful introduction) and Angel Hernández (for his assistance in gathering the photographs for the book).

Also, I need to acknowledge that the sections of *The Birth of a Nation*, *Manhatta*, *The Outlaw* and *Titicut Follies* first appeared on *Film Threat* and *Angelica's Dreams* first appeared on the Secondary Marketing Executive website – they are reprinted here through the good graces of both media outlets.

In creating this text, I learned a great many facts about independent cinema that I never previously knew. Researching and writing this book was a wonderful discovery for me, and I hope the enthusiasm I experienced in putting this together will be shared as you start to turn through these pages. I would also like to dedicate the book to the memory of the many pioneers who created the independent film industry. Without those brave, audacious and prescient men and women, I would be at a significant loss for words ... and you would be reading another book!

– Phil Hall

FOREWORD: WHAT IS MEANT BY INDEPENDENT CINEMA?

By Mike Watt

"The creative is the place where no one else has ever been."   *– Alan Alda*

I'm not sure when the concept of "independent film" entered my consciousness. Movies have always been my first joy and my earliest memory is of watching a movie: George Pal's *Doc Savage: The Man of Bronze*, at a drive-in with my parents. I was two. So I never really made a distinction between glossy Hollywood movies like *Star Wars* or *Sinbad and the Eye of the Tiger* and lower-budgeted Saturday-afternoon TV things like Roger Corman's *It Conquered the World* or *The Little Shop of Horrors*.

As I got older, the more subversive movies on cable started to attract my attention. The "Scream Queen" movies like *Slave Girls from Beyond Infinity* and *Sorority Babes in the Slimeball Bowl-O-Rama* came onto my radar. For obvious reasons. And when I needed a hit of gore, I turned to *Evil Dead II* and *Re-Animator*. And, since this was the age of the mom 'n pop home video rental industry, I'd bring home stacks of VHS tapes from stores who didn't care how old you were, so long as you had the money. That's when I discovered things like Tim Ritter's *Truth or Dare?: A Critical Madness* and Leif Jonker's *Darkness*. The Internet was still uncharted territory, so I relied on *Fangoria Magazine* and *Film Threat* (back in its paper magazine days) to tell me that these movies had been produced by guys on their own, using money they'd raised, with no more connection to Hollywood than I had.

By the time I graduated high school with my eye on studying film and filmmaking in college, the idea of independently-made films had finally captivated me. Inspired by Quentin Tarantino, Spike Lee and Kevin Smith, all of whom were canonized in the early '90s (on the heels of Steven Soderbergh a few years earlier), it was understood by many of us that we, too, could make movies with our own means, as long as we understood the mechanics, principals and, more or less, the business.

Our naiveté aside, the theory was sound. By the mid-'90s, the Internet had opened up a whole new world; independent filmmakers could not only make their own films in their own backyards (literally and figuratively), but now had a brand-new outlet to advertise and show their work. The feasibility increased as did hard-drive capacity, operating systems and modem speed. iFilm gave way to YouTube and MySpace. The 16mm film and S-VHS formats gave way to digital video. Suddenly – very suddenly, it seemed – everyone was an independent filmmaker. Economics was hardly an issue thanks to off-the-shelf editing software and equipment.

The pendulum swung back, of course. You rarely hear about a new indie movie becoming a blockbuster these days. But that isn't stopping new people from trying their hand at creating their own movie masterpieces, or even just screwing around for their own amusement and MySpace pages.

And while the "serious filmmaker" in me resents the "kids" from swimming in my pool, as it were, my less-curmudgeonly self has to admit that the liberation of the film medium – taking filmmaking out of the hands of the studio elite and putting it affordably into the hands of "the people" – is very satisfying. There's something to be admired in even the lowest-budgeted, inept "Jackass" stunt caught on video. If you look at all those YouTube videos with a Dadaist sense of humor, you'll find more than just the idiocy of the moment. You'll find the very idea that "anything created by man is art," whether you agree with that sentiment or not.

As for those who seriously hope someday to make a living as film-makers, the digital revolution has enabled them to hone their craft, to stretch and grow. And if their earlier attempts pale in comparison to the big-budget blockbusters, we can at least tip our hats to the fact that the films were completed. Often, that's the sum of the battle right there.

My exposure to independent filmmaking was, at first, relegated primarily to the horror genre, because that's where my interests lay. And that's pretty much holding true today. But along the way, through my travels, I discovered the likes of Stan Brakhage, George Kuchar, Maya Deren, Alex Cox, Tim Ritter, Kevin Smith, Ron Bonk, J.R. Bookwalter, Scooter McCrae, William Kaufman, Lloyd Kaufman – countless others, all playing in the same "indie" pool, but making very different movies. Different from each other and cosmically different from the slick Hollywood offerings.

Filmmaking is, at its core, telling a story visually and aurally. The folks who make the greatest contributions to pushing the form further will be doing it for the love of the medium, not for the paycheck. That's the way art works – any art. It's the artists who redefine the art and turn it into craft for the craftsmen.

I didn't always like what I was watching. I wasn't always satisfied with the obscure thing I'd spent months seeking out. But I can't say that any independent film I've ever seen was a complete waste of my time. Even the worst movie – technically, thematically – had a soul behind it. It wasn't a film made by committee with numerous test screenings and rewrites and reshoots. What you saw is what they got, if not exactly what they set out to get.

And even the most inept filmmaker earned the right to say to his harshest of critics, "Oh yeah? Where's *your* movie?" Now that the economic field has been leveled, the critic really has no excuse for talking, rather than doing. To paraphrase Lloyd Kaufman, president and co-founder of Troma Entertainment, the world's oldest completely independent movie studio, there is really no reason that anyone – anyone – can't go out and "make their own damn movie."

"Independent film" is a broad, deep pool. Plenty of room for everyone already there and plenty of room for more. Dive in. Try and make something worth watching. It's not easy. But afterwards, you'll never watch another movie the same way.

(Mike Watt is an award-winning filmmaker, author and journalist. He is the editor of *Sirens of Cinema Magazine* and has written for *Cinefantastique, Femme Fatales, Film Threat, Pretty/Scary, The Dark Side and Draculina*. In 1997, he co-founded Happy Cloud Pictures with his partners, Amy Lynn Best and Bill Homan, in order to produce the feature film *The Resurrection Game*. He has written four novels, including the novelization to the aforementioned film, and has directed and produced several independently produced films.)

INTRODUCTION:

The View from the Outside

By Leslie Dallas

"History, real solemn history, I cannot be interested in.... I read it a little as a duty; but it tells me nothing that does not either vex or weary me." – Jane Austen

The day after I was bounced by the Disney Fellowship, I received notice that I'd made the finals of the Austin Film Festival. I returned home from the three-day festival with all sorts of possibilities for getting my script made. The big buzz at Austin was a small, low-budget picture that took forever to get made, ran out of financing at one point, but was finally picked up by Miramax for something like $10 million dollars. *Sling Blade* was exactly the kind of story I wanted to tell. Suddenly, aspiring screenwriters and filmmakers of small, personal films seemed to have a real shot at a career. *Sling Blade* went on to be nominated for Academy Awards and win the Oscar for Best Screenplay, demonstrating that good writing and compelling characters could find success.

That was 1996. Today, I've been asked to examine the current state of independent film. What are its parameters? Is it still a vehicle for non-commercial artistic expression, more so than mainstream film? Good questions, particularly as they highlight a problem in the definition of their subject.

There now exists a full library of American films that do not rely on big budgets or distribution, do not use star talent, and do not follow the rules of Hollywood storytelling. But another case can be made for other, smaller films, with unknown casts and directors that cross lines into mainstream Hollywood status.

So what makes a film an independent film? "Robert Rodriguez, David Lynch, Paul Thomas Anderson, Quentin Tarantino, Kevin Smith." That's how the eight college seniors in my Advanced Screenwriting class responded to a question about the independent filmmakers who have inspired their own work. No surprises there until one of them asked, "Wasn't the first *Terminator* an independent?"

There's the question. And maybe the answer.

I once understood the definition of an independent film as any film whose viewing required a midnight bus ride to a dicey part of a city to view. *Eraserhead* and *Pink Flamingos* quickly come to mind. But that is obviously no longer true. The New Hollywood Films of the 1970s have been described as the beginning of the current wave of smaller, "indie" films. But independent films have become much more than that.

In their college text, "Film Art: An Introduction," David Bordwell and Kristin Thompson identify the 1970s as the age of the "movie brats," filmmakers who came up through film schools and not through the Hollywood system. Unlike strictly independent filmmakers, the movie brats made highly personal films using traditional Hollywood techniques. Think of the stylistic differences between *Mean Streets* and Andy Warhol's *Sleep*.

Bordwell and Thompson characterize this period as the financial decline of the studio system and the rise of films aimed at a young, counter-culture audience, cheap to make and distribute but following the same narrative conventions of big-budget studio films. Steven Spielberg, a movie brat of the '70s, is quoted in Bordwell and Thompson: "I love the idea of not being an independent filmmaker. I've liked working within the system. And I've admired a lot of the older directors."

As an educator, the graduate and undergraduate film majors I've encountered have a general knowledge of independent film. The Internet and all its avenues give them a mainline to everything produced and about to be produced. From YouTube to Current TV to shorts made by online gamers, this generation has access to more cutting-edge filmmaking than many film professionals. And more access to film, video and pirating, too

Most students name classic directors and works such as Stan Brakhage's *Mothlight*, Andy Warhol shorts and *Meshes of the Afternoon* as influences on their own work. But just as many name *Sideways* and *Little Miss Sunshine*. Here, again, is the notion of the independent film as a hybrid of a small film making the transition into the mainstream.

So, as Howard Suber says, the question about the "so-called independent film" is: "Independent for what? Independent from what?"

Suber is someone to listen to in these matters. He's been part of the UCLA faculty for 44 years, helped establish and chaired the UCLA Film Archive, the Critical Studies and Ph.D. Programs, and the UCLA Film and Television Producers Program.

Suber traces the birth of independent American film to the Filmmakers' Cooperative founded in the early 1960s by Jonas Mekas, Stan Brakhage and others, as an artist-run center for distribution of independent film: "As is true for most self-declared 'movements' in the arts, politics, religion, etc., it was very good at defining what it was against, since it was inherently insurrectionist/revolutionary, but wasn't very good at defining what it was for. Most of the world's film 'movements' have been against the same thing: Hollywood and/or the 'well-made' fiction film (you know – those that use a script and actors)."

Consider the case of Paul Thomas Anderson, writer and director of *There Will Be Blood* (2007), who began as an "independent filmmaker" with his debut film, *Hard Eight* (1996), developed and financed through the Sundance Lab. Anderson is known for having dropped out of NYU Film School after only two days, reportedly after submitting material written by David Mamet, and having it returned with a "C" grade. Sundance, NYU, for two days? Mamet? Sounds like the definition of the ultimate independent filmmaker. And, yet, Anderson's latest film competed for all the top Oscar awards last year. Anderson's IMDb biography compares him with Truffaut, Ophuls, Renoir and Scorsese. Scorsese, like Anderson, began as an independent (*Mean Streets*) and developed into a mainstream filmmaker, winning the Best Director Oscar in 2006 for *The Departed*.

In addition to financing Anderson's first film, Sundance launched many "indie" projects, including Quentin Tarantino's *Reservoir Dogs*, Jim Jarmusch's *Stranger Than Paradise*, the Coen Brothers' *Blood Simple* and Robert Rodriquez's *El Mariachi*. The festival is still a major vehicle for new filmmakers.

In 2008, the Sundance Lab received nearly 4,000 films for consideration for only 121 festival slots. There are countless other festivals and plenty of material fueling them. Most major filmmakers started early and couldn't make films. Festivals, the Internet, independent and niche cable channels all add to the mix for the new definition of the independent film. Even the major studios are getting into the act. Fox Searchlight made *Little Miss Sunshine* and *Juno* and Lionsgate made *Hard Candy* and *The Cooler*. So if a studio is making it, does it qualify as an independent film?

Let's revisit the question of *The Terminator*. When James Cameron wrote the movie in 1984, he originally envisioned Lance Henriksen playing the title character. Cameron even had Henriksen dress-up as the character and attend an Orion Pictures meeting in character. The budget for the film was definitely "low" – $6.5 million – but went on to gross $78 million worldwide. Independent or blockbuster?

For me, the definition of an independent film still goes back to *Sling Blade*, and the fact that a small, character-based feature could attract the attention of multi-million-dollar investors, critics and neighborhood Cineplex audiences alike. But rule-breaking isn't true of all independent films, not anymore.

Suber explains: "More often, the term is used for films that have small budgets of necessity, and a good proportion of 'Independent' filmmakers move as quickly as they can into Hollywood studio productions

(Soderbergh, for example). Few independent films in recent years differ from the standard Hollywood product in terms of either style or content. The most well-known and financially successful independent films, like *My Big Fat Greek Wedding* and *Juno*, break no significant rules (or break them insignificantly). And films that do break the rules – *There Will Be Blood*, for example, may be 'independent' in 'spirit' but are firmly within the orbit of mainstream filmmaking."

So what is the difference between independent films and ones that aren't? Suber and I are in agreement here: "Damned if I know." The concept is evolving as I write this. And I think that's a good thing. A very good thing, especially if you're an aspiring filmmaker.

(Leslie Dallas is a screenwriter, story editor and poet. She has been awarded the Samuel Goldwyn Writing Award, the Disney Fellowship and the Jack Nicholson Prize in Screenwriting. She is the Managing Director of the New Haven Underground Film Festival and an adjunct instructor of cinema studies at the University of Hartford in Connecticut.)

CHAPTER ONE:
The Roots Of Independent Cinema

"All great deeds and all great thoughts have a ridiculous beginning."   – Albert Camus

The motion-picture industry did not originate in the United States. In 1888, French photographer Louis A. A. Le Prince photographed what is now called *Roundhay Garden Scene*, a two-second piece of movement based on a strip of film paper. But in the U.S., motion pictures took shape under the guidance of one of the most important inventors of the 19th century: Thomas A. Edison.

In the waning years of the 19th century, the American film industry was directly created by Edison and his merry band of technology wizards. However, what Edison initially planned didn't quite occur. In fact, the film world we know today, particularly the sector that became independent filmmaking, was the raucous result of Edison's well-considered plans gone hopelessly awry. And it is a bit of a long story – but, as with many long stories, there is a great punch line.

For starters, Edison did not envision film appreciation as a communal happening. The projection of film in an auditorium setting was not part of the master's plan. Instead, Edison figured the future of movies rested in something called the Kinetoscope, which consisted of a large and bulky cabinet with a viewing window. As designed, people would approach the Kinetoscope, drop a coin into a slot, peer into the viewing window and watch a short film playing in a continuous loop. By "short," this meant less than one minute.

At first, the novelty of the Kinetoscope had great appeal with Americans. From 1894 to 1896, Edison successfully promoted the product and people found its flickering images to be highly amusing.

But in order to keep people coming back to the Kinetoscope, Edison wisely packed his brief films with many celebrities of the day. Thus, people who only heard about personalities such as German strongman Eugen Sandow or the Wild West sharpshooter Annie Oakley were able to see them in motion – albeit in mute, monochromatic, fleeting images.

Across the Atlantic, however, things were progressing rather differently. The concept of projected film took off in Europe, thanks in large part to the efforts of France's Lumiere Brothers, who proved that film viewing could be a communal and commercial effort. Edison, who never enjoyed admitting when he was in error, glumly realized the one-coin-at-a-time approach to Kinetoscope viewing could not compete against a packed auditorium of people happily forking out money for admission at a front door. As 1896 rolled along, the Kinetoscope was assigned on a one-way trip to oblivion.

Beyond film projection, Edison also picked up another European trend: creating narrative films. Rather than offering static filmed records of people engaged in some unusual activity, such as Eugen Sandow flexing his muscles or Annie Oakley firing her six-shooters, the challenge arose to create an original production using performers working from a script. To supply content that would keep his young film business active, Edison found himself wearing a new hat: he became a movie producer.

It should be noted that Edison was not personally responsible for directing, writing scripts, or even serving in a supervisory producer function. In fact, there is no evidence that Edison actively sought to be in show business. However, under his aegis the American film business began to blossom. In 1903, the Edison production *The Great Train Robbery* created a sensation with audiences. This inventive tale of a daring heist and its raucous aftermath captivated audiences. Even today, *The Great Train Robbery* is still highly entertaining (particularly if one watches the film realizing that the Wild West setting was actually a location near Edison's headquarters in New Jersey). With this and other films Edison was the acknowledged first king of the nascent film industry.

But Edison's power was not solid, primarily because he was unable to maintain omnipotent control of the tools required to create motion pictures. In the early years of the 20th century, the filmmaking technology and equipment quickly became available, mostly through means that could charitably be called "dubious," and other entrepreneurs who were inspired by or jealous of Edison's success sought to get a toehold in this market.

Edison, who had no qualms of vigorously pushing competition aside, initially sought to prevent other would-be producers by unleashing volleys of lawsuits against the competition that alleged violations of his patents relating to the movie camera and projection equipment. Had Edison and his lawyers succeeded in their legal pursuits, the film industry may have been far different than it turned out.

But the Edison strategy failed to work. In fact, it was an expensive disaster that did not stop a single non-Edison film from being made. Facing acute financial challenges from both his competitors (who showed no signs of quitting their pursuit of the movie mania) and his lawyers (who showed no signs of winning, despite being paid handsomely for their services), Edison opted to drop the courtroom pursuit in favor of a Plan B: If one man cannot hold the reins alone, then the power should be shared by a selected few.

In January 1909, Edison reached out to his major competitors of the day with the offer to join a new organization that would consolidate control of the film industry into the hands of an exclusive cabal. This organization would be called the Motion Picture Patents Company, and only those entities that were members could enjoy the profits being generated through film exhibition.

Edison's invitation extended to seven American production companies – Biograph, Essanay, Kalem, Kliene, Lubin, Selig and Vitagraph – plus two French production companies, Méliés and Pathé, who were the leading creative and financial forces across the Atlantic. Edison, naturally, took charge at the helm of this new group, which insisted that only its member companies held the exclusive rights for motion picture production under U.S. and European patent laws.

In concept, it was a bold idea and it could have succeeded – had Edison left things alone at this level (or at least until some muckraking anti-trust advocate decided to go on the attack against the blatant monopolistic nature of this endeavor). But luck was still not on Edison's side. Incredibly, he kept overplaying his hand with shameless abandon. In doing so, he directly sped the demise of his cinematic empire; by default, he indirectly created what became the American independent film industry.

Through the Motion Picture Patents Company, Edison devised a subsidiary called the General Film Company. This entity was named as the sole source the distribution of the films created by Edison's tight circle of corporate cronies. During this period, there were no national theater chains. Instead, there were constellations of independent motion-picture exhibitors who ran their own standalone venues. A few savvy individuals were able to string together a small chain of theaters within limited regions, but for the most part they were single screen owners and operators.

The nation's exhibitors received word from the Motion Picture Patents Company that going forward, they could only book films through the General Film Company. Adding insult to injury, they needed to pay a license of two dollars per week to the General Film Company in order to stay in its good graces. At this point in time, two dollars was a considerable sum of money.

This development did not sit well with most exhibitors, but their options were limited. Although there were some producers working outside of Edison's circle, their output was spotty and they lacked the quantity and quality of titles to keep exhibitors satisfied. In comparison, the production companies within the Motion Picture Patents Company were churning out highly appreciated films by the truckload. Most exhibitors felt they had no choice but to grit their teeth and fork over two dollars a week to the General Film Company.

But one man felt otherwise. He was a German immigrant named Carl Laemmle and he ran what was known as an "exchange" – basically a wholesale operation that purchased films from producers and rented them to individual exhibitors. Laemmle quickly realized the General Film Company would put him and other exchange operators out of business, and he tried to negotiate with the Motion Pictures Patent Company in private meetings. But Laemmle had no leveraging advantage – as an exchange operator, he was at the mercy of the production companies that supplied him with films that he required to stay active.

Unable to quietly agitate for a solution, Laemmle then took a bold step in making his complaints public. He took hostile and threatening letters sent to him by the Motion Pictures Patent Company's lawyers and published them in the film industry's trade journals. This news, in turn, began to spill into the mainstream newspapers, which marked the first time that most people were aware that there was actually an industry responsible for creating those diverting amusements that played at the local picture show venue.

Edison's cabal, who were becoming irritated by what they saw as Laemmle's insubordinate behavior, turned up the proverbial heat: they decided to run Laemmle out of business by refusing to sell his exchange any of their titles. Without films, Laemmle had no livelihood. Edison and his pals expected Laemmle to retreat. That did not happen – and that is the aforementioned punch line. By provoking Laemmle, Edison inadvertently helped spark the beginning of the independent film industry.

Laemmle decided to become a producer and create his own movies. He formed the Independent Motion-Picture Company (IMP) and began providing them directly to exhibitors. However, Laemmle needed a gimmick to make his films stand out from the Motion Pictures Patent Company elite. To achieve this, he recalled the selling point that first made the Edison Kinetoscopes a hit: the appearances of Annie Oakley, Eugen Sandow and other big names of the late 1890s entertainment circuit in the brief Kinetoscope films. However, once Edison moved his films up on the big screen, the famous stars vanished from his movies. Part of this was due to the reluctance of established actors to appear in the seemingly lowbrow world of movies, and part of this was based on Edison's refusal to create big stars that would inevitably demand big salaries.

Laemmle lacked the funds to attract any well-known stars to appear in his films, but he felt he could do something that was never done before and create his own star on a tight budget. The gamble paid off in the form of Florence Lawrence, a pretty young Biograph contract player who toiled anonymously on screen. Laemmle took the lovely Miss Lawrence away from Biograph and prominently played up her presence in all of his marketing materials.

The most provocative aspect of this strategy came in identifying the star. The name "Florence Lawrence" was highlighted on the title cards of the Laemmle films, and the indefatigable producer even created an outlandish publicity stunt where he feverishly denied rumors – allegedly planted by his rivals – that Miss Lawrence was killed in a St. Louis streetcar accident. Laemmle actually planted those rumors and it was no secret within the media, but the press happily played along with the story.

While this was going on, a second man who had his own beef with Edison took a different plan of assault. He was Adolph Zukor, an independent exhibitor. In 1912, he found himself with a chance-of-a-lifetime business opportunity of securing the U.S. rights to a four-reel film of the French stage production, *Queen Elizabeth*, starring Sarah Bernhardt, arguably the world's most famous theatrical star.

The outsider Zukor openly challenged the Motion Picture Patents Company to allow this movie to be sold via the General Film Company. There was no good reason to deny Zukor's request for inclusion. In fact, refusing the offer would have seemed very peculiar, given the presence of Sarah Bernhardt in a film and the fact that *Queen Elizabeth* was generating attention (and profits) across the Atlantic. Permission was reluctantly granted by the Motion Picture Patents Company for Zukor to proceed with the release.

When *Queen Elizabeth* came to the U.S., Zukor took the unprecedented step of renting a Broadway stage theater for the New York premiere (this tactic would be used for many years afterwards as "four-walling"). Sophisticated Broadway audiences, who would never dream of going to see a movie, paid one dollar per ticket (a princely sum for that time) to see the silent, black-and-white "photoplay" production. The engagement was a major success that rivaled the other cultural events of the day. Zukor created a distribution company called Famous Players in Famous Plays and booked *Queen Elizabeth* in a city-by-city reserved-seat road show distribution pattern – a strategy that continued well into the 1970s.

Zukor, like Laemmle, began creating his own films and selling them directly to exhibitors. Other men followed their lead, and from that moment the Motion Picture Patents Company was doomed. Edison tried to put up a fight in the courts, but he could not prevent the inevitable and by 1915 his organization was dead.

In 1918, Edison acknowledged total defeat and quit the film business, angry and confused that he was unable to maintain control over what he created. By that time, the other companies who were part of his would-be monopoly either went out of business or were acquired by faster-growing rivals.

As for Laemmle and Zukor, they went on to launch Universal Pictures and Paramount Pictures, respectively. The independent film outsiders became the consummate Hollywood insiders – a pattern that repeated itself endlessly over the years.

Birth of a Film Movement

While Edison's power waned and Laemmle and Zukor's power ascended, another figure began to emerge as a creative force in filmmaking. Through him, the modern independent film movement was created. The man was D.W. Griffith and the production that pushed independent film into the national culture was his 1915 epic, *The Birth of a Nation*. Yes, *that* film.

It is impossible to discuss *The Birth of a Nation* today without being tripped by the film's grueling racism and wildly misguided sense of history. So let's put the obvious out front – *The Birth of a Nation* represents the most malignant example of an American artist's use of motion pictures to promote racial hatred. The film's value as a work of art is damaged by its vituperative intellectual corruption.

But to ignore *The Birth of a Nation* and Griffith is to ignore the fundamental development of independent film production and distribution. For better or worse, it all started here.

The Birth of a Nation, not unlike many contemporary independent films, was a combination of its creator's artistic pretensions and pie-in-the-sky concept of getting rich by filling a cultural void. In the nascent years of silent movies, failed stage actor David Wark Griffith somehow wound up behind the camera at the Biograph studios. From 1908 through 1913, Griffith directed hundreds of one-reel and two-reel films for Biograph - the exact number is uncertain, since Griffith did not receive on-screen credit for his work and many of the films are now considered lost.

Despite his prolific output and growing proficiency in the direction of films, Griffith was stifled at Biograph. He wanted to emulate the growing success of feature-length films being imported from Europe, including the aforementioned *Queen Elizabeth* and the Italian epic *Quo Vadis?* from 1912. But Biograph did not wish to expand into feature films. The company enjoyed its take on American capitalism, making the greatest amount of profits from the lowest level of investment, and balked at the expense of financing longer movies. Furthermore, Biograph strictly saw itself as an entertainment outlet while Griffith was growing interested in using film as a tool to expound his notion of social injustice.

Griffith left Biograph in 1913 to join the Mutual Film Corp., an independently-operated film production and distribution company. But, again, Griffith faced the same problem that he encountered at Biograph: an executive's unwillingness to devote time and money to creating epic

American features. Within a year of joining Mutual, Griffith began work on the film that would change both his life and his industry.

The Birth of a Nation was culled from a pair of novels written by Rev. Thomas A. Dixon, *The Clansman* and *The Leopard's Spots*. The project was originally called *The Clansman*, but its title was changed after the production was completed. Dixon's work had limited popularity and there should not have been problems in obtaining the properties for a film. But Griffith's attempts to purchase the screen rights to Dixon's books were stymied when the author demanded a $25,000 advance and 25 percent of the film's box office receipts. The Mutual executives refused to agree to that, citing Griffith's projected budget on the film was a total of $40,000.

Griffith then took an unprecedented step that other filmmakers would duplicate for years to come: he began to raise his own funds for his film. His pass-the-hat routine was extremely successful, and Griffith's salesmanship helped shake loose money from the individual members of the Mutual executive team and even his production staff (cinematographer G.W. Bitzer reportedly gave Griffith his $7,000 life savings). To ensure his new venture would be guaranteed theatrical distribution, he aligned his new production venture with a pair of well-known producers, Thomas Ince and the Keystone Studios' Mack Sennett, to create the Triangle Pictures Corp.

Dixon, for his part, lowered his advance asking price to $2,000, but insisted on 25% of the box-office take. Griffith agreed, and *The Birth of a Nation* began shooting in July 1914. The finished film came in at over $110,000 (the highest budget for an American film) and a running time of three hours (projected at 16 frames per second), making it the lengthiest U.S. production up to that point.

The Birth of a Nation also influenced modern independent cinema by its daring to address themes that the so-called mainstream film companies were too afraid to consider. The film's view of the Civil War from the Southern point of view and its retelling of the socio-economic abuses heaped on the former Confederate states during the Reconstruction period were still controversial in Griffith's era, even though five decades passed since the Civil War ended. After all, no one ever presented a history lesson from the perspective of the conflict's losing side – Griffith, in his film, took a broad assault on popular history as written by the victors of the Civil War.

Of course, Griffith's grasp of history was highly subjective, and that also influenced independent filmmakers who still use their medium to present highly subjective and deeply personalized visions of events and issues. Before *The Birth of a Nation*, movies were seen as a vehicle for entertainment and not provocation. Griffith, by championing the Ku Klux Klan and depicting the freed black slaves as a force of evil, was taking an outsider's perspective and daring to challenge American society to accept his political opinions as facts. Filmmakers continue to take this route, both in narrative features and (increasingly) in non-fiction films.

Griffith also pioneered the use of publicity to stir debate over his work. Prior to *The Birth of a Nation*, no American film ever generated controversy at a national level. In fact, no American film generated *any* conversation at a national level. But Griffith, with surprisingly vigorous support from Dixon, helped to push the film front and center through the media and even into the upper levels of the federal government. Dixon arranged a screening for President Woodrow Wilson at the White House, which marked the first time a movie played at the presidential residence. By doing this, *The Birth of a Nation* sought out a specific audience endorsement in an attempt to give the film prestige-by-association. (Mel Gibson would do the same thing when he brought *The Passion of the Christ* to the Vatican as a private screening for Pope John Paul II in 2004 – a screening that was also very heavily publicized.)

The Wilson White House screening also created the first "blurb" to go with the marketing of a film: Wilson's alleged claim that Griffith's work was "like writing history with lightning, and one regret is that is all so terribly true." Actually, there was no evidence Wilson said anything of the sort – Dixon initiated the claim of that quote and, years later, his widow continued to insist on its authenticity despite no independent verification. (Ironically, Mel Gibson pulled the same stunt by claiming Pope John Paul II approved his film, despite claims by Vatican officials to the contrary.)

The impact of *The Birth of a Nation* was without precedent. Attempts to censor the film and halt its release only added to its mystique and drummed up further box office. Public leaders ranging from Jane Addams to Booker T. Washington chimed in on the controversy. Many white moviegoers became too caught up in the film's story and were inspired to follow the example of the film by launching their own violent attacks against African Americans. The Ku Klux Klan, which was dormant prior to the film's release, was inspired to regroup thanks solely to the movie.

Finally, Griffith's greatest impact on independent cinema was elevating the filmmaker's visibility as the driving artistic and emotional force behind the production. Before *The Birth of a Nation*, Griffith was unknown to the general public. With the film, he became a public figure and established the concept of the director as the intellectual driving force in popular culture.

There is no possible way to determine the financial success of *The Birth of a Nation*. Griffith also had another trait that independent filmmakers would adopt for years to come: a terrible sense of financial management. In his case, *The Birth of a Nation* was sold on a states right basis to regional salesmen who, in turn, played the film in theaters within defined territorial parameters. One of the states right distributors for *The Birth of a Nation* was Louis B. Mayer, who used his box-office receipts to launch a production career that eventually culminated in his rule over the studio that became Metro-Goldwyn-Mayer, Hollywood's most influential company during American cinema's so-called golden age. Griffith made a profit, but he never truly enjoyed the fullest returns of the film's release.

The Birth of a Nation was still being shown theatrically as late as the 1950s, but during its long run the movie was frequently bootlegged. Today's circulating prints are all based on dupes that are several generations removed from the original source material – Griffith's original negative deteriorated from the high number of prints required for its release, so subsequent distributors (authorized and otherwise) simply made dupes that devalued the pristine visual quality of the original cinematography.

Had Griffith never made the film – indeed, had Griffith been absent from films altogether – it is impossible to imagine how the American movie industry would've progressed. Granted, the movie is an embarrassing ancestor. However, to ignore *The Birth of a Nation*, at least from a historical standpoint, is to ignore the beginnings of independent cinema and its impact on society.

What happened next to Griffith also signaled new directions for American cinema, albeit with far less satisfactory results for the filmmaker and his financiers. Griffith fell into the trap that too many successful filmmakers would emulate in the years to follow: trying to top a box-office hit with an even greater hit.

Harping on his obsession with social injustice, Griffith created an unorthodox epic that spanned the centuries to tell four interweaving stories from different eras that detailed man's cruelty to his fellow beings. To the casual observer, the stories barely seemed connected: the fall of Babylon, the crucifixion of Jesus, the slaughter of the French Huguenots in the 1572 St. Bartholomew's Day Massacre and a modern tale of corrupt capitalists and hypocritical morality in urban America. Connecting the stories was an image of a woman (played by Lillian Gish) rocking a cradle.

The resulting production, *Intolerance*, staggered the film industry with its grandeur, most notably the 12-story set depicting ancient Babylon (complete with colorful, if anachronistic, elephants) and its budget ($2 million). Epic productions of this scale, let alone experimental filmmaking of this scope, did not exist in 1916 and nearly everyone was baffled by what the filmmaker was trying to accomplish. But Griffith explained this experimental storytelling technique in this manner: "The stories begin like four currents looked at from a hilltop. At first the four currents flow apart, slowly and quietly. But as they flow, they grow nearer and nearer together, and faster and faster, until in the end, in the last act, they mingle in one mighty river of expressed emotion."

The resulting film overwhelmed audiences – and, sadly, alienated them. Few people in 1916 could relate emotionally to the scale and scope of Griffith's epic. Even worse, the film's perceived pacifist sentiments seemed wildly outdated by the time it was released – American public opinion was progressing toward involvement in the World War raging in Europe.

The independently-financed *Intolerance* was a commercial failure of unprecedented proportions. Triangle Pictures Corp. went bankrupt due to the film's anemic returns. Griffith attempted to salvage the wreckage by re-editing and re-releasing the Babylonian and modern chapters as standalone features, but those works also failed to win box-office success in all but one market.

The only audiences who understood what Griffith was trying to accomplish were in the Soviet Union. But it was hardly a triumph for Griffith, as the Soviet audiences were viewing bootlegged prints that were created and distributed without Griffith's knowledge.

The failure of *Intolerance* created an artistic setback for Griffith, who would not direct another film until *Hearts of the World* in 1918. It also created acute financial difficulties, as Griffith was saddled with debts from this failed epic that would take years to pay off.

Yet, Griffith would not be stopped. Within three years of the doomed release of *Intolerance*, he would again reshape the concept of independent film distribution. This time, he had assistance from three of the most important figures in the film industry.

Introducing United Artists

Following the death of Triangle Pictures Corp., Griffith aligned himself with two other production companies, Artcraft (a forerunner of Paramount Pictures) and First National (which was later absorbed into Warner Bros.). Neither partnership was satisfactory to Griffith's needs. As luck would have it, he did not find himself isolated in chafing at the limitations created by studio executives.

On February 5, 1919, Griffith was joined by the three reigning stars of the film world – Charlie Chaplin, Mary Pickford and Douglas Fairbanks – to announce the creation of their own production and distribution company, to be called United Artists. Actor William S. Hart was initially part of the venture, but he dropped out before the final paperwork was signed. William S. McAdoo, the son-in-law and Treasury Secretary to President Wilson, provided the legal guidance for the effort. As a result, the original stakes in United Artists were divided five ways: 20% each for Griffith, Chaplin, Pickford, Fairbanks and McAdoo.

Richard Rowland, head of Metro Pictures, sneered that United Artists was a case where "the inmates are taking over the asylum." It was a funny line, but completely off-base. United Artists, in concept, enabled Griffith and his partners to produce and distribute their own films, thus ensuring they enjoyed both artistic control over the finished product and a full harvest of the box-office returns. While Griffith had a taste of being in charge of his own production and distribution with *The Birth of a Nation* (and enjoyed the profits that came with it), it was without precedent for actors like Chaplin, Pickford and Fairbanks to shoulder the multiple burdens of star, producer and distributor (Chaplin, of course, was also his own writer and director).

It was a great idea, but almost immediately things went horribly wrong. In the original agreement, the four stellar talents behind United Artists were supposed to create five feature films per year. Griffith, still fixated on epic productions, failed to meet his quota. Although his first United Artists feature, *Way Down East* (1920), was a big hit, his subsequent features, including *Dream Street* (1921), *Orphans of the Storm* (1922), *One Exciting Night* (1922) and *America* (1924), were major commercial flops.

Why Griffith lost his touch remains something of a mystery. One could speculate he was either unable to adapt to changing audience tastes in movies, or he was foolishly fixated on trying to create a star out of his protégé, Carol Dempster (a curiously charmless and less-than-photogenic performer), or he needed a producer to rein in his budgets. Whatever the reason, by 1924, he was forced to sell his shares in United Artists to recoup his mounting debts. Griffith retreated to a contract at Paramount Pictures.

If Griffith's films were flopping, at least he was making films. Chaplin didn't produce his first United Artists feature until 1923, and his initial effort shocked his partners: a dramatic movie called *A Woman of Paris* that centered around Edna Purviance, the leading lady of his classic comedy shorts. Chaplin wanted to launch Purviance as a star in her own right. But repeating Griffith's error with Carol Dempster, he failed to realize that Purviance lacked the star power (let alone the talent) to carry a movie. Chaplin only turned up in *A Woman of Paris* in an unbilled bit role as a railroad porter, but his face was obscured from the camera.

A Woman of Paris was a huge failure. Had it not been the resounding success of his next United Artists feature, the classic *The Gold Rush* (1925), the studio may have crashed and closed.

Incredibly, Chaplin made the same mistake with Purviance again when he produced *A Woman of the Sea* in 1926. Directed by Josef von Sternberg, this dramatic film turned out so poorly that it was never released; Chaplin destroyed the film's negative in 1933 to accommodate a tax write-off. Purviance made one last film, the French production *Education of a Prince* in 1927 – but Chaplin did not acquire it for United Artists. Chaplin's final silent-era film for United Artists was *The Circus* (1928), a second-tier effort that enjoyed box-office success.

If Chaplin's output was erratic, Douglas Fairbanks enjoyed more consistency – albeit with a relatively limited output. Fairbanks' United Artists efforts focused on action-packed adventure epics, with the star-producer inevitably cast as the good-humored athletic hero. Fairbanks' films were expensive, requiring far more time to create than the average silent film drama. But they were worth waiting for; productions such as *The Mark of Zorro* (1920), *The Three Musketeers* (1921), *Robin Hood* (1922), *The Thief of Bagdad* (1924), *Don Q, Son of Zorro* (1925), *The Black Pirate* (1926), *The Gaucho* (1927) and *The Iron Mask* (1929) were hugely popular with audiences.

Compared to her male partners, Mary Pickford was a veritable pillar of stability. She was no stranger to independent production, having left her Paramount contract in 1918 to release her self-produced films through First National prior to the creation of United Artists. Maintaining her screen persona of the plucky young girl with the bountiful curls,

Pickford created a highly successful skein of films, including *Pollyanna* (1920), *Suds* (1920), *Little Lord Fauntleroy* (1921), *Tess of the Storm Country* (1922), *Rosita* (1923), *Dorothy Vernon of Haddon Hall* (1924), *Little Annie Rooney* (1925), *Sparrows* (1926) and *My Best Girl* (1927).

The expense of running a studio was clearly too great a burden for the United Artists team, however, and, a decade after its creation, United Artists faced peril when its four founders were abruptly forced to face the challenge of switching to the sound film medium. Griffith, who returned to United Artists after a disastrous spell at Paramount Pictures, made two sound films – *Abraham Lincoln* (1930) and *The Struggle* (1931) – that were commercial flops; his career was effectively over when those titles were withdrawn from circulation. Fairbanks could not adapt his silent film swashbuckler style to the sound films, and he abandoned motion pictures after a few desultory and forgettable endeavors. Pickford seemed poised to make the transition without problem, abandoning her little girl persona for adult roles. Her first effort, *Coquette* (1929), showed a strong mastery of dialogue and won her the Academy Award as Best Actress. But audiences were not eager to accept this new mature Pickford and the star wisely realized it; her film acting career was effectively over by 1933 with *Secrets*, though she continued to produce films (mostly of an undistinguished nature) well into the 1940s. As for Chaplin, we'll consider his post-1920s career in the next chapter.

Fortunately for the United Artists founders, help came along in the form of Joseph Schenck, an independent producer who wielded the power of nepotism to bring star wattage to the studio. Schenck was married to one of the leading actresses of the era, Norma Talmadge. She was the sister of two prominent stars, Constance Talmadge and Natalie Talmadge. Natalie was married to another big name, Buster Keaton.

The Talmadge sisters are barely recalled today beyond the realm of film historians, and perhaps for good reason: their films were (for the most part) corny, silly, forgettable melodramas. It is difficult to understand what audiences in the 1920s saw in their work, but for the decade they were able to enjoy considerable success and help grow United Artists.

Ironically, Buster Keaton's United Artists output was not well considered in its time. The master comedy star's graduation from two-reelers to feature films created films that failed to connect with audiences. Although movies such as *The General* (1927), *College* (1927) and *Steamboat Bill Jr.* (1928) are considered classics today, they were box-office duds in their initial releases. In 1928, Schenck sold Keaton's United Artists contract to Metro-Goldwyn-Mayer. Keaton's loss of control over his work, coupled with the fraying of his marriage to Natalie Talmadge, sped him to a professional and personal decline from which he never truly recovered.

Other artists briefly found their way to the United Artists stable. Rudolph Valentino brought his production output there, offering *The Eagle* (1925) and *The Son of the Sheik* (1926) before his tragically premature death. Gloria Swanson enjoyed a commercial success with *Sadie Thompson* (1928), but clashes with director Erich von Stroheim prevented a U.S. release of her 1929 feature *Queen Kelly*. Up-and-coming producers such as Howard Hughes and Samuel Goldwyn also came to United Artists in the late 1920s.

Schenck, who became president of United Artists in 1924, was also wise enough to build a theater chain that operated under the United Artists umbrella. This enabled the studio to release its films without having to haggle, bargain or plea with exhibitors. No other independent production entity followed that lead.

By the end of the decade, United Artists was the leading force in the presentation of independently produced films.

L. Frank Baum and the Film Franchise

At this moment, we should pause and pay tribute to a man whose contributions to the world of independent cinema are usually ignored, which is strange since he created a concept that remains with us to this day: the film franchise. But maybe it is not so strange, since the first attempt at creating a film franchise was a quick and painful dud. The man responsible for this was L. Frank Baum.

Yes, this is the same L. Frank Baum who sent a Kansas farm girl and her little dog over a rainbow. Baum's 1900 book *The Wonderful Wizard of Oz* brought forth a flurry of Oz-related books, creating one of the most lucrative literary properties of the early 20th century. Baum expanded his view to the stage, and in 1902 a musical version of the novel, called *The Wizard of Oz*, opened in Chicago in 1902. The show moved to Broadway in 1903 and was a huge hit. The production later became a successful road show presentation.

In 1910, Baum permitted the Selig Polyscope Company to create a 13-minute production called *The Wonderful Wizard of Oz*, which boiled down the 1902 musical for the short silent film format. Selig quickly created three sequels to this title, but these films are now lost (the initial 1910 film was considered lost for many years, but it has been located and preserved). In 1914, however, Baum thought it would make sense if he tried to bring the Oz stories to the big screen. As a business concept, this made sense – the popularity of the movies had grown substantially in the four years since the first attempt at an Oz-related film. Rather than license the rights to his stories to others, Baum took the bold step of being in charge of the film adaptation of his work. This marked the first time that a writer demanded full artistic control over the film versions of his work.

Baum and three business partners (Louis F. Gottschalk, Harry M. Haldeman and Clarence R. Rundel) created the Oz Film Manufacturing Company in Los Angeles. Curiously, the first production from this new independent film venture was not based on the original classic *The Wonderful Wizard of Oz* (the Selig film did not make that kind of an impact as to rule out a new film version). Instead, Baum chose to create a feature-length film based on a later book called *The Patchwork Girl of Oz*.

The resulting film could charitably be described as a mess. It is also not clear why Baum jettisoned much of that book's plot and nearly all of its gentle charm in favor of a raucous, Mack Sennett-style romp. The film is wall-to-wall madness, with knockabout acrobatics, chases and slapstick animals (played by Fred Woodward, who turned up in the Oz films playing animal characters in conspicuously raggedy costumes).

Based on the high name recognition of the Oz books, *The Patchwork Girl of Oz* was picked up for release by Paramount Pictures. But the film was a commercial disaster – audiences that loved the book hated the film, and those who didn't know the book weren't particularly impressed by the frenetic knockabout. The film's failure was a lethal blow to Baum and his partners, and they struggled to recover from their error.

The next film was *The Magic Cloak of Oz*, and its inclusion in the Oz film series was even more puzzling since this was not part of the Oz book series, but was adapted from another Baum book, *Queen Zizi of Ix*. However, Baum was quoted as saying that this was the best book he ever wrote, which may explain how it got on film.

Actually, it didn't stay on film very long. The Oz Film Manufacturing Company turned out a five-reel production. Yet, the film followed *The Patchwork Girl of Oz* as a box-office failure. Paramount withdrew the film and resubmitted it for theatrical release in 1917 as a three-reel version called *The Magic Cloak* (apparently, the word "Oz" in the title was becoming box-office poison). For the film's British release, it was cut up into a pair of two-reelers, *The Magic Cloak* and *The Witch Queen*. One reel from the original print was jettisoned and remains lost to this day. Even in this truncated state, the film found no favor.

Baum and his partners decided to give their film venture another shot, and this time they brought in the characters that everyone associated with Oz. *His Majesty, the Scarecrow of Oz* found the Yellow Brick Roadsters in a new adventure written especially for the screen (the first and only time Baum created an Oz story that was not meant for publication). This tale involved King Krewl, the autocratic ruler of the Emerald City, who tries to force the beautiful Princess Gloria to marry against her will (she's in love with a gardener's son). The story gets fairly complicated and (by contemporary standards) strange: the Tin Man decapitates the Wicked Witch with his axe (she reattaches her head), the Wicked Witch turns the gardener's son into a kangaroo, the Wizard of Oz traps the Wicked Witch in a giant can, the Scarecrow flirts with a mermaid and engages in a jaunty jig with a giant bird, and everyone winds up in King Krewl's castle, where the mean leader is tied up and dragged off to be executed.

By this point, Paramount didn't want anything to do with Baum's films and declined to distribute *His Majesty, the Scarecrow of Oz*. The Oz Film Manufacturing Company tried to self-distribute the movie, but their efforts were not successful.

The Oz Film Manufacturing Company sought to switch gears to a different side of the rainbow. Subsequent films included a feature based on Baum's non-Oz *The Last Egyptian* and a series of comic-fantasy shorts. The company re-released *His Majesty, the Scarecrow of Oz* under the title *The New Wizard of Oz*. Sadly, none of these worked. Baum's son took over operations, changed the company's name to Dramatic Feature Films, and made two films: a slapstick short called *Pies and Poetry* and a melodrama based on the then-current World War I called *The Gray Nun of Belgium*. The films were flops. By the end of the 1915, Baum's connection to the movie world end. He died in 1919, recalled for his literary contributions but not his cinematic output.

The failure to establish a film franchise based on the Oz stories was, in retrospect, not surprising. In the silent movie world, these stories came across like weird and silly riffs. The charm and delight of Baum's writing were lost, and the resulting void was filled with chaos that bore little resemblance to the beloved adventures of Dorothy and her friends. The same problem bedeviled comic Larry Semon, whose 1925 independent feature *Wizard of Oz* was little more than an excuse for lame slapstick at the expense of a Baum-inspired plot.

Film franchises, of course, managed to take off despite Baum's shortcomings. And while few people may realize his pioneering work in this sector of the movie world, he is deserving of recognition and tribute for setting us off on the road (yellow bricked or otherwise).

Bringing in Sound and Color

It was never the intention of the pioneers of the early cinema to present a medium that existed as a monochromatic pantomime of real life. Unfortunately for these men, the technologies initially at their disposal were inadequate in providing the solutions they required to make motion pictures a true mirror of the human experience.

Thomas Edison, in developing his aforementioned Kinetoscope machines, had planned to incorporate an aural element into the viewing experience. In Edison's plan, a cylindrical phonograph would be in the base of the Kinetoscope-viewing cabinet. The viewer, after depositing his coin into the machine, would pick up a telephone receiver and listen to a soundtrack that accompanied the film loop playing in the Kinetoscope machine.

Alas, Edison failed to consider the problems in synchronizing his very fast film loops (some ran 30 fps) with his very slow and clumsy cylindrical phonographs. Offering synchronized dialogue was out of the question, and even the problem of keeping musical cues and film action in unison eluded Edison and his engineers. Edison shipped his Kinetoscopes without the sound equipment and, at first, no one seemed to mind.

If Edison couldn't bring sound to his film-viewing experience, he could at least bring color – if only by cheating. Color film stock did not exist, so it was decided to paint the color directly on the film. This was also being done by the French film production pioneers who rivaled Edison's output in the nascent cinema period. Hand painting films was a costly and time-consuming process, having to apply with painstaking accuracy the correct dabs of color in the areas of the film frames. There were ways of getting around that – color would be reserved for limited sections of the film, usually to highlight unusual or dramatic movement. For example, many of the early prints of *The Great Train Robbery* used painted-on color to dramatize the fiery bursts from revolvers and dynamite. The result was often fey, but at least it saved the films from being strictly black-and-white affairs.

Surprisingly, audiences did not mind the absence of sound and color during the early years of the silent movie. In essence, the viewing experience was never totally silent – when films moved out of peep show Kinetoscopes into venues with screen projection, live music would be performed along with the film. At first, the music came from a single source, usually a pianist at an upright piano or an organist. As the popularity of the art form grew, so did the size of its musical accompaniment. Original music scores replaced the hodgepodge collections of popular tunes, ballads, hymns and forgettable original compositions that gave musical accompaniment to the earliest films. And the lone person at the piano or organ was soon joined by ensembles or (in the case of prestige productions playing the larger venues) small orchestras.

Even if there was a clamoring for sound, there was no way to offer it. The original sound film experiments from the first two decades of the 20th century attempted to synchronize the actors on the screen with dialogue and music recorded on phonograph discs. Unlike Edison's cylindrical concept, the disc format enabled engineers to achieve a better (though not flawless) synchronization with the actions on the screen. That was the first good news in the development of sound on film.

The bad news, however, came in recording and projection. The earliest attempts at recording spoken dialogue and music were hit-and-miss, but mostly "miss." The first microphones were unable to capture the full vibrancy of sound waves, resulting in efforts that sounded crackly, too deep or just plain inaudible. The latter situation reportedly befell ragtime legend Scott Joplin, who was the subject of a sound film experiment that was shot during the 1904 World's Fair in St. Louis. The playback on Joplin's piano playing was considered so dismal that the project was scrapped and the footage was thrown away. Since this was also the only known film footage and sound recording of Joplin in performance, the extraordinary nature of that loss cannot be measured.

As for the projection of what was recorded, the sound discs could only be played on Victrola-style machines that did not offer vibrant sound projection. Anyone sitting at the front of a theater would be able to hear (to a point) the sounds and music emanating from these machines. Those seated toward the rear, however, would need to strain in order to catch any possible noise. Audiences were not impressed, and early sound experiments were doomed to being little more than experiments.

Likewise, audiences were not complaining about the absence of color in their films. There was no evidence that hand-colored films enjoyed more commercial popularity than the black-and-white variety. And as the cost of film production increased when motion pictures began stretching into features, the idea of paying people to dab paint onto thousands of celluloid frames was neither cost-effective nor practical.

A compromise was reached in tinting films to suggest either times of day or individual emotions (blue tints for evening, yellow for day, red for dangerous situations). But, again, the filmmakers were primarily pleasing themselves with such actions – audience anger was non-existent at these circumstances, and movie theater attendance steadily rose without the bother of sound and color. Indeed, the power players who came to run the film industry saw no reason to tinker with a successful formula.

But, of course, no one told the independent filmmakers. As usual, being on the outside gave the independents a nothing-to-lose determination as they sought to remake film technology to suit their needs. Working outside of the power circles, they labored to take on the challenges of incorporating sound and color into films. When they were able to perfect what they sought, the power players took a new look and brought their innovations into the film industry.

Outside of a belated and poorly received 1913 attempt by Thomas Edison to integrate sound and film via a new version of the Kinetophone (this one involved a phonograph hooked by a complicated pulley system to a film projector), the American film industry was content to offer silent motion pictures. But a few malcontents buzzed along the fringes and were determined to crack the challenge that kept human speech out of the cinema. Perhaps the most determined of this tiny group was Dr. Lee DeForest.

DeForest was an engineer who invented the audion tube in 1906. This device helped to amplify the transmission of wireless telegraph signals, and it was later incorporated into the development of radio broadcasting. DeForest realized the primary problem in bringing sound to movies was amplification – it was possible to achieve perfect synchronization with a sound-on-disc system (as Edison achieved in his few 1913 Kinetophone shorts), but the limitations of the phonograph system in that era made it impossible for the recording to be heard throughout a theater.

DeForest reportedly was tinkering with a new approach, a sound-on-film concept, as early as 1913. However, his efforts did not begin to coalesce until he came upon sound-on-film experimental work that was developed and patented in Finland by inventor Eric Tigerstedt and in Germany by the Tri-Ergon company. DeForest expanded upon this work and pushed it forward, not only in terms of technical polishing but as a corporate entity. In 1922, he created the Phonofilm Corporation and began shooting one-reel films featuring prominent celebrity performers and politicians of the day.

DeForest's system worked, although the aesthetic aspects of his films left something to be desired (a static, stationary camera and people speaking a LITTLE TOO LOUD). Nonetheless, the idea worked and he was able to snag the participation of many prominent figures of the day, including President Calvin Coolidge. However, there were several problems that halted DeForest's progress.

The main problem was DeForest himself. Whatever his genius as an inventor (or as one who improved on existing inventions, as in this case), he was a terrible businessman. DeForest wound up getting into legal squabbles with Theodore Case, who was working on his own sound-on-film process. Case enabled DeForest to use some of his patented technology for the Phonofilm presentations, but later expressed anger that DeForest failed to provide proper recognition for such generosity.

Case responded by refusing to allow DeForest to have access to his inventions. DeForest realized too late that his Phonofilm was heavily dependent on Case's technology. By 1926, unable to obtain outside financing and incapable of expanding the sound-on-film technology fur-

ther by his own creativity, DeForest was forced to shut down the Phonofilm Corporation by declaring it bankrupt.

There was also the uncomfortable fact that Case's technology, on
its own merits, was superior to what DeForest was cobbling together.
In his book, *The Speed of Sound*, historian Scott Eyman notes that when
comparing the test films shot by the two men, "Case's sound system is
amazingly clean, a considerable improvement over the fuzzy DeForest
system, and far superior to any sound-on-film disc system."

Then there was the lingering problem of sound-on-disc technology
– many people in the industry still considered it to be the correct course
of action. Even D.W. Griffith registered in that school of thought, recording a sound prologue for his 1921 feature *Dream Street* that was
presented via a sound-on-disc system invented by Orlando Kellum.

A major player in the sound-on-disc technology was Western
Union, which previously had no connections to the motion picture industry. The company jumped into the race to bring sound to movies in
1922 by creating a one-reel animated short designed to explain how
sound transmission worked. Whether the company intended to slap
both DeForest and Case for their sound-on-film work or whether it was
a mere coincidence is unclear, but that film was called *The Audion* (by
then, DeForest's financial problems forced him to sell the patent rights
to his invention) and it was premiered at Yale University in New Haven,
Connecticut (where Case was a prominent alumnus).

Western Union also had a major advantage over DeForest and
Case – it perfected a public address system that would enable broadcasts to be heard far and wide. This solved the problem of transmit-
ting cinema-based sound from a single, small source on a phonograph.
Thus, theaters could now be wired for sound in a way that enabled
every member of the audience (not just those close to the phonograph)
to hear the presentation.

Not surprisingly, Western Union got to the Hollywood studios
first. The small but scrappy Warner Brothers studio partnered with

Western Union. In 1926, Warner Brothers presented the John Barry-
more costume drama *Don Juan* with a synchronized music score via the
sound-on-disc process that the studio dubbed Vitaphone. The following
year, a so-so Broadway show about a young man breaking away from
his Orthodox Jewish family to pursue a vaudeville career was presented
with an expanded use of the Vitaphone process. The film was called *The
Jazz Singer* – further comment isn't required.

Theodore Case, however, was not one to be trumped. He brought
his sound-on-film technology to the Fox Film Corporation, which incorporated it to provide synchronized sound in their prestige release
Sunrise (1927). Fox dubbed this process Movietone.

In the end, of course, sound-on-film won out over sound-on-disc
(which lingered until about 1930 before being retired). But the efforts
of the independent outsiders who tinkered, squabbled and patiently
pursued these efforts are often forgotten. Actually, that's not entirely
true – the movie industry *did* offer a brief, after-the-fact tribute to one
pioneer. In 1959, Lee DeForest received an honorary Academy Award
for his work in the field. (Case, who died in 1944, never received any
industry tribute.)

Simultaneous to this effort was the rise of color films. It was never
the intention of the pioneers of cinema to offer monochromatic visions.
But they had no choice – color film stock did not exist in the late 1890s
and the first decade of the 20th century. Nonetheless, the celluloid
dreams were always in color.

At first, the only viable solution was to hand paint the prints that
were offered for viewing, first in the Kinetoscopes and later on the projected screen. This was a tedious and expensive process, to be certain,
with each frame of film receiving its own coat of paint. As a means of
speeding up the process, a unique compromise was offered in which
certain parts of the film would receive color treatment while the majority of the screen scene was reserved for black and white. The results of
such a strategy were often enchanting and entertaining, most notably
the hand-colored version of *The Great Train Robbery*, where the ban-

dits' gunfire fusillade and the dynamite explosion were illustrated in rich bursts of red and orange.

When hand painting became too burdensome, another compromise involved tinting the film print. A limited mix of colors was used to signify specific emotions portrayed on the screen. But this, ultimately, was an unsatisfactory strategy. Instead of having films in consistent black and white, audiences were watching films that switched from black-and-yellow to black-and-blue to black-and-red, with portions reserved for the original black-and-white format. No one ever credited the tinting process with enhancing the actual film; in fact, it appeared to add confusion and eyestrain rather than adding color.

A new solution was needed, one that did not rely on accessorizing monochrome film. A British process called Kinemacolor was presented in 1908, but its attempts to capture hues on film were unsatisfactory. In 1915, Technicolor Corporation was created by Herbert Kalmus, Daniel Comstock, and W. Burton Wescott. The company created a special camera to record red and blue-green images through a single lens. The print itself was black and white, but it was shown through a special projector consisting of twin apertures and lenses (not unlike the twin-projector system that was used for showing 3-D movies). Color filters were attached to the projectors to bring out the visual vibrancy.

It was a great idea that did not work. The Technicolor Corporation produced its own film, *The Gulf Between*, in Florida in 1917, and presented it in New York to highlight the wonders of this new system. Alas, the projectionist had no clue how to coordinate the screening and the film was reportedly a blurry mess. The company's leaders returned to the proverbial drawing board; *The Gulf Between* is now considered a lost film, with only a few frames surviving.

By 1922, a second version of Technicolor was ready. This time, problems relating to cinematography and projection were ironed out. Known both as a two-color and two-strip system, this second version of Technicolor was tested with an independent feature called *The Toll of the Sea* (1922). The film's exotic storyline (a derivative of *Madame*

Butterfly set in China) and remarkable leading lady (newcomer Anna May Wong, who became the first Asian-American film star) helped sell the concept. *Toll of the Sea*, unlike *The Gulf Between*, had no problems being projected. Based on its success, studios began calling Technicolor Corporation to save their films from black and white.

But Technicolor was an expensive solution, requiring a special camera and more intensive lighting. Thus, it was limited to special sequences within mega-epics, such as the original Cecil B. DeMille version of *The Ten Commandments* (1923), the Lon Chaney version of *The Phantom of the Opera* (1925) and the original MGM version of *Ben-Hur* (1926). It was not until Douglas Fairbanks, in his United Artists production of *The Black Pirate* (1926), that a full-length Technicolor feature was shot.

The coming of sound did not hamper the viability of the Technicolor process. In fact, the mixture of sound and color seemed like a great selling point. Many sound films included color sequences, but many others were shot entirely in Technicolor. In the 1930s, the process was improved again with the so-called three-color system. The first successful offerings of this process were the 1933 Walt Disney animated short *Flowers and Trees*, followed by the 1934 short *La Cucaracha* and the 1935 feature *Becky Sharp*, both created by the independent production company Pioneer Pictures.

Technicolor was not the only attempt to bring color to films. Other processes were created by independent companies, but few enjoyed any genuine success. Today, all we have are their names: Colorcraft, Kellycolor, Photocolor and Sennet Color came and went. The most successful rival to Technicolor began its life under the name Multicolor in 1929 and was purchased by Cinecolor Inc. in 1932, which changed the process' name to Cinecolor. But Cinecolor was limited for the 1930s and early 1940s primarily to shorts and cheaply-made independent Westerns.

By this period, the film industry became solidified into a specific environment. A hierarchy of major studios, minor studios, prominent independent producers, and frenetic outsiders buzzing at the fringes defined motion picture output.

The 10 Most Important
Independent Films of All Time:

Eric Stanze, filmmaker (*Savage Harvest, Ice from the Sun, Scrapbook*)

Q: If you were to look over the span of the history of U.S. independent cinema, from the silent era to today's output, what would
you list as the 10 Most Important Independently-Produced Films of All
Time ... and why?

I'd like to call attention to a key term in this question. This is *not*
my list of the best independent films of all time. It is my list of the Top
10 most important independently-produced films of all time. There is
a drastic difference. That stated, here they are, in chronological order:

1. *Fred Ott's Sneeze* (1894).This was an actuality film of
   the Edison Kinetoscope library. The Edison Manufacturing Company produced this 35mm film, shot by
   William K.L. Dickson. The film (appropriately) starred
   Fred Ott. Only a few seconds long, *Fred Ott's Sneeze*
   will represent the birth of American cinema in my Top
   10 list. However, this very short film must share credit
   for launching the most important and stimulating art
   form of the 20th century. The film was not produced
   for Kinetoscope distribution, but as a publicity stunt
   for a magazine. The tremendous attention the film received sealed its place in film history. Some call it the
   world's first cult film and Fred Ott later joked that he
   was the world's first film star. This was also the first
   motion picture to be copyrighted in the U.S.

2. *The Great Train Robbery* (1903). Directed by Edwin S.
   Porter, it is included here due to its impact on audiences upon initial release and its lasting relevance as a
   pioneering commercial film. Though it was not the first

film to use these innovative techniques, *The Great Train Robbery* introduced many American cinema patrons to cross-cutting, location shooting, and basic camera movement. The movie also contains the famous shock gimmick of an actor firing his gun into the audience by aiming his weapon directly at the camera, a memorable trick that terrified early filmgoers. The movie has its place in cinema history as the first narrative film. This particular claim is erroneous. However, it may indeed have been the most financially successful American narrative film at that time. It is on my list because it signaled the commercial demise of the actuality film, and it ushered in the era of the American fictional narrative film, which dominates the industry to this day.

3. *Meshes of the Afternoon* (1943). The short experimental film directed by Maya Deren and Alexander Hammid can be seen as a bookend companion to *The Great Train Robbery*. While *The Great Train Robbery* may have introduced the formula for the mainstream narrative film, *Meshes of the Afternoon* may have been the first widely received film to deviate from this standard and offer audiences an alternative. Taking some inspiration from French avant-garde cinema, it filled a void for film fans bored of repetitive Hollywood product. Emotionally tinted by the unique and turbulent atmosphere of World War II- era America, *Meshes of the Afternoon* explored artistic terrain not traversed by the Hollywood narrative film. The film's co-creator, Maya Deren, spawned the subsequent east coast experimental film movement known as the New American Cinema, which continues to inspire filmmakers (most notably David Lynch) to this day.

4. *Night of the Living Dead* (1968). George A. Romero's film almost single-handedly re-defined the American horror genre. This somber zombie film managed to shock and impress with its groundbreaking displays of gore. It was also an unblinking peek into the soul of America at that time (whether the filmmakers intended this or not). The production and distribution of the film opened a lot of eyes. *Night of the Living Dead* was shot in Pittsburgh, not Hollywood, and was produced by private investors, not a feature film studio of any sort. The fact that such a small and fragile base could support a movie that would go on to be seen by a great many people (and, in fact, achieve a certain level of cultural impact in the years that followed) was exciting. On the negative side, copyright issues spawned an infamous battle to collect the money being made by the successful movie. Everyone was profiting except for the filmmakers and investors. This incident became a warning to other independent filmmakers that without the protective walls of a major Hollywood studio, anyone could take a piece out of you at any time.

5. *Easy Rider* (1969). Dennis Hopper wrote, directed, and starred in *Easy Rider*. This movie is often cited as the beginning of New Hollywood wherein adventurous avant-garde filmmakers, using lower budgets, and targeting a more youthful audience, essentially began saving Hollywood. The standard studio output was failing to attract audiences and the studios were floundering financially. Studio executives began putting up with these loose-cannon filmmakers as a last resort. The gamble paid off and the studios began to thrive again. Ironically, *Easy Rider* gave rise to the Film School Gen-

eration which would soon dominate Hollywood. Generating the first blockbusters (most notably *Jaws* and *Star Wars*) the Film School Generation again changed Hollywood by greatly altering the studios' perception of what a successful film was. The independent film (and any film of any budget that did not meet mass audience expectations) was all but doomed from that point forward.

6. *THX 1138* (1971). This only barely makes the list because it was produced with the support of major studio Warner Brothers. However, it is exactly this hook into a major studio (among other reasons) that makes *THX 1138* a notable entry into America's history of independent cinema. Directed by George Lucas and produced through Francis Ford Coppola's American Zoetrope Studios, this film is primarily important because of what Coppola was attempting to do with his Zoetrope organization: put the money and the creative power in the hands of the artists instead of the studio executives. *THX 1138* was a blending of disparate cinema styles: the experimental and the narrative. It began its life as a short experimental student film by Lucas, which was heavily inspired by a Canadian experimental film called *21-87*, directed by Arthur Lipsett. *THX 1138* tells a narrative story, though many of its sequences are designed to not propel the plot, but to summon tone, cinematically indicating love, lust, and paranoia. This is noteworthy in its attempt to blend a style of cinema that is decidedly non-mainstream with a standard style of filmmaking embraced by the mainstream. Lastly, it is important to note that it was the debut feature film from a director who has become arguably

the most successful independent filmmaker in history. Ironically, George Lucas is also criticized for playing his part (along with Steven Spielberg) in castrating the American independent film by introducing the block-buster mentality to the film industry.

7. *Deep Throat* (1972). The hardcore pornography film appears on this list for its impact on national attitudes about porn films, for becoming the most profitable movie in porn film history, and for being the porn film with the most significant and long lasting cultural impact. Though not a well-made film, it invaded public consciousness to the point where most adults had at least heard of the film, even if they'd never seen it. The title was used as a pseudonym for an informant during the Watergate scandal, a pseudonym that was later resurrected for a character on television's *The X-Files*. The film's star, Linda Lovelace, added fuel to the film's fire by flip-flopping her public statements about the making of it, first calling the experience liberating and then later stating that she was forced to have sex in the movie by her abusive husband. A tempest of obscenity litigation surrounded the film, hampering its release while simultaneously generating free publicity for it. Adding more depth to the shadowy *Deep Throat* legend, the movie was produced by "made" mobsters and distributed by mafia-connected enterprises, including the many mob-run theaters which exhibited the film. Mobster book-cooking made it difficult to determine just how profitable it was. Today, the film is estimated to have grossed 4,000 times its production budget at the box office, despite being banned in 23 states.

8. *Dawn of the Dead* (1978). This sequel to *Night of the Living Dead* is directed by George Romero (the only film-maker to be represented twice on my list). It is notable for evading the blockbuster mentality of the time and becoming a world-wide hit without the aid of a Hollywood studio. Independently financed by investors in the U.S. and Italy, and produced in Pittsburgh, Romero shot the film in an actual mall – he simply asked the owners of the mall if he could shoot his movie there. The mall's owners agreed, even though they knew they would not profit from the arrangement. Today, malls are owned by huge corporations that would not even consider such an event (as their insurance and legal representatives would advise against it) and they most certainly would not allow such an event on their property without substantial compensation which few independent producers could afford. The producers chose to break virtually every rule of a successful film release at the time. They left the movie's run time longer to keep the character development intact, they refused to censor the high-impact violence of the film, and they released it without an MPAA rating. The producers searched for and found a distributor who would give the film proper support, despite the fact that it was not designed to have mainstream blockbuster potential. Worldwide, *Dawn of the Dead* had a theatrical run that grossed 85 times its production budget - a claim that cannot be made by blockbusters *Jaws* or *Star Wars*.

9. *Blood Cult* (1985). This is not on this list due to any specific merits of the movie, but instead because of what I feel it represents. Directed by Christopher Lewis and shot in Tulsa, Oklahoma, it is not a well-made movie

and it has had no discernable cultural impact. However, *Blood Cult* is historically significant for two reasons. It was the first motion picture produced specifically for home video distribution and it was the first commercially released motion picture to be shot electronically, on video instead of on film. Evaluating the current landscape of indie cinema, it is easy to see *Blood Cult* as the doorway filmmaking stepped through to become what it is today. From big-budget Hollywood features shot on High Definition video, to consumer digital camcorders and home editing systems, *Blood Cult* paved the way that eventually led to a boom of shot-on-videotape productions released to home video in the 1990s. Around the end of the 1990s digital video formats emerged that gave low-budget filmmakers a boost in picture quality and tape format reliability.

10. *Reservoir Dogs* (1992). It can be said that the chasm between the financial resources of the Hollywood studios and the artistic ambitions of the independent filmmaker was mended, to a certain degree, by Quentin Tarantino's *Reservoir Dogs*. It did not break new ground in the craft of filmmaking, nor was it even a well-made film. In fact, Tarantino's gifts as a writer/director lay not in any significant grasp of the craft, but in his ability to gleefully patchwork together concepts and sequences from older films that he appreciates as a fan. This fan-boy style of film direction translated easily over to students of film who were eager to mimic their filmmaking heroes, and less interested in exploring the full spectrum of tools and techniques offered by the craft. For a decade and a half now, film students and film hobbyists have been obsessed with making movies

about gun violence, lippy gangsters, and pop-culture references, almost entirely thanks to Quentin Tarantino. Thus, based on its cultural impact and influence on up-and-coming directors, one could say that *Reservoir Dogs* drove independent filmmaking right into an insipid rut where it spun its wheels for many years.

CHAPTER TWO:
Parallel Worlds

"It was the best of times, it was the worst of times."
— Charles Dickens

During the 1930s and the first part of the 1940s, Hollywood experienced what film scholars would later call its Golden Era. For the realm of independent cinema, however, this period was marked by the formation of two separate and unequal realms of creation.

On one hand, there were savvy producers who functioned as de facto independents, but who were actually very much a part of the Hollywood system. They ran their operations like mini-studios, complete with keeping key talent under contracts. While their output was limited and they relied on other companies to actually get their films into theaters, they were still, for all intents and purposes, Hollywood players.

On the other hand, there were smaller production groups that lacked the access to the Hollywood orbit. Some of these focused solely on specialized niche markets, while others gamely attempted to mirror the studio output on significantly smaller budgets.

Viewed from today, both sectors of the independent film world created works that are still celebrated for their daring, audacity, skill and entertainment value. In many ways, this period could also be seen as a Golden Age.

The Hollywood Indie Insiders

Within Tinseltown, a number of prominent men set themselves up as independent producers. Separately, they were responsible for extraordinary productions. Viewed as a whole, they arguably offered the most dynamic gathering of artist/businessmen in the history of 20th-century show business.

Samuel Goldwyn

Perhaps the most successful independent producer of Hollywood's Golden Era was Samuel Goldwyn. Just a casual listing of the films produced by Goldwyn over a 25-year period can confirm the depth and scope of his versatility as a producer: *Whoopee!* (1930), *Street Scene* (1931), *Arrowsmith* (1931), *The Dark Angel* (1935), *These Three* (1936), *Come and Get It* (1936), *Dodsworth* (1936), *Stella Dallas* (1937), *Dead End* (1937), *The Hurricane* (1937), *Wuthering Heights* (1939), *The Westerner* (1940), *The Little Foxes* (1941), *Ball of Fire* (1941), *The Pride of the Yankees* (1942), *The Princess and the Pirate* (1944), *The Best Years of Our Lives* (1946; the second independently-produced film to win the Best Picture Oscar), *The Secret Life of Walter Mitty* (1947), *The Bishop's Wife* (1947), *My Foolish Heart* (1949), *Hans Christian Andersen* (1952) and *Guys and Dolls* (1955).

The key to Goldwyn's success was both simple and complex: offering high-quality productions. The simplicity was obvious: people associated the Goldwyn name with the finest in motion picture entertainment. But the complexity bedeviled many of Goldwyn's competitors – and even today, many film historians are baffled at how this rather unlikely individual could have been the driving force behind some of the greatest American films ever made.

Samuel Goldwyn was born Schmuel Gelbfisz in Warsaw in 1879 to a Polish Jewish family. At the age of 15, with no money or connections, he emigrated to Birmingham, England, where he reinvented himself as Samuel Goldfish and found work in a blacksmith shop. By 1898, he made his way to America by way of Nova Scotia (why he decided not to come directly into America is not certain). He found his way to Upstate New York, where he successfully began a career as a glove salesman.

The young man's fascination with the new film medium inspired him to pursue business opportunities within that environment. As luck would have it, his brother-in-law was a successful stage producer, Jesse L. Lasky, and this family connection helped bring about an independently-produced 1914 feature-length endeavor called *The Squaw Man*. That production was significant on two counts: it was the first film produced in Hollywood, and it marked the directing debut of Cecil B. DeMille. Goldfish's role in *The Squaw Man* was concentrated in selling the film to exhibitors, but after its success (and Lasky's subsequent partnership with Adolph Zukor to create Famous Players-Lasky, later known as Paramount Pictures), Goldfish desired to become involved in the production side of the business. Neither Lasky nor Zukor welcomed his involvement there, so Goldfish partnered with the Selwyn family of theatrical producers in 1917 to create a new company called Goldwyn Pictures (a combination of their surnames). Goldfish obviously liked the way that sounded, as he changed his surname to Goldwyn in 1918.

Again, clashes of personality created problems and Goldwyn left the company prior to its 1924 purchase by Marcus Loew, who also purchased the independent Metro Pictures and Mayer Pictures to form Metro-Goldwyn-Mayer (commonly known as MGM). Although his name was part of the corporate moniker, Goldwyn never had anything to do with MGM until 1955, when the studio agreed to distribute his production of *Guys and Dolls* starring Marlon Brando and Frank Sinatra.

On his own, Goldwyn created the Samuel Goldwyn Inc., and for the next three decades he turned out an extraordinary canon of films. To his credit, Goldwyn surrounded himself with the finest talent available: director William Wyler, writers that included Sidney Howard, Ben Hecht, Lillian Hellman and Robert E. Sherwood, and actors like Gary

Cooper, Danny Kaye and Virginia Mayo. Even studio-supported stars that would normally balk at appearing in independent films eagerly accepted roles in Goldwyn films, most notably Bette Davis in *The Little Foxes*, Bob Hope in *They Got Me Covered* and *The Princess and the Pirate* and Myrna Loy in *The Best Years of Our Lives*.

Perhaps to diffuse his admittedly irascible (some might say crude and overpowering) personality, Goldwyn's company sought to promote the producer as a somewhat zany character with a tortured command of the English language. So-called "Goldwynisms" were leaked to entertainment media, which in turn built a softer and somewhat comic reputation for Goldwyn. Nutty comments such as "A verbal contract isn't worth the paper it's written on" and "Gentlemen, include me out" have been credited to Goldwyn, though it is widely assumed that many of these aphorisms were the result of talented ghostwriters. (A recording survives of Goldwyn's appearance on Jack Benny's radio show in 1946, and the producer was clearly capable of speaking flawless English without any perceived assault on the syntax.)

Goldwyn initially released his films through United Artists, switching over to RKO for distribution purposes in the 1940s until a dispute with the Howard Hughes-run studio in 1952. By that time, Goldwyn's output began to slow considerably. After *Guys and Dolls* in 1955, he only produced Otto Preminger's 1959 film adaptation of *Porgy and Bess*, which was released through Columbia Pictures. By then, however, Goldwyn's critics accused him of being old-fashioned and out of touch with changing audience tastes. In retrospect, this may have been a cruel dissection – although, admittedly, *Porgy and Bess* seemed like an odd offering during the period when agitation for civil rights was beginning to gather full force across Jim Crow America.

Goldwyn passed away in 1974, and today his finest productions are still treasured as classics of film art. While contemporary film scholars may seek to assign credit to the directors or writers of these works, it is obvious that Goldwyn was the force that made these productions possible. His films were, literally, the gold standard of Hollywood's peak years – even today, few independent producers could dream of duplicating the depth and scope of his output.

David O. Selznick

After Goldwyn, the most recognizable independent producer of the Golden Era was David O. Selznick. He is primarily remembered today as the producer of *Gone with the Wind*, which is not an independent film (though it was initially planned as such). During the 1930s and 1940s, Selznick was among the most tenacious independent producers in Hollywood. While his output was spottier and less prolific than Goldwyn, and his well-publicized persona lacked Goldwyn's broad comic undertones, the quality level of Selznick's best work was peerless.

Selznick was somewhat unique, compared to his peers, in that he was a second-generation film executive. His father was the Ukrainian-born Lewis J. Selznick, who entered the movie business during its early days as the general manager for the East Coast Universal Film Exchange. The elder Selznick moved into production and became a significant force in both the creation and distribution of films. He enjoyed considerable success until a string of bad breaks (complicated by the ruthless machinations of his competitors) forced him into bankruptcy in 1923. His son David was aware of the perilous business that saw his father's rise and fall, and he felt he could conquer it.

And for many years, he did. Selznick gained entry into the studio systems and rose quickly to the level of producer. He worked at RKO (most notably as the producer of the 1933 landmark *King Kong*) and at MGM (as the producer of *Anna Karenina* and *A Tale of Two Cities*). The MGM connection brought Selznick into another Hollywood power family: while he was there, he married Irene Mayer, the daughter of studio mogul Louis B. Mayer. The marriage didn't particularly bolster his standing at MGM (Mayer never seemed to like his daughter's brash husband), but cynics insisted otherwise (the Hemingway-inspired Hollywood wisecrack "the son-in-law also rises" came from the Selznick-Mayer marriage).

By 1935, Selznick decided to become an independent producer. To his credit, he lined up a considerable number of deep-pocketed investors and began operations on a $3 million budget. United Artists signed Selznick International Pictures to an eight-picture deal, based solely on his reputation and funding.

As a producer, Selznick got off to a strong start: *A Star is Born* (1937), *Nothing Sacred* (1937), *The Prisoner of Zenda* (1937), *The Young in Heart* (1938), *Made for Each Other* (1939) and *Intermezzo: A Love Story* (1939) were produced by Selznick International Pictures.

The fact Selznick felt he could pull off *Gone with the Wind* as an independent film could be seen as either a tribute to his jaw-dropping daring or as evidence of his rampant megalomania. He purchased the book's screen rights in 1936 for the then-princely sum of $50,000. Yet his initial plans to launch a film version hit two road blocks: the proposed grand epic was far beyond the scale of his production company, and the star power needed to sell the film was outside of his grasp. Unable to independently produce *Gone with the Wind*, Selznick reluctantly partnered with his father-in-law. For its part, MGM provided reigning box-office star Clark Gable to play Rhett Butler, $1.25 million toward the film's production costs (which ultimately soaked up $4 million), and its studio facilities. In return, MGM obtained the full distribution rights to the film and 50% of the profits. Those last two requirements sat very poorly with United Artists, which made its own *Gone with the Wind* production financing proposal to Selznick (who was still under contract with United Artists for the release of his company's films).

Of course, *Gone with the Wind* went on to be the most successful commercial release of Hollywood's Golden Age. Selznick was honored by the industry during the Academy Award ceremonies, and his share of the box-office profits enabled him to keep Selznick International Pictures flourishing. The year after *Gone with the Wind*, he scored another major success with *Rebecca*. That film won the 1940 Academy Award as Best Picture, making it the first independent production to be so honored.

At this point, however, the Selznick story starts to veer off course.

Selznick began to develop a wealth of projects that never took root. He also became obsessed in turning a B-movie actress named Phylis Isley into a major star. He achieved that, renaming her Jennifer Jones, and aggressively campaigning for her to receive plum roles. In that campaign, he succeeded – it helped that Jones was a genuine and distinctive talent – but it wrecked his marriage to Irene Mayer. After the couple divorced, Selznick wed Jones.

But, as a producer, Selznick seemed to lose his touch. Complicating matters was his desire to top *Gone with the Wind*– this actually became something of an obsession, as he feared he would be identified solely with that film. His much-ballyhooed 1944 release *Since You Went Away* (which he, amazingly, marketed as being on par with *Gone with the Wind*) didn't resonate in the manner that he desired. Selznick's increasingly abrasive behavior soured his relations with United Artists.

In 1946, Selznick split with his long-time distributor and took the daring move of becoming his own distributor (an unprecedented action for an independent producer). Selznick Releasing Organization got off to a rough start with the oversized Western *Duel in the Sun*; although a commercial success, it was widely derided by critics and it still holds the stigma among many film scholars of being a failure. Subsequent productions, such as *The Paradine Case* (1947) and *Portrait of Jennie* (1948) were better received by the critics, but audiences stayed away. For the most part, Selznick never truly enjoyed success as a distributor; his only genuine hit was the 1950 U.S. theatrical release of *The Third Man*, in which he had a nominal production stake (his contract players Joseph Cotten and Alida Valli were the film's leading actors).

But *The Third Man* was not enough to float Selznick's boats. The lack of overall commercial success took its toll, and the late 1940s required Selznick to raise cash by selling away the rights to *Gone with the Wind* for $400,000, a move that he would rue for the remainder of his life. Most of his income came in loaning out talent he had under contract, especially actors Joseph Cotten and Ingrid Bergman and director Alfred Hitchcock. In this manner, Selznick seemed more like a talent broker than a producer.

In the 1950s, Selznick was something of a shadow of his former self. Financial limitations prevented him from achieving his dreams of grand productions, while attempts to create star vehicles for Jennifer Jones – most notably two Italian-based productions, *Indiscretion of an American Wife* (1953) and *A Farewell to Arms* (1957) – were embarrassing failures. He died in 1965, with *Gone with the Wind* recalled as his crowning achievement.

What went wrong for Selznick? Perhaps it was the curse of not being able to improve on perfection. After all, if someone is the producer of *Gone with the Wind*, how can you do better than that? But perhaps Selznick made the mistake of trying to outdo himself rather than expand into new territories. Unlike Goldwyn, whose output varied from drama to comedy to musical, Selznick in the post-*Gone with the Wind* period lacked the notion of presenting versatile offerings. Even after winning his second Best Picture Oscar for *Rebecca*, he only produced two films with Alfred Hitchcock as the director (*Spellbound* in 1945 and *The Paradine Case*), preferring to loan out Hitchcock to other studios (who, in turn, profited from the master filmmaker's talents).

Ultimately, Selznick's experience is one that can be found across the spectrum of the film industry and throughout other sectors: when you reach the top of your profession, where do you go from there? It's a puzzle that is still teasing and tormenting those who are ensnared in its thorns.

Walter Wanger

Today's average moviegoer will probably not recognize the name of Walter Wanger. But during Hollywood's Golden Era, Wanger was among the most prominent independent film producers.

Wanger came to independent cinema after spending much of the 1920s and early 1930s as an executive at Paramount, Columbia and MGM. Unhappy at working within the studio system, he managed to secure a unique opportunity in 1934 that enabled him to function as an independent producer whose films would be released by Paramount.

Wanger's Paramount films are barely recalled today; *The President*

Vanishes, Private Worlds, the Technicolor feature The Trail of the Lonesome Pine and The Moon's Our Home are his best known, and that's not saying much. Nonetheless, his films were profitable and his standing within the industry grew.

In July 1936, Wanger signed a ten-year contract to produce films for release through United Artists. His first effort was the highly regarded You Only Live Once, directed by Fritz Lang and starring Sylvia Sidney and Henry Fonda.

During the course of his decade with United Artists, Wanger's output was strictly hit-and-miss. The misses have drifted into obscurity (Vogues of 1938, I Met My Love Again, Stand-In, 52nd Street). But the hits are the reason Wanger is recalled today.

As a producer, Wanger brought moviegoers such classics as William Dieterle's Spanish Civil War drama Blockade (1938), Algiers (the 1938 Americanized version of Pepe Le Moko), John Ford's 1939 Stagecoach and 1940's The Long Voyage Home, Alfred Hitchcock's (1940) Foreign Correspondent and Fritz Lang's 1945 Scarlet Street.

Within the Hollywood establishment, Wanger was no one's idea of an outsider. He served as president of the Academy of Motion Picture Arts and Sciences from 1939 to 1945 and received an honorary Oscar in 1946 in tribute to his output. In addition to his producing, he created the 16mm educational company Young American Films Inc. and organized his own distribution company with Edward Nassour.

But continued success in the post-World War II film world proved strangely elusive. His production output did not generate any considerable box-office success: A Night in Paradise (1946), Smash-up: The Story of a Woman (1947), The Lost Moment (1947) and Tap Roots (1948) did not resonate with audiences.

Things took a turn for the worse when Wanger's mania to create a monster hit with the 1949 feature Joan of Arc proved to be a major embarrassment that helped derail his career. The film was blasted by critics and proved to be an expensive commercial failure, despite an elaborate promotional campaign and an Oscar-nominated performance by Ingrid Bergman as the doomed Maid of Orleans. Wanger was bitter by the film's poor reception and his behavior was borderline unprofessional. He created a great deal of animosity in Hollywood by refusing to accept an honorary Oscar, which was considered very bad form, since the tribute was admittedly presented as a consolatory honor to compensate for the film's failure to score a Best Picture nomination (a failure that Wanger openly denounced). But Wanger's rage didn't stop with the Academy: he publicly blamed of RKO for mismanaging the *Joan of Arc* release. That didn't endear him with his peers, especially when the studio itself lost money in the film's failure.

In 1951, Wanger found himself in the wrong spotlight when he accused his wife, actress Joan Bennett, of having an affair with agent Jennings Lang. Wanger confronted Bennett and Lang with a gun, shooting Lang in groin. Lang survived (in one piece, thank you), but Wanger was arrested and charged with attempted murder. Fortunately for Wanger, his attorney Jerry Giesler successfully pushed for a temporary insanity defense. The producer received a four-month sentence at the Castaic Honor Farm outside of Los Angeles.

After his release, Wanger was able to resume his career and actually created three films that are considered classics of independent cinema: *Riot in Cell Block 11* (1954), *Invasion of the Body Snatchers* (1956) and *I Want to Live!* (1958). Oddly, Wanger concluded his career with one of the most notorious studio films of all time: 20th Century-Fox's mammoth 1963 epic *Cleopatra*. For his role in the *Cleopatra* debacle, he was fired by the studio toward the end of the film's troubled production and became part of the morass of lawsuits that persisted long after that tired mess of a film slumped out of the theaters.

Wanger's name holds recognition with film scholars, who are aware of his role in the creation of many movie classics. Yet, unlike many of his peers, Wanger's name does not connect with the average moviegoer, even though films such as *Algiers, Stagecoach, Foreign Correspondent* and *I Want to Live!* are immediately recognizable. However, those films are recognized for the contributions of other artists: Hedy Lamarr's astonishing beauty in *Algiers*, John Wayne's star-establishing charisma in *Stagecoach* under John Ford's vigorous direction (Orson Welles claimed to have watched *Stagecoach* repeatedly to learn the language of cinema before making *Citizen Kane*), the Hitchcockian brilliance of *Foreign Correspondent* and Susan Hayward's brilliantly no-holds-barred Oscar-winning performance in *I Want to Live!*

The problem with Wanger, it would seem, was inconsistency. For every *Stagecoach*, there were too many forgettable pieces like *Salome, Where She Danced* (1945), with Yvonne De Carlo as an Austrian ballet star in the Old West. Wanger, unlike Selznick or Goldwyn, did not have a specific style that one immediately associated with his creative focus – everything from Westerns to frothy romantic comedies to prison movies to science fiction to historical epics; he was literally an anything-goes producer.

Of course, Wanger, in his capacity as producer, was the force that brought these memorable films together. If his name-recognition value is low today, the classics within his canon show no signs of losing their allure.

Walt Disney

During the silent-movie era, a number of animators set up independent production companies. In this period, animated films were strictly one-reel affairs designed to be distractions and fillers. Even though the market was limited, several talented individuals rose to the occasion. Winsor McCay, best known for *Gertie the Dinosaur*, led the way among cinematic animators, followed by the likes of Paul Terry, Amadee J. Van Beuren, Pat Sullivan, J.R. Bray, Willis O'Brien and Max and Dave Fleischer.

Also in the mix was an aggressive young man originally based out of Kansas City named Walt Disney. Today, most people do not think of Disney as an independent filmmaker. Indeed, after the early 1950s, Disney graduated from independent production to being the head of an entertainment conglomerate that rivaled and later surpassed the reigning studios of Hollywood. But for the period from the 1920s until the early 1950s, Disney occupied a unique position as being the leading independent producer of animated films.

Success wasn't always part of Disney's trade. During the silent era Disney was among the least successful of this sector – but not for lack of trying. Disney had the foresight to try to differentiate himself from his peers by creating films of significant style differences, starting with the *Alice* series in the 1920s. These shorts integrated live action (in this case, a little girl, vaguely inspired by Lewis Carroll's Wonderland-bound Alice) into a skein of adventures involving wacky animated characters.

However, the *Alice* films were fairly weak. Three different child performers played Alice during the course of the series (Virginia Davis, Margie Gay, Lois Hardwick), none earning anything in the way of viewer affection. The limitations of the early animated film technology made the mix of live action and animation visually crude – it was obvious the child was badly plopped in front of the cartoon characters. As for content, most of the action involved Julius, a feline character who bore more than a passing resemblance to Pat Sullivan's Felix the Cat. In most of the films, Alice barely appeared – and when she did turn up, it was usually in a reactive mode to Julius' antics.

From a business standpoint, Disney was at a disadvantage by working with Margaret J. Winkler, one of the few women working as an independent distributor in the 1920s. Winkler specialized in the distribution of animated shorts, but her enthusiasm for Disney's work was not measured by any success in bringing fame or fortune to the young animator. Winkler retired from the distribution business after marrying one of her competitors, Charles B. Mintz. And from here, Disney's story gets thorny.

Mintz hated the *Alice* films and wanted a new series that focused entirely on animated comedy. Disney, working with Ub Iwerks, developed Oswald the Lucky Rabbit. Mintz successfully sold Universal Pictures on acquiring Disney's Oswald cartoons for distribution, and Disney appeared to be on the fast track for success.

However, Disney was derailed when he discovered that Mintz orchestrated his contract with Disney in a way that he, not Disney, controlled the rights to the Oswald character. Correctly suspecting the animator would be pissed off, Mintz also went out of his way to hire most of

Disney's animation staff to continue the Oswald series without Disney's input. Needless to say, Disney was crushed and walked away from Oswald in 1928 – but, as we all know, something better was on the horizon.

That something better was Mickey Mouse, and Disney created two cartoons in 1928, *The Gallopin' Gaucho* and *Plane Crazy*. At first, Disney was stuck without distribution; no studio was interested in the character, which seemed too similar in personality to the well-known Oswald. But Disney finally hit pay dirt with a third Mickey Mouse cartoon, *Steamboat Willie*, which introduced the new sound technology to animated films in 1928.

At first, no distributor wanted to gamble on a talking cartoon film. Disney lucked out by gaining screen time at New York's Colony Theater without having a distributor for his short film. The strong audience reaction was enough to interest the studios, and Disney began receiving offers – including one, ironically, from Universal, which seemed oblivious to the damage it previous exacted with the Oswald fiasco.

Curiously, Disney chose to sign with Columbia Pictures, which at the time was a small yet scrappy studio that was eager to challenge the larger Hollywood power players. Having Disney's cartoons helped bring Columbia prestige and profits it was otherwise lacking. Disney, for his part, reconfigured the previously silent *The Gallopin' Gaucho* and *Plane Crazy* with sound effects and synchronized music, and began working exclusively on sound cartoons.

Other animation houses quickly followed suit by adding sound to their films, but they were too late to curry audience favor. Disney, in his ability to be the first to offer vocal dimension to his animated characters, opened new possibilities for the animation genre. Virtually overnight, Mickey Mouse became a global sensation, and Disney was able to build a mini-studio of new animated characters that possessed their own distinctive vocal and emotional personalities. (We don't really need to run an inventory of those characters.)

Yet, as an independent filmmaker, Disney never truly had a successful relationship with distributors. He severed ties with Columbia in 1932 over problems relating to the profits (or the lack thereof) from the release of his animated shorts. Disney took his output to United Artists, and that distribution company helmed the release of Disney's groundbreaking forays into three-strip Technicolor production with *Flowers and Trees* (1932). But that relationship soured with problems similar to the Columbia situation, so Disney then moved to a new partnership with RKO Radio Pictures, which broke new ground in the distributed of Disney's landmark feature-length filmmaking debut, *Snow White and the Seven Dwarfs* (1937).

Disney released films through RKO until 1953, when an abrupt series of disagreements over the content of films and distribution strategies ruptured the relationship between the producer and the studio. By this time, however, Disney had expanded far beyond exclusive animation work. During the 1940s, the studio enjoyed successful commissions from the U.S. and Canadian governments to create wartime propaganda films. Private sector corporations also hired Disney for promotional and industrial film production. Disney ventured back into live-action filmmaking, putting actors under contract and releasing films that mixed live action and animation (*So Dear to My Heart, Song of the South*) and then pure live-action films (beginning with *Treasure Island*). Disney also ventured into documentary filmmaking, which will be discussed later in this book.

By creating Buena Vista Pictures Distribution to bring his productions to theaters, Disney effectively ceased being an independent producer and was officially a full-fledged studio that handled the creation and release of its exclusive product. To date, no other independent animation production company has ever been able to duplicate that aspect of the Disney success story.

Disney's position in the history of independent cinema is somewhat anomalous. As the only major independent animation producer, he enjoyed success that his peers never hoped to achieve. That he was able to transcend the outsider position of independent producer into the ruling elite of studio power broker (and, later, head of the most important entertainment conglomerate in the U.S. that still bears his name) was a tribute to his tenacity and daring as a business innovator. That few people connect him with independent cinema is a sign of how far Disney's company traveled; the distance is so extraordinary that few can recall where the journey actually commenced.

Howard Hughes

The mysterious and elusive Howard Hughes first arrived in the movie world at the tail end of the silent era. Serving as a producer and working with United Artists as his distributor, he brought forth commercially successful films, including *Two Arabian Knights* (1927) and *The Racket* (1928). In 1930, Hughes tried his hand at directing with *Hell's Angels*. The World War I-inspired film ran over budget and was widely predicted by many industry cynics to fail, but audiences enjoyed Hughes' epic – particularly his exciting aerial battle scenes and his choice of leading lady, a little-known actress named Jean Harlow.

Hughes didn't appear to savor the life of a director and went back to producing after *Hell's Angels*. He put his money behind successful features, including the two features that are regarded as being his finest achievements as a producer: *The Front Page* (1931) and *Scarface* (1932). By the mid-1930s, however, Hughes withdrew from independent films to focus on other endeavors.

By the beginning of the 1940s, however, he came back to the sector with the movie that most people remember him for: *The Outlaw*. Thanks to aggressive publicity, this Western earned a level of notoriety unparalleled in Hollywood history. Even at this late date, the PR myths surrounding *The Outlaw* dominate with such fury that spin continues to be mistaken for truth.

As a public service to serious film lovers, let's clear the air on many myths surrounding *The Outlaw*.

MYTH: Jane Russell, Hughes' buxom protégé, is the title character in *The Outlaw*.

FACT: Although Jane Russell was the focus of the film's wonderfully tacky advertising, she is not The Outlaw of the title. That honor goes to one Jack Buetel, a former insurance clerk who plays Billy the Kid. Russell plays Rio, a half-breed girl who becomes Billy's lover.

If you've never heard of Buetel, that's because *The Outlaw* was the only significant film he made. Howard Hughes kept him under contract but off screen until 1951 (no public reason was ever given for this decade-long exile). Hughes even kept Buetel from being cast in *Red River* (Montgomery Clift got the role and became a superstar through his performance). By the time Buetel was able to work steadily on screen, he was unable to move beyond B-movies and TV guest appearances.

MYTH: Howard Hughes designed an aerodynamically superior bra to show off Jane Russell's 36D cleavage.

FACT: Yes, Hughes created such a bra. But Russell never wore it for *The Outlaw*. Russell would later complain that Hughes' bra was so painfully uncomfortable that she only wore it for a few seconds. But the legend of the bra became so prevalent that in later life Russell would express undisguised irritation at having to talk about it.

MYTH: *The Outlaw* is laced with seething homoeroticism between the male leads, Jack Buetel (as Billy the Kid) and Walter Huston (as Doc Holliday).

FACT: No, Howard Hughes didn't beat Ang Lee to *mano-a-mano* cowboy territory. For some queer reason (sorry about that pun), several writers insist that the Billy the Kid-Doc Holliday relationship in *The Outlaw* has gay undercurrents. It is unclear where this notion originated or how it could be supported, since the men spend the bulk of the film arguing about the ownership of a horse and the love of a girl – in that order. If any genuine emotion, even latent, was evident in the screenplay, it was certainly flattened on the screen due to the non-chemistry between Huston (who shamelessly overacts) and Buetel (who, sadly, was not very talented as an actor). While gay viewers may enjoy Russell's presence as old-style camp, they won't find any homo on the range in *The Outlaw*.

MYTH: Hughes, originally the producer of the film, fired director Howard Hawks and took over the direction of *The Outlaw*.

FACT: The exact nature of the Hawks-Hughes blow-up will probably never be determined. Some sources claim Hawks quit due to Hughes' meddling in the film. Other sources claim Hawks jumped ship to helm a superior production called *Sergeant York*. And others claim Hughes was angry that Russell's breasts weren't being given the attention they deserved on camera. In any event, Hughes was clearly not comfortable as a director and *The Outlaw* went wildly over budget due to his insistence on endless takes (a reflection both on his obsessive-compulsive behavior and his insecurity in not getting the right shots). Screenwriter Jules Furthman eventually took over for Hughes as director, but he did not receive screen credit for that work.

MYTH: *The Outlaw* generated major censorship problems.

FACT: In reality, much of the censorship problems were strictly of Hughes' creation, since Hollywood's censorship board cleared the film for theatrical release in May 1941. However, many state and municipal censors demanded cuts that Hughes initially refused to make. So Hughes shelved *The Outlaw* until February 1943, when he self-released the film in San Francisco. Local censors demanded that Hughes cut a 20-minute love sequence with Buetel and Russell, but he balked and shelved the film again for three years.

In 1946, Hughes agreed to re-release the film in San Francisco with the local censor's cuts, but apparently he provided the uncut print and the owner of the theater playing *The Outlaw* was arrested on morals charges.

United Artists, which had the distribution rights to the film, released it on a city-by-city road-show basis in order to deal with local censorship boards. The film didn't play in New York until September 1947.

Needless to say, the squabbles with the local censors created a publicity gold mine and *The Outlaw* was a major hit in every city where it played, becoming one of the most commercially successful independent films of Hollywood's Golden Age.

Despite the film's success, Hughes opted never to direct again. He produced two unsuccessful films, *Behind the Rising Sun* (1943) and Preston Sturges' ill-fated *The Sin of Harold Diddlebock* (1946), which he later re-edited and re-released (without success) in 1950 as *Mad Wednesday*. (Most critics believe the Hughes revision was superior to the Sturges original.)

In 1948, Hughes left the independent film world completely through his purchase of RKO Radio Pictures. His reign was widely regarded as disastrous, from both an artistic and commercial viewpoint. He sold the studio in 1955, but he left it in such a precariously weakened state that it folded within three years of his departure.

Through the string of commercial hits he enjoyed in the late 1920s and early 1930s and thanks to notoriety of *The Outlaw*, Hughes occupies a niche in independent cinema history.

Hal Roach

Among the independent producers of the Golden Age, Hal Roach was something of a curiosity. He was the sole producer who survived the silent era with an exclusive emphasis on comedy. His chief rival, Mack Sennett, was already running out of steam by the mid-1920s and hit the sound era as an enervated shadow of his former self. By the mid-1930s, Sennett was considered something of a has-been, churning out cheap shorts for low-rent production companies.

Roach, however, sailed through the silent-into-sound transition fairly easily. The 1930s were a boom time for him, and he was actually poised to go further in dramatic directions before World War II broke his stride (not to mention his operations).

Roach reportedly showed up in Hollywood in 1912 as an extra in silent film. Working in anonymity, he became friendly with another struggling movie-struck youth, Harold Lloyd. Roach was rescued from extra work thanks to a conveniently-timed inheritance, which enabled him to produce films starring Lloyd.

Success for Roach and Lloyd was slow in coming, but their persistence paid off. By the early 1920s, Lloyd was a major comedy star through Roach-produced efforts such as *Grandma's Boy* (1922) and *Safety Last* (1923). Lloyd then decided to become his own producer, leaving Roach without a star for his small independent studio.

Fortunately, Roach enjoyed a second lightning strike with a series of short comedies featuring a band of mischievous children. *The Our Gang* series was unique at several levels: the child ensemble was unusual for its era, and the characters were obviously the products of working-class homes (even back in the 1920s, the working class rarely saw themselves on film). Even more progressive was the racial integration of the ensemble; despite occasional lapses into stereotype humor, the black children in the cast were treated as equals to their white playmates.

Our Gang was a hit, but for a while it was Roach's only hit. He attempted to build other series around solo comics and even a group of trained chimps called the Dippy Doo-Dads. He even brought in over-the-hill dramatic stars, including Herbert Rawlinson and Theda Bara, to star in two-reel comedies, but that proved to be a poor idea.

Then lightning struck a third time: the accidental pairing of Stan Laurel (a British comic who never quite found a niche as a comedy star) and Oliver Hardy (a Georgia-born character actor relegated to playing comic villains for second-tier funnymen like Billy West and Larry Semon) in a 1927 short called *Duck Soup*. The result of that serendipitous accident was ... well, do you really need more information on that?

By the late 1920s and the early 1930s, everything seemed to be going right for Roach. With his distributor, the U.S. branch of Pathé, Roach signed a lucrative deal with MGM. (Sennett, ironically, was also using Pathé for his distribution needs, but failed to secure a mooring elsewhere.) The success of Our Gang and Laurel and Hardy enabled Roach to expand his output with the likes of Charley Chase, Max Davidson and Thelma Todd (who was teamed with ZaSu Pitts and, later, Patsy Kelly in a series of sadly-forgotten shorts). Behind the camera, Roach gave big breaks to young directors, including Leo McCarey, George Marshall and George Stevens.

Roach concentrated on short film production until the early 1930s, until he slowly began to edge toward sound features. By the mid-1930s, he was ready to jettison the short subjects completely. He also decided to take a very unusual turn away from his tried-and-true formula, pursuing higher-budgeted prestige offerings.

His gamble paid off, with films like *Topper* (1937), *Of Mice and Men*

(1939), *Captain Fury* (1940) and *One Million B.C.* (1940). Roach sold the *Our Gang* franchise to MGM in 1938 and then cut ties with the studio, signing United Artists to handle his distribution.

Somewhat controversially (at least in retrospect), he allowed Laurel and Hardy to leave his fold. Despite the commercial popularity of their films, Roach and the comics always had a strained relationship. Endless problems on contract renewals and disagreements on the content of the comedy films took its toll on both sides – Roach wanted to move away from the lowbrow comedy in favor of classier fare, while the duo were eager for a new beginning. Laurel and Hardy left Roach in 1940 and signed with 20th Century-Fox, which actually turned out to be a major mistake for them (they were slotted into undistinguished B-level fare and their careers sped to a close by 1945).

Roach seemed to be on a winning formula, but World War II disrupted his stride.

Although he was 50 when war broke out, he was called to active duty and put his production work aside. Roach's studio was leased to the U.S. Army Air Forces, where the First Motion Picture Unit made 400 training and propaganda films.

In Roach's absence, his production company attempted to stay afloat by producing featurettes that were billed as "Streamliners." Running an awkward 40 to 50 minutes, they found no favor with audiences and exhibitors.

After the war, Roach was not able to regain his success. Lacking financing, he was forced to produce cheap features with undistinguished casts. The advent of television saved Roach, as he refocused his studio's facilities to accommodate the production of TV shows. He also syndicated his old short films, most successfully the Laurel and Hardy comedies and the original *Our Gang* capers (the latter was renamed "The Little Rascals").

If Roach, as a producer, has not quite received the level of stature and praise that he deserves, at least his canon cannot be ignored. Of all the independent producers of his era, he certainly brought the most happiness to movie audiences.

Charles Chaplin

Of all the major independent filmmakers of the Hollywood Golden Era, Chaplin had the most tumultuous career. His output was limited – five feature films between 1931 and 1952 – and public sentiment toward the artist veered wildly from gushy adoration to seething anger during this period.

Chaplin released *The Circus* in 1928, which coincided with Hollywood's turmoil over the arrival of sound-recording technology. Comedy was being redefined through the introduction of dialogue, sound effects and song – the brilliant pantomime of the silent era's comedies were suddenly seen as passé.

By 1929, the studios began importing comedy headliners from Broadway and vaudeville to star in both features and shorts. The idea made sense: bringing in talent who could use dialogue to generate laughs, but the resulting efforts were often filmed plays where the comic timing was marred by stagnant production values. Only the Marx Brothers became bigger stars after leaving the stage for the screen. Others, such as Fanny Brice, Jack Benny and the team of George Burns and Gracie Allen, used their less-than-memorable Hollywood films as a stepping stone to a more lucrative future in radio. And others, including the comedy teams Wheeler and Woolsey and Clark and McCullough, turned out dreadful films that are barely recalled today by anyone except masochistic cinephiles.

This commotion over funny people with adequate voices was actually not necessary, since most of the reigning comedians of the silent screen had no problems handling dialogue. Harold Lloyd, Buster Keaton, Harry Langdon and Laurel and Hardy all had fine voices that recorded well. Only Raymond Griffith was left behind; he had suffered a vocal cord injury in his youth that left him with a raspy whisper of a voice. After a brief role as a silent dying soldier in the classic drama *All Quiet on the Western Front* (1930), he retired from the screen and concentrated the remainder of his career in writing and producing.

But the problem that emerged had nothing to do with the quality of the comics' voices, but rather their ability to adapt their well-known styles of a medium that incorporated sound into the mix. A few cases were successful. Laurel and Hardy maintained their slapstick knockabout while keeping dialogue to a relative minimum, which worked wonders for their brand of comedy. W.C. Fields, who had a significant (if desultory) silent film career, found the deeper texture to his on-screen persona through the imaginative use of his highly distinctive voice. Marion Davies, who scored respect as a light comedienne in the final stretch of the silent era, worked hard to overcome a slight stammer and emerged with hitherto unexpected talent for both dialect humor and songs. Even the blacklisted Roscoe "Fatty" Arbuckle was able to return to the screen as the star of a series of two-reelers that revealed his deft handling of dialogue.

Instead, the problem required a new consideration of framing screen comedy. Sound forced new requirements on direction and editing, and the dizzying pace of silent comedies could not be duplicated during the early years of the talkies. Harold Lloyd and Buster Keaton learned that the hard way in their unsuccessful attempts to duplicate their classic silent-era sight gags into their sound films.

Even more complex, from a business standpoint, was exporting sound films to international markets, particularly countries and regions where English was not spoken. Silent movies were the closest thing the world experienced to a lingua franca – intertitles could easily be changed, thus offering the entertainment to audiences in any part of the globe. But sound suddenly localized movies to a particular country. Dubbing and subtitles were slow in coming to the new talkies, and some studios made an effort to appease their overseas audiences by creating multi-lingual versions of their major films. This didn't always work, particularly when the American stars were forced to speak uncomfortable phonetic approximations of unfamiliar languages. (Spanish-speaking audiences reportedly laughed at Laurel and Hardy's misguided slaughter of their language.)

Not every country's cinemas were immediately wired for sound – China and Japan were producing and showing silent films well into the mid-1930s – and many silent movies were re-released in the early 1930s with new synchronized music scores and goofy sound effects added to compensate for the lack of dialogue. But for the most part the world had forsaken the silent movie by the late 1920s.

Except for Chaplin. As his own producer and (through his stake in United Artists) his own distributor, he was comfortable in setting his own rules. But Chaplin's rules put him in conflict with his Hollywood peers, who invested considerable money into the erasure of silent movies in favor of an all-talking medium. When word seeped out that Chaplin was following the silent production *The Circus* with another silent production, as opposed to a sound film, many people in the industry were aghast. There were more twitters as Chaplin's production dragged on; not only was he making a silent movie, but it was turning into a highly expensive one.

There was also another matter. Chaplin's output rested solely on films where he was the star. As mentioned earlier, he made two attempts to create serious dramatic features designed to elevate his long-time leading lady, Edna Purviance, to standalone stardom. Not willing to risk his money in any venture where he was not front and center in his familiar Little Tramp persona, Chaplin was forced to make himself his own star.

Chaplin also didn't see how his Little Tramp creation would possible exist in the sound medium. Without a specific accent or idiom, the persona was literally a universal character. His strength was physical agility coupled with an indefatigable spirit. Putting jokes on his lips would limit his appeal and keeping him mute in an all-talk world (as with Harpo Marx amidst the Marx Brothers' lunacy) was not a feasible solution.

Three years passed between the release of *The Circus* and the premiere of *City Lights*, which cost a reported $1.5 million to create and was plagued by delays and disruptions, including Chaplin's rash firing of non-professional Virginia Cherrill as his leading lady in favor of Georgia Hale, his star of *The Gold Rush*, only to require Cherrill's return at a much higher fee when Hale proved unsatisfactory in the role.

City Lights was ready for screenings in 1931, but exhibitors balked at putting a silent movie in their venues. Even though Chaplin was still considered the world's greatest comic star, a silent movie in 1931 was considered commercially suicidal. United Artists was repeatedly rejected by New York's major theaters when it tried to book the *City Lights* premiere, forcing Chaplin to rent a run-down stage theater, install a projection booth, and present his movie in a four-wall format.

Of course, Chaplin proved everyone wrong with the astonishing commercial success of *City Lights*. While not a silent film, per se (it had a synchronized score and sound effects, including the effective instrumental mimicking of vocal patterns), its lack of dialogue did not keep audiences away. But at the same time, it didn't make Hollywood stop and reconsider the viability of silent movies. Chaplin's triumph was an anomaly and the industry was sore over his one-upmanship (to the point of excluding *City Lights* from Academy Award nominations).

But Chaplin realized he could not hold out in solitary silence. His next film, *Modern Times* (1936), incorporated ingenious slices of dialogue into its soundtrack of synchronized music and sound effects. Chaplin finally acquiesced to the microphone's presence and made his voice heard, albeit in a song consisting of gibberish lyrics. Yet at this time, problems began emerging. Some audiences were uncomfortable with perceived left-wing political statements that permeated the film's sequences about striking factory workers. Self-appointed moral custodians were more concerned over the nature of Chaplin's relationship with leading lady Paulette Goddard; no one was certain if they were married, and neither performer was willing to confirm or deny such a union. The U.S. box office for *Modern Times* was weaker than *City Lights*, though favorable reaction overseas boosted the film's commercial success.

But the overseas market disappeared by the time Chaplin was ready with his next film, *The Great Dictator*. As with *City Lights*, the film industry was apprehensive about an overt satirical slam at Hitler and what it would mean for exports to the German market (Hollywood films were still playing in Germany until America's entry into World War II). Hitler controlled most of continental Europe by 1940, when *The Great Dictator* was ready, and the film was obviously not welcome in Nazi-controlled cinemas. (Reportedly, Hitler acquired a print and saw the film twice, but his reactions were never recorded.) The film was unseen by most

Europeans until 1946, at which time the film was painfully dated for audiences who survived wartime's ravages.

However, there was no apprehension about Chaplin's ability to adapt to the sound film medium. In *The Great Dictator*, he was able to maintain brilliant pantomime routines where music and sound effects complemented the visual gags. But then there was a dialogue concern. In his dual-role performance as the faux-Hitler and a victimized Jewish barber within *The Great Dictator*, Chaplin became the last star of silent era to make the transition to sound (13 years after the debut of *The Jazz Singer*). His voice was perfectly fine, yet a new problem arose: Chaplin suddenly seemed to fall madly in love with the sound technology and the concept of reciting dialogue. Great heaps of dialogue, to be specific. *The Great Dictator* is an extremely verbose movie, and for the remainder of his career Chaplin would field complaints that his films became wall-to-wall talk.

This was initially raised in 1942 when Chaplin re-released *The Gold Rush* with a new narration that he delivered in deeply plumy tones that did not mesh with the hardscrabble action in the film. This version of *The Gold Rush* is difficult to endure because of its irritating narration, but Chaplin insisted on keeping this in circulation as the official version while removing the silent original from circulation. (Perhaps mercifully, the original silent edition of *The Gold Rush* fell into the public domain and is the more widely-seen version.)

Verbosity also crushed the appreciation of Chaplin's last two American films, *Monsieur Verdoux* (1947) and *Limelight* (1952). But other issues helped create problems that Chaplin could not easily elude.

Post-World War II attitudes hardened in relation to left-wing politics, and anyone who was even vaguely considered to be sympathetic to the Communist cause was viewed as a traitor. While *Monsieur Verdoux* was basically a black comedy about a man who marries and murders rich women, the film's brazen negative commentary on the connection between capitalism and war seemed seditious to many right wingers. Coupled with ill-conceived public notions of Chaplin's alleged political philosophies, the comedy of *Monsieur Verdoux* generated few laughs in 1947 America.

As with *City Lights*, Chaplin needed to four-wall a legitimate New York theater to premiere *Monsieur Verdoux*, but, in this case, public hostility to Chaplin was at such a virulent pitch that the film's opening grosses were astonishingly low. Despite a sympathetic Oscar nomination for its screenplay, United Artists barely released the film in the U.S. Once again, the world came to Chaplin's rescue and favorable international response saved *Monsieur Verdoux* from total financial ruin.

Chaplin attempted to turn the tide back in his favor with the 1950 re-release of *City Lights*, and the film was able to enjoy a better release than *Monsieur Verdoux*. Even *Time Magazine* (not exactly a fan of left wingers) praised *City Lights* in re-release, proclaiming it the greatest film of the first half of the 20th century. But it was a minor and fleeting victory. *Limelight*, although thoroughly non-political with its benign tale of an aging London music hall star's belated comeback, was blocked from wide release due to excessive pressure by right-wing political groups.

United Artists was unable to secure any West Coast exhibitions for the film, and in the rest of the country it only played in theaters in major metropolitan sectors. A final injurious insult took place when Chaplin sailed to England in October 1952 for the *Limelight* London premiere – the U.S. State Department announced it would not allow his return (Chaplin never took out American citizenship).

Time eventually proved to be Chaplin's ally. Twenty years after the *Limelight* debacle, Chaplin returned to Hollywood to receive an honorary Academy Award. And *Limelight* finally enjoyed a full U.S. theatrical, including a two-decades-late Hollywood premiere (which enabled it to be eligible for, and win, an Oscar for its charming music score). By that time, however, Chaplin had long since sold out his interest in United Artists and *Limelight* was released theatrically by Columbia Pictures.

William Randolph Hearst

William Randolph Hearst was one of the most famous – though least successful – independent producers during Hollywood's Golden Age. The newspaper magnate found himself in the middle of the Hollywood vortex thanks to a frenzied but futile attempt to sell the movie-going public on Marion Davies.

Most people only know of Hearst and Davies through Orson Welles' *Citizen Kane*, which offered a thinly veiled caricature of Hearst. While few people would rush to Hearst's defense against the way Welles presented him, it needs to be stated that Welles's film offered a cruelly distorted slander of Davies (something Welles admitted years later). Unlike the shrill, miserable and talent-free woman played by Dorothy Comingore in *Citizen Kane*, the real Marion Davies was a warm, generous and genuinely talented individual. The problem, however, was not Davies' ability but her connection to Hearst, who was a polarizing, controversial and (quite frankly) megalomaniacal personality. He was also a married man who lived in an openly adulterous relationship with Davies, which flaunted the taboo against non-monogamous unions in Hollywood.

Hearst founded Cosmopolitan Productions in 1918 with the original mission to create the Davies-starring feature *Cecilia of the Pink Roses*, and for the next two decades Hearst financed a long series of Davies vehicles. What many people fail to realize is that Davies might have been able to advance in films without Hearst's backing – her first feature film was actually 1917's *Runaway Romany*, which was written by Davies and directed by George W. Lederer, a Broadway producer and her brother-in-law.

Having Hearst's backing was a blessing *and* a curse for Davies. Hearst's publishing power enabled him to secure distribution deals for the Cosmopolitan-produced titles with Paramount, MGM and Warner Bros. Since the studios were eager to curry favorable press coverage from the Hearst newspapers, they put great effort into the promotion of the Cosmopolitan films.

However, the films were often not worthy of such sweetheart deals. Hearst's spare-no-expense approach to producing drove up budgets, to the point that many of his films were unable to recoup their expenses. There is a story, perhaps apocryphal, where Hearst is conversing with a stranger at a Hollywood studio. "You know," the stranger allegedly said, "there's plenty of money in movies."

"I know," Hearst reportedly replied. "Mine "

It also didn't help that Hearst lavished Davies with a eleven-room portable bungalow, which was transported between the studios where Cosmopolitan Productions had distribution deals. In an industry where one-upmanship was a finely-tuned craft, such a display (particularly on an actress who was not among the top box-office stars of the day) could have easily created more than a little resentment.

Then there was the problem of the content of Davies' films. Hearst had a passion for period epics and emotional melodramas. Davies was simply an adequate presence in these films, providing great beauty as a screen presence but rarely connecting on an emotional level with the hackneyed screenplays and the one-dimensional characters she was asked to play.

But if Davies treaded water in melodrama, she thrived in light comedies. Indeed, films such as *Show People* and *The Patsy* (both directed by King Vidor in 1928) showed Davies had a natural, charming appeal that did not require highlighting via expensive costumes or excessive set design. Davies displayed a wonderful sense of comic timing, bringing effervescence and spirit to her farcical surroundings.

In the transition to sound films, Davies also showed a fine flair for musicals, particularly in *Going Hollywood* (1932), where she held her own opposite Bing Crosby. This should not have been a surprise, since her career first took root in stage revues.

Alas, a combination of failing box-office returns, Hearst's antagonistic relationships with the studio chieftains, and Davies' health problems relating to alcohol addiction (reportedly brought on by the stress of her Hearst-driven film career) brought Davies' career to a close with *Ever Since Eve* in 1937.

Strangely, many people assume Cosmopolitan Productions existed solely to present Marion Davies films. In fact, the company was responsible for some fairly remarkable productions that had nothing to do with Davies: *The Mask of Fu Manchu* (1932), *Gabriel Over the White House* (1933), *Men in White* (1934), *Manhattan Melodrama* (1934), *The Thin Man* (1934), *The Story of Louis Pasteur* (1935), *Captain Blood* (1935),

Howard Hawks' *Ceiling Zero* (1936), *The Story of Alexander Graham Bell* (1938) and John Ford's *Young Mr. Lincoln* (1939). It should be noted that Hearst was not directly involved in the making of these films – instead, the executives in his much-maligned production company were the driving force in their creation. There is no small irony that the best of Cosmopolitan Productions had one thing in common; Marion Davies was not in their casts

Clearly, Hearst and Davies register a footnote in the development of independently-produced cinema. But it would be unfair to their memory if one judges their contributions solely by the fiction of *Citizen Kane*. Hearst's inability to turn Davies into America's favorite movie star was evidence that even the greatest financial power cannot dictate popular taste. And Davies' career shows that she is more than deserving of a fresh look.

Outside of the Walls

Beyond Hollywood's power elite was another independent cinema. These films lacked the budgets, prestige and distribution outreach enjoyed by the likes of Goldwyn, Selznick and company. In their day, they received little attention from the mainstream media and, to some extent, the mainstream movie-going public. Today, however, they are seen as important parts of both the overall development of the American cinema and American sociology.

Race Films

One of the more unfortunate aspects of popular culture in the first part of the 20th century was the role that motion pictures played in reinforcing racism against African Americans. Negative stereotypes did not begin in the movies, of course, but the power of the medium helped reinforce notions designed solely to demean and humiliate an entire demographic – not only at home, but to global audiences who had no interactions with African Americans and, thus, only knew what they saw in the movies.

In the early years of the film industry, African Americans were rarely welcomed before the cameras. A very few prominent entertainers managed to secure some camera time: ragtime composer Scott Joplin in a now-lost experimental sound film shot during the 1904 World's Fair in St. Louis and vaudeville headliner Bert Williams in a couple of short comedies.

But for films where African-American characters were present, scurrilous depictions were par for the course. Granted, the presentation was designed for comic effect, albeit gag-filled silliness that relied too heavily on racial stereotypes to secure a laugh. Offerings such as *Who Said Chicken?* (1900) and *A Nigger in a Woodpile* (1904) used white actors in blackface to depict African Americans as oafish miscreants. Even the relatively few films that attempted to show some degree of maturity to the subject, such as the various film adaptations of *Uncle Tom's Cabin*, inevitably diluted their effectiveness through the use of white performers in blackface (usually cartoonish minstrel show-worthy make-up, as opposed to a genuine effort to achieve transracial identity).

Needless to say, African Americans were acutely aware of the power and influence of motion pictures in shaping racial attitudes. The early years of the 20th century were marked by the nascent stirrings of the civil rights movement, and the demands of social and economic equality were not helped by movies showing African Americans as harmless and silly imbeciles. There was very little pleasure among black audiences in viewing this type of entertainment.

But that led to another problem – being able to actually *see* these films. Segregation prevented African Americans from enjoying equal access to cinemas. In the Deep South, African Americans found movie going limited to theaters that either catered exclusively to blacks or to white-run theaters that set either aside specific times of the week for black-only audiences. Some theaters tried to appear progressive by keeping black patrons seated apart from their white counterparts (usually in balconies). Of course, it is unfair to state theater segregation was unique to the Deep South, since more than a few theaters above the Mason-Dixon Line also enforced such miserable practices. Some black-owned theaters existed in some predominantly black neighborhoods across the country, but these were usually small venues that rarely received the choice quality of film titles.

Due to this social environment, the African-American community in the early 20th century lacked the political and economic leverage to agitate for a positive on-screen depiction (calling for the integration in the filmmaking process itself would have been asking too much at this period). But as a result of this situation, something strange and unusual began to take root: a parallel universe of films made exclusively for black audiences, featuring all-black casts in settings where racial humiliation did not take place. They were known as the "race" films.

From the early 1910s to the mid-1950s, at least 500 race films were produced. It is believed that only 100 survive, though some titles may still be extant in undiscovered corners of archives and private collections. Most of the lost films come from the silent era, which disrupts any attempt to trace the genre's beginnings, although some sound-era titles are also missing and presumed lost. Feature films, short subjects, and even black-oriented newsreels were created, mostly by white production companies and white filmmakers. However, there were cases where black-owned companies and African-American creative artists were able to bring their own vision to the screen.

No one is entirely certain just where the race films began, though most scholars point to 1910 when William Foster, an African-American press agent based in Chicago, created the Foster Photoplay Company and made a short comedy called *The Pullman Porter*. The film is considered lost today, but it is believed to be a slapstick comedy with an all-black cast. A similar film, *The Railroad Porter*, was made in 1912, and a short called *The Butler* was made in 1913. Alas, commercial success eluded Foster when he attempted to serve as his own distributor, and his output ended with *The Butler*.

Foster's lead inspired other black entrepreneurs to follow suit. A flurry of black-owned film production companies began to open during the mid- and late-1910s: the Peter P. Jones Photoplay Company, the Afro-American Film Company, Haynes Photoplay, Lincoln Motion Picture Company and Whipper's Reel Negro News. The companies primarily focused on shorts and newsreels, with a fairly strong emphasis on coverage of prominent civil rights leaders and African Americans in military service.

The most ambitious of these companies was the Lincoln Motion Picture Company. Founded by Noble Johnson (an actor) and his brother George (a postal employee), the Los Angeles-based company boldly stated its mission was "to picture the Negro as he is in his every day, a human being with human inclination, and one of talent and intellect."

The company's first production, a three-reel drama called *The Realization of a Negro's Ambition* (1916), was unusual in that it offered a mixed race cast. The film followed the adventure of a Tuskegee Institute engineering graduate who rescues the daughter of an oil company owner from a vehicular accident. As a reward, he is given a job with the oil company's exploration team and helps his new employer locate a new oil field.

Lincoln Motion Picture Company made five more films after *The Realization of a Negro's Ambition* before folding in 1921. As with William Foster's effort, distribution problems limited the endeavor's commercial viability.

Also complicating matters was the unusual good fortune of founder Noble Johnson, who broke the color line in Hollywood and enjoyed a long career in feature films as a supporting character actor. Contemporary audiences will probably know him best as the island tribal chieftain in *King Kong*, but Johnson often played characters of varied races – in the course of his career, he turned up as an American Indian, Arab, Latino and a Pacific Islander (he played Qeequoq in the 1930 version of *Moby Dick*).

Johnson's company may have enjoyed a longer life had a fateful encounter with a brash, aggressive aspiring filmmaker gone differently. The filmmaker in question was named Oscar Micheaux.

Oscar Micheaux

Oscar Micheaux was not the first African-American filmmaker, and few people will argue he was the most talented. But his indefatigable spirit and groundbreaking work in production and distribution earned a place of historic significance not only within the race film genre, but in the full realm of independent cinema. Sadly, many people only think of Micheaux within the narrow fringe of race films, unaware that his achievements continue to resonate in the lives of independent filmmakers of all colors.

Micheaux was the ultimate example of a self-made man: a onetime shoeshine boy and Pullman porter who enjoyed his first financial success as a farmer in an all-white section of South Dakota. Without training as a writer or connections in the publishing industry, Micheaux authored a novel called *The Conquest* in 1913 and self-published the text. For distribution, he sold it door-to-door across his state, which must have come as something as a surprise to white South Dakotans in 1913, having a self-confident African American show up unannounced at their door offering copies of a black-themed novel for sale.

A turn of very bad luck in 1915 (the loss of his farm due to financial mishandling by his father-in-law) was actually a new opportunity in disguise: Micheaux relocated to Sioux City, Iowa, to start his own publishing company. He authored the books and sold them door-to-door across the Midwest. Many doorbells later, Micheaux was able to recoup his fortune.

In 1918, he received an offer from the Lincoln Motion Picture Company to make a film of his novel *The Homesteader*. Micheaux, who had no connection to the film world prior to this invitation, welcomed the offer but insisted that he direct the film. Since he had no experience in filmmaking, Micheaux's request was summarily rejected. Undaunted, Micheaux created his own production company, raised funds, returned to South Dakota with an all-black cast and crew, and created an eight-reel version of *The Homesteader*.

No print of *The Homesteader* survives, so it is impossible to offer opinions on its artistic value. What is known, however, was Micheaux's success in making it a commercial hit. Serving as his own distributor, he traveled city-to-city with a print and advertising materials for *The Home-steader*. Realizing that exhibitors would not be welcoming of a one-shot distributor, Micheaux also traveled with publicity stills of what he stated was his next production and a contract for the exhibitor to have the first rights to show this new film. The inconvenient fact that the next film only existed as publicity stills did not faze Micheaux; the exhibitors were not wise to this. In using this technique, Micheaux was able to self-finance and self-release 30 feature films during the 1920s.

Even more interesting was Micheaux's ability to get his film released in Europe. There are unconfirmed reports that he opened an office in London, but it is known that he sailed to Europe to sell his films in over-seas markets. This was highly unusual, since race films were virtually unknown outside of the African-American community and their com-mercial value to foreign audiences were considered nil. In retrospect, Micheaux's European foray helped preserve his legacy since two of his most notable productions, *Within Our Gates* (1920) and *Symbol of the Unconquered* (1921) were considered lost in the U.S. but were later recovered in European archives.

Micheaux was also an uncommonly daring filmmaker who tackled subject matter that was considered highly inflammatory in its day: lynch-ing, interracial romance, social and economic injustice against African Americans, prostitution, and corruption among African-American com-munity and religious leaders. Micheaux's willingness to fight censorship boards and present provocative films put him beyond the narrow limits of race films and decades ahead of his time.

Sadly, Micheaux's success skein hit a major obstacle with the intro-duction of sound technology to motion pictures. While he could quickly and cheaply churn out silent movies, the inclusion of sound created higher production costs. This was coupled with the abrupt collapse of many independent cinemas catering to African-American communities and the rise of better-financed white-run companies specializing in race film production.

Yet, Micheaux did not give up, and he proceeded into the 1930s by averaging one or two films a year. By the 1940s, however, his output was exhausted and the decade only saw two features from Micheaux: *The Notorious Elinor Lee* in 1940 and *The Betrayal* in 1949. Ironically, *The Betrayal* broke the color barrier and was booked in a New York theater with a predominantly white clientele. It was a critical and commercial flop, and the film disappeared; seemingly forever (it is now considered to be a lost film). Micheaux died two years after the release of *The Betrayal*, but his passing was barely noted in the African-American media and completely ignored by the white-run press.

Viewed from today's safe distance, Micheaux's value to independent cinema rests in his business skills and his daring to challenge the white establishment by creating and maintaining a successful commercial operation. One wishes that praise could be lavished on his films, but even Micheaux's most ardent supporters would blanch at that notion. Quite frankly, his artistic output left a lot to be desired.

Admittedly, it is impossible to enjoy a complete appreciation of his canon since the majority of his films are considered lost and many of the surviving films are not extant and require proper restoration. What does survive, however, is on the shaky side, and Micheaux the creative artist is consistent by putting forth movies that are riddled with garbled storylines, uneven acting, threadbare productions and lethargic direction.

Perhaps the greatest compliment to racial equality (and the greatest criticism of the man's creative aspirations) is to judge Micheaux's films on their artistic merits, rather than their sociological value. *Time Magazine's* Richard Corliss, who is not given to hyperbole, said of the filmmaker: "Micheaux was the D.W. Griffith of race cinema. And also its Edward D. Wood, Jr. ... Micheaux's work represents the apogee or nadir of Bad filmmaking. His close study of Griffith's visual lexicography got him through the silent period, but the demands for realism in sound films harshly exposed his inadequacies of technique ... The director seems not only to have learned nothing from 30 years of filmmaking, but also to have seen no other films."

Village Voice critic J. Hoberman was even crueler: "The longer Mi-

cheaux made films, the badder they got ... Micheaux's films define objective badness. His camera ground relentlessly on while the key light
wandered, traffic noise obliterated the dialogue, or a sound man's arm
intruded upon the frame. Actors blew their cues, recovered and continued ... Thirty years before Warhol, Micheaux approached *mise-en-scene*
Degree Zero. Left stranded in scenes that are grossly overextended, his
performers strike fantastic poses, stare affectingly into space or gaze
casually off-camera."

But Eric Monder, a Micheaux scholar and a reviewer for *Film Journal International*, sums up Micheaux's importance succinctly: "Oscar Micheaux inspires me personally as the first true 'indie' feature director
and the first real 'hyphenate' director-actor-producer-writer-distribu-
tor. Moreover, Micheaux has probably influenced and inspired many
filmmakers who have never even heard of him. The more I learn about
Oscar Micheaux and what he achieved, the more impressed I become.
His visionary approach also extends to the sensitive and often controversial topics he tackled, probably at considerable professional and personal risk. I am amazed by his frank, unflinching perspective about race,
religion and gender, among other subjects."

The Race Film Comes of Age

During the 1920s and 1930s, Micheaux was the only active African-
American filmmaker to work regularly. During this era, black directors were relatively few and exclusively limited to black-owned production companies. Nearly all of the black directors were male, but a
few women were able to get time behind the camera: Tressie Souders
became the first black female to direct a film with *A Woman's Errors*
in 1922, followed by Maria P. Williams in 1923 with her direction of
Flames of Wrath. Eloyce Gist was the first black female director of the
sound era with *Verdict Not Guilty*, made in 1933. Zora Neale Hurston,
the celebrated novelist and playwright, could be considered the first
black female documentary filmmaker; she shot a few 16mm shorts in
the Deep South during the late 1920s and again in 1940 as a record

for ethnographic studies; these films, however, were not theatrically released and are primarily known today only to sociologists and not general audiences.

By the 1920s, there were more than thirty production companies that focused exclusively on producing race films. As mentioned earlier, Oscar Micheaux's films were notable for addressing controversial social and political issues that related to African Americans. But in this case, Micheaux's taste for controversy made him an exception to the genre.

The race films, for all intents and purposes, were strictly all-black versions of the all-white films that dominated the cinemas. The productions followed the basic conventions of melodrama, light comedies, gangster films, Westerns, horror movies and (following the coming of sound) musical revues. The focus was on entertainment, not provocation. While Micheaux would dare to address lynching or interracial relations, the vast majority of race films were created without any underlying socio-political agenda.

But that's not to say the films did not carry their own coded messages. From today's perspective, the hidden language of the race films is difficult to decipher. One needs to put these productions in their proper time frame and to understand the circumstances of their exhibition. The original race film audiences were, overwhelmingly, working class or (at best) lower middle class. Many of these people were only recently relocated from rural isolation of the South to the urban environment of the North. Discrimination, both overt and casual, were a daily occurrence – employment, schooling, housing, healthcare, banking and leisure activities were strictly and callously defined along racial lines, and African Americans suffered humiliation on an almost daily basis in their interactions with white America.

This is not to say there wasn't a black elite in regard to politics, business, culture or education. But the elite represented a slender fraction of the general black population. For every Langston Hughes that achieved success in literature or Madam C.J. Walker who earned millions in business, there were millions of African Americans struggling to keep their lives intact.

The race films, not unlike the Hollywood fare of the Great Depression years, created a parallel universe of escapism. The poverty, discrimination and turmoil that plagued the real world was absent from the reel world. A very different world existed in the race films, populated by beautiful people in well-tailored clothing who enjoyed fine surroundings and were able to command their careers and activities. It was a world where black people didn't answer to the white man – if only because white men almost never walked through this realm. (One of the very few appearances by a white performer in a race film took place in the 1947 comedy *Boy! What a Girl!* In a jarring sequence, drummer Gene Krupa turned up to jam with a black jazz band. Krupa's presence was referred to strictly in a jokey manner – he invited the band members to visit him in his next movie – but the odd appearance of a white performer in an otherwise all-black world was never remarked upon in that film. Freddie Bartholomew, the one-time MGM child star, also made a guest appearance in a race film, the 1947 *Sepia Cinderella*, where he played himself in a nightclub scene.)

But many of the race films went beyond fluffy diversion. Some productions placed an emphasis (sometimes subtle, more often not) on the value of education and hard work, with the goal of achieving economic self-sufficiency. Integration and social equality in a broader context were alien concepts to this genre. If anything, the race films drove home a subtle message of a separate society.

Indeed, the separateness created a wealth of black screen characters that had no equivalent in mainstream movies. Within the race films, African Americans assumed the roles of doctors, lawyers, judges, police officers, private investigators, businessmen, nurses, teachers, cowboys, mobsters, beauty queens, secretaries, soldiers and classical musicians. Compared to the Hollywood formula that presented African Americans strictly as maids, servants or valets, the race films offered the sole cinematic source of black role models.

But there was also, sadly, a crass distinction of color as the determining factor that separated the haves and have-nots. The race films fell into a strange and sad pattern where the lightest-skinned performers enjoyed the romantic leading roles while the darker-skinned performers were limited to playing villains or comedy relief. Even Micheaux fell into the trap repeatedly with his color-based casting decisions. The irony of the situation is difficult to understand today: creating subdivisions within a community that, based on racial prejudice, was dislodged from the fabric of American society.

Yet the greatest challenge to the race films was not the color line, but the bottom line. In the 1930s, the financial problems created by the Great Depression, coupled with the expense of sound film technology, created a financial seismic event that shook many producers out of business and discouraged others from seeking a foothold in this genre.

Oddly, the mainstream film industry that kept African Americans off its screens during the reign of the silent movie suddenly did a drastic turnaround when sound entered the filmmaking process. Two studios rushed to create all-black sound features in 1929: MGM, at the prodding of director King Vidor, created *Hallelujah!* while Fox produced *Hearts in Dixie*. Both films relied heavily (and clumsily) on racial stereotypes, and both suffered distribution problems when many theaters (particularly in the South) refused to present them. A glimmer of hope existed when MGM signed on its *Hallelujah!* star, the vivacious Nina Mae McKinney, to a contract, a first for an African American (though, sadly, her Hollywood career went nowhere fast and she was reduced to uncredited bit parts as maids a decade later).

Independent cinema also chimed in, with a 1929 short sound film starring blues singer Bessie Smith. *St. Louis Blues* also trafficked in stereotypes in its tale of a woman abused and abandoned by a cruel lover. But it created a sensation in bringing the distinctive sound of the blues (then dismissed as "race music" by white audiences) to the screen and by providing the only filmed record of Bessie Smith in full-throttle performance.

In 1933, the independently-financed adaptation of Eugene O'Neill's *The Emperor Jones* broke ground as the first film where an African-American star enjoyed star billing in a racially-mixed production. The

star, of course, was Paul Robeson, who repeated his Broadway performance for the film version.

By the 1940s, an unlikely event occurred out of an unlikely corner
of the film world. Down in Dallas, Texas, an African-American creative
artist was given the chance to get behind the camera and create a series
of race films. His name was Spencer Williams.

Spencer Williams

No serious appreciation of this genre can be complete without paying
tribute to Spencer Williams, the only prolific African-American filmmaker of the 1940s. Working for Dallas-based Sack Amusements, Williams served as director and writer (and, in most of the films, as an
actor) for eight films in a six-year period.

Williams truly stood out in this period. By the 1940s, black-owned
production companies vanished, with Micheaux as the last holdout. The
white producers of the race films were not eager to create a racially-
mixed environment among the film's crew and even if they were, the
unions that determined membership of the various trades (cinematography, editing, etc.) excluded blacks from being members. There may
have been black input on screenplays and music scores, but that was it.

Except for Spencer Williams.

Williams began his career behind the camera back in the late 1920s,
snagging bit parts in movies (most notably in Buster Keaton's *Steamboat
Bill, Jr.*) and creating scripts for the early two-reel talkies produced by
Al Christie's independent comedy studios. The Christie films were all-
black burlesques that relied heavily on malapropism and the perceived
pretensions of upwardly mobile African Americans trying to secure middle-class standards. These films were not particularly amusing in their
day and are painful to endure now, but at least they got Williams into
movies.

But Williams' time at the Christie studio only lasted a year, from
1929 to 1930. For most of the 1930s, Williams was primarily involved
in bit parts as an actor. He didn't return behind the camera until 1939,

when he wrote the screenplay for the all-black Western *Harlem Rides the Range*. The following year, he wrote and co-starred in the horror-comedy *Son of Ingagi*, also an all-black feature.

Son of Ingagi was no one's idea of a great movie, but it attracted the attention of Alfred Sack, whose company Sack Amusement Enterprises acquired the title for a states rights release to the segregated theaters in the South. Sack invited Williams to come to Texas with the astonishing offer of writing and directing his own films. It was a generous offer at all levels – except for the financial element. Even by the shoestring budget standards of the race films, Sack provided little in the way of financial support: for the first film under Williams' direction, Sack provided a mere $5,000 budget.

That film was the 1941 feature *The Blood of Jesus*. By contemporary standards, it is a deeply flawed production: production values are crude, editing is choppy, the music soundtrack was clearly lifted from old 78rpm records, and the non-professional cast either muffed their lines or were so inadequate that their performances had to be re-recorded with other actors.

Yet in two key areas, *The Blood of Jesus* stood out from the race film genre. First and foremost, the film was an overt celebration of fundamentalist Baptist theology. The race films were, for the most part, strictly secular. If religion entered into the plots, it was either in a marginalized manner or, in the case of Micheaux's *Body and Soul*, in a negative storyline.

But *The Blood of Jesus*, with its story of a dying woman's soul being tempted by Satan (played by a man in a Halloween devil costume), wore its faith on its sleeve. The impact of Christ on the woman's life plays so prominently in the story that one can think of Him as being a character. Indeed, the film's most striking moment finds the heroine lying at a crossroad sign that transforms into the Golgotha cross, where she witnesses the Crucifixion anew while blood drips down on her face.

The other main difference in *The Blood of Jesus* was its setting, a rural Southern village. The race films were strictly bourgeois, offering urban environments where African Americans strived for sophistication and wealth. The poverty of the rural residents in *The Blood of Jesus* stands in striking contrast to other all-black productions of the era. Considering that many African Americans in the 1940s either still lived in rural settings or were only recently removed from such surroundings following the great Negro Migration, *The Blood of Jesus* resonated with uncommon poignancy and immediacy.

The Blood of Jesus was the race films' equivalent of a blockbuster, playing for years in both theaters and (on 16mm) in black churches. Sack recalled the production as "possibly the most successful of all Negro films," and he encouraged Williams to direct and write additional features (though the budgets never increased).

Ideally, it would be a joy to cite how Williams followed *The Blood of Jesus* with a series of equally imaginative and bold films. Sadly, that didn't quite happen. Williams never quite topped his debut feature, either in the audacity of concept or in the execution of the production. In fact, his films, from a technical standpoint, seemed to grow cruder over time. In fairness, his later work offered interesting ideas and some remarkable moments, but on the whole they were not special.

Williams returned to the theme of religion in two films, *Brother Martin* (1942) and *Go Down Death* (1944). No print of *Brother Martin* is known to exist, so it is impossible to determine its artistic value; there is no evidence that it appealed to audiences. *Go Down Death* is, quite frankly, an embarrassment, with Williams giving an uncharacteristically bad performance as a gangster who is haunted by conscience when he tries to discredit a new preacher. *Go Down Death* includes an extended fantasy sequence that depicts Hell through a hodgepodge of zany and frenetic clips from silent movies; it is an unbearable sequence, but not for the reason that Williams envisioned.

Williams' other films tested several genres. *Marching On!* (1943) was the rare race film that focused on the World War II military. It is jolting only for a quick moment when one black defends his military service (in a segregated army, of course) by stating, "It's my country, too." Beyond that, however, the film is lethargic and monotonous.

Of One Blood (1944) is unintentionally funny today, owing to a white-bearded Father Time figure who presides over a connect-the-dots drama of fraternal fate. Williams turns up as an undercover FBI agent, a plot twist that took the film into the realm of fantasy (J. Edgar Hoover's FBI had no black agents). Dirty Gertie from Harlem U.S.A. (1946) was an unauthorized remake of Somerset Maugham's Rain and is notably only by providing a rare starring role for the beautiful black theater actress Francine Everett. (Williams turned up, incredibly, as a female fortune teller.)

The melodrama The Girl in Room 20 (1946) and the comedies Juke Joint (1947) and Beale Street Mama (1947) were undistinguished films that were so poorly made that one could not help but wonder if The Blood of Jesus was a fluke.

Sack's company went out of business shortly after Beale Street Mama was released and Williams did not receive offers from other companies to continue in filmmaking. Williams retired from the entertainment world and invested in a business school in Tulsa, Oklahoma. In 1951, however, he made a stunning comeback with his first and only role in Hollywood: as Andrew H. Brown in the controversial Amos 'n' Andy television series.

Williams' films were unknown to white audiences during his lifetime (he died in 1969). Even today, his contributions to race films are barely acknowledged, owing to both the uneven quality of his filmmaking and the relative obscurity of his post-Blood of Jesus output.

Even if Williams only rates a curio footnote in the history of independent cinema, his presence behind the camera was highly unusual for its time. As a pioneer black filmmaker, he deserves recognition and respect.

The End of the Race Films

In the late 1940s, the race films took an unusually strong focus on diversion. The melodramas and social advocacy films of the 1920s and 1930s gave way to frothy, often silly musical comedy revues. The vices of the genre remained in place: low budgets, sluggish direction, weak screenplays, but they were superseded by the virtue of having a wealth of talent to showcase.

Since revues relied on a series of acts to fill the bill, the race films of this era combed the chitlin' circuit vaudeville houses and swanky nightclubs for their star power. Top-of-the-bill performers were attracted to appear in these productions. Sometimes entire films were wrapped around their oversized personas, such as *Hi-De-Ho* (1947), starring Cab Calloway, and *Reet, Petite, and Gone* (1947), starring Louis Jordan and His Tympany Five. In other cases, prominent guest appearances were secured: Dizzy Gillespie was the hip master of ceremonies for *Jivin' the Be-Bop* (1946), while the King Cole Trio, starring a 29-year-old Nat "King" Cole, performed a trio of tunes in *Killer Diller* (1948).

On the comedy side, the race films offered the very rare opportunities for the stand-up stars of the day to enjoy starring roles; Hollywood was still not ready for African-American comedy headliners. Chitlin' circuit legends like Tim Moore, Moms Mabley, Dusty Fletcher and "Pigmeat" Markham enjoyed a unique opportunity to strut their stuff as the front-and-center stars.

Even in cases where a straight drama was being presented, accommodations were made for song and mirth. *Miracle in Harlem* (1948), a murder mystery (a rarity for the race films), managed to shoehorn the oddball antics of Stepin Fetchit (playing a clumsy porter) and a diverting tune by Juanita Hall (as a singing confectioner).

In retrospect, this strategy made perfect sense. The postwar cinema faced considerable challenges from television; many theaters, particularly independently-owned and -operated neighborhood venues, saw their attendance drop dramatically once Milton Berle and company secured a place in America's living rooms. Having star power, particularly well-known recording artists and stage performers, was an excellent strategy to ensure audiences would return.

But also, in retrospect, these actions seemed strangely out of touch with the state of the African-American community. The postwar years saw a new stirring for civil rights protection. African-American veterans returning from World War II were understandably bitter over the shabby treatment they received from their country's military, and the prospect of resuming a second-class-citizen status after fighting to secure liberty in other countries was too grotesque to endure.

Complicating the matter was the sudden interest in Hollywood to acknowledge that America had very serious race relation problems. Studio productions like *Pinky* (1949), *Intruder in the Dust* (1949) and *No Way Out* (1950) dared to bluntly address questions of racial inequality with a frankness that was previously unknown to the film industry. Independent productions also raised the stakes. *Home of the Brave* (1949), produced by Stanley Kramer, addressed the debilitating effects of racism on black soldiers in the wartime military. (The film was based on a Broadway drama that originally had a Jewish character as the alienated and suffering soldier.) *Lost Boundaries* (1949) presented a drama, based on a true story, of the personal upheaval that affects a New England family when their community discovers they are light-skinned blacks passing for white. *The Quiet One* (1949) took its cameras to the gritty streets of Harlem for a neorealist presentation of the circumstances that led a 10-year-old boy to require psychiatric care. (*The Quiet One* was so boldly effective in detailing daily life in Harlem that many people actually mistook it for a documentary.)

Even foreign filmmakers chimed in with their opinions of America's race problems. The father of neo-realism, Roberto Rossellini, included the story of a maladjusted African-American soldier struggling against his personal demons amid the wreckage of wartime Italy in the 1947 classic *Paisan*. And Richard Wright's explosive 1940 novel, *Native Son*, was the basis of a French-financed production shot in Argentina, of all places, with Wright starring as his doomed antihero, Bigger Thomas.

It is difficult to determine if the disconnect between the race films and the changing times alienated African-American audiences. Arguably, audiences of that period, regardless of race, primarily saw motion pictures as a form of diversion and not a forum for political and social provocation. But at the same time, the heavy emphasis on song and jokes may have struck some people as being too distracting. It almost seemed that the films made a self-conscious effort to ignore the real world.

Whatever the case, the race films came to a swift and abrupt halt by 1950. It seemed that almost at once, production on these features ceased. A few isolated revues managed to get filmed, and an independent company kept up production on newsreels highlighting African-American achievements and issues. But otherwise, the production companies that churned out the race films closed up shop. No one stepped in to fill their void.

The collapse of this corner of the motion picture industry created significant problems for the fate of their films. With no one around to preserve them, damage began to permeate. Some films vanished amidst the neglect; Spencer Williams' *Brother Martin* (1942) and Oscar Micheaux' final film, *The Betrayal* (1949) are among the most prominent missing titles. Those that survived were separated from their original elements, which became lost. Thus, the surviving prints came down through the years as scratchy, splicey, bootlegged offerings. Many of these films are difficult to watch today because their visual and audio quality is so unsatisfactory.

The race films were rediscovered in the 1970s, and over the years they enjoyed grudging admiration from film scholars; perhaps more for their sociological value than for any artistic merit. Today, they occupy a curious niche in the appreciation of independent film. If the genre produced too few genuine classics, it did provide us with a permanent reminder of how the socially and economically isolated African-American community created its own film entertainment in the dismal days of Jim Crow. For that reason, they are among the most valuable assets of both independent cinema history and American history.

Yiddish-language films

America's multicultural demographics have been reflected in the output of independent cinema. Beginning in the silent era and working well into today, different racial and ethnic groups have created films reflective of their unique experiences. But due to the costs of film production and the challenges in distributing films designed for niche markets, this output has often been limited.

For example, the Japanese actor Sessue Hayakawa produced and starred in a series of films during the 1920s that were designed to provide a positive influence on Asian culture. During that period, these films were highly successful and Hayakawa enjoyed the very rare privilege of being among the few non-white Hollywood movie stars. But Hayakawa's example was truly a fluke, and he enjoyed the financial wherewithal to create these films. Other filmmakers lacked access to capital and distribution, and their work suffered accordingly. One of the more remarkable examples involved *The Curse of Quon Kwon*, a 1916 feature created by Marion Wong. This would have been the first Chinese-American feature film, except that Wong ran out of funds and the film was never finished or released. Considered lost for many years, it survives today with only two reels of extant footage.

The coming of sound to film made multicultural productions more difficult to produce and market. The Hollywood studios in the early sound era made parallel versions of some of its major movies to be shown in foreign markets (a German-language *Anna Christie,* with Greta Garbo reprising her English-language role, and a Spanish-language *Dracula*, with Carlos Villarias in the Bela Lugosi part, are the most famous examples of this multilingual switch). But, ironically, these films were not targeted at America's ethnic communities; if you wanted to see the German-language *Anna Christie*, you had to go to Germany rather than the German immigrant neighborhoods in America.

Independent producers sought to fill that void, but there were obvious problems with financing and distribution. Over the years, there were several one-shot domestic flicks created in the U.S. that featured Italian-language, Ukrainian-language and Spanish-language soundtracks. These films, however, were not known outside of their relatively small target markets.

But for roughly a dozen years, one demographic group was able to maintain its own separate cinema with films created in its own language: Jewish Americans and the Yiddish-language movies.

Yiddish was the lingua franca of the Ashkenazi Jewish diaspora that spread throughout Europe and across the Atlantic to both North and South America. The language enabled Jews to maintain their own heritage and identity, even in societies where assimilation was welcomed and encouraged.

Yiddish-language theater had a rich tradition stretching into the latter part of the 19th century in Eastern Europe. As waves of European-Jewish immigrants arrived in the U.S. during the late 19th and early 20th centuries, Yiddish theater came with them. As the nascent motion picture industry began to take shape, it seemed like a natural extension to have films made by and for Jewish audiences who were conversant in Yiddish.

Yiddish-language cinema began in the silent era, with European-based productions dating back to 1911. The first American-based effort was the 1926 *Broken Hearts*, directed, produced and starring Maurice Schwartz, the great star of the Yiddish stage. The film featured Yiddish intertitles, the only time that appeared in an American silent production. The resulting work was not considered to be successful and no further silent Yiddish films were made in the U.S.

In 1931, Yiddish-language cinema was able to take root in America with its first sound production, a feature called *His Wife's Lover*. Shot in New York on a shoestring budget, the film was a very light musical comedy built around theater star Ludwig Statz, who made no further films beyond this production. *His Wife's Lover* was not particularly distinguished in content or style; it was adapted from a stage farce and bore the stagnant visual elements that were too common for many films of the early sound era. Nonetheless, it had commercial appeal both with Jewish audiences in the U.S. and in other parts of the world, and its success encouraged other producers to move forward.

During the 1930s, a small but steady number of Yiddish-language features and shorts were created in the U.S. The films came at a curious time in Jewish-American culture: it was a period when the immigrant community and the first generation of native-born Jews found themselves straddling the worlds of their European heritage, with its traditions and rigidly defined protocol, and the American happening, where traditions were not enforced and protocol gave way to redefining how men and women carried on their lives. A few films tried to address the sharp differences between these two cultural spheres. *The Feast of Passover* (1931) provided a 15-minute consideration of the traditional Seder by comparing a then-contemporary American approach versus the traditional Russian approach. *Uncle Moses* (1932), another Maurice Schwartz film, used uncommon frankness to detail the problems facing Polish-Jewish immigrants who left their rural shtetl for a new life in New York's Lower East Side.

But, for the most part, the Yiddish-language films either placed themselves solely in a romanticized European past or firmly in an electric American present. As with the race films, these films presented a self-segregated isolated world populated solely by Jewish men and women.

The European-flavored films mostly focused on the rural environment, which was often very easy to recreate on American farms (New Jersey's agricultural environment often filled in for Poland or Lithuania). One producer, however, broke new ground by taking his independent production company to Europe. Joseph Green brought theatrical star Molly Picon to Poland to shoot *Yiddle with a Fiddle* in 1936 on a $60,000 budget. The film, a musical comedy about a woman who poses as a man in order to join a klezmer music troupe, was the closest thing that Yiddish-language cinema had to a crossover hit: an English-subtitled version enjoyed a wide theatrical release in the U.S. (it was picked up by the Loew's chain, a first for a Yiddish-language film). Even the Nazi government allowed the film to be imported in 1938 for theatrical screenings to the Jewish population that still lived in Berlin.

Green remained in Poland after the completion of *Yiddle with a Fiddle* and quickly created three more films: *The Jester* (1937), *Mamele* (1939, with Picon returning for the starring role) and *A Letter to Mother* (1939). Fortunately, Green was able to leave Poland prior to the beginning of World War II.

Oddly, the Yiddish-language cinema virtually ignored the rise of Nazism and the peril it brought to Europe's Jewish population (in the same way the race films rarely explored the state of Jim Crow America). Outside of a 1933 feature version of *The Wandering Jew*, the situation facing Europe's Jews in the 1930s was not put on the screen.

What did show up, however, often mirrored the Yiddish theater both in subject (adaptations of well-known plays) or personality (works that were heavy in raw emotion or airy in comic flippancy). Classics of that entertainment experience, such as *The Yiddish King Lear* (1935), *Mirele Efros* (1939, sort of a Yiddish "Queen Lear") and *Tevye* (1939, a non-musical forerunner of *Fiddler on the Roof*, directed by and starring Maurice Schwartz) were major films of the genre.

As for the Yiddish-language films based in contemporary America, the focus was mostly on farce and music. Leo Fuchs, known as "Yiddish Fred Astaire," and Moishe Oysher were the leading men of these frothy offerings, which put logic on the sidelines while focusing heavily on song and the stars' charisma.

Many contemporary film scholars focus on Yiddish-language cinema today because the genre attracted the work of Edgar G. Ulmer, the prolific and peripatetic filmmaker. Ulmer, who was Jewish but did not speak Yiddish, directed four feature films for Yiddish-speaking audiences: *Green Fields* (1937), a love story set in rural Lithuania, *The Singing Blacksmith* (1938), a musical starring the legendary Moishe Oysher, *Fishke the Lame* (1939, later retitled *The Light Ahead*), a story of two young lovers seeking to leave a shtetl for a new life in urban Odessa, and *American Matchmaker* (1940), a Leo Fuchs comedy.

Ulmer's work is considered by many to be the peak of the Yiddish cinema. But one can question whether this is a grand tribute to Ulmer in view of his overall canon or whether the films are, in fact, superior to the rest of the genre. For example, an argument can be made that Joseph Green's work is less static and more emotionally involving than Ulmer's work, or that Maurice Schwartz's *Uncle Moses* brought a greater sense of honesty to the screen. In fairness, there is nothing wrong with Ulmer's Yiddish-language output, but, at the same time, it is not cruel to say the films would not enjoy the same level of attention had they been created by a filmmaker of far less retro prominence than Ulmer.

As with the race films, it is difficult to offer harsh criticism. Yes, these works were mostly cheaply made and the production values were often shaky. And many of the productions were presented as little more than filmed records of Yiddish theater, complete with the fairly over-wrought acting that was compelling when viewed on a stage but which became excessive under magnification by the camera's lens.

For the 1930s, the Yiddish-language films were able to eke out a small but steady profit. As long as there were Yiddish-speaking audiences around the world, the films were able to get on a screen. But, of course, that came to a tragic end with World War II. As the European market was blocked off, the producers of these films could not maintain operations with distribution limited to the domestic market. They had no alternative but to shut down completely for the course of the war.

In the postwar years, a couple of attempts were made to revive the Yiddish-language films. American productions such as *Catskill Honeymoon* (1949) and *God, Man and Devil* (1949) tried to reignite the old magic, and a few European-based Yiddish-language productions were also filmed. But by that period, it was too late. The Holocaust decimated Europe's Jewish population, and many of those who survived either emigrated to the Holy Land, where the new State of Israel vigorously sought to sup-press Yiddish in favor of the revival of the Hebrew language, or to other countries where they sought to assimilate and learn the new language of their adopted homes. For the Jews who remained in Europe, the socio-political climate of the late 1940s (particularly in Eastern Europe) did not encourage attempts to resurrect the Yiddish-language culture.

In the U.S., there was no longer a market for these films. Jewish Americans, particularly the first and second generation born after the great immigration wave, moved away from the old world language in favor of English. The younger generation coming of age was not being educated in the language, as the Jewish religious schools across the U.S. focused on Hebrew rather than Yiddish.

Even the stars of the Yiddish stage and screen found themselves increasingly working in the English-language entertainment world. They had no choice, as it would have been financially impossible for them to exist solely in a Yiddish-exclusive environment. Sometimes these stars turned up in very unlikely places: Maurice Schwartz, for example, earned an unlikely reputation as a camp icon for his role as "The Kahuna" in the 1951 Polynesian tropical epic *Bird of Paradise*, while David Opatoshu, the star of Ulmer's *The Light Ahead*, will probably be forever recalled as Anan 7 in the *Star Trek* episode "A Taste of Armageddon."

By 1950, Yiddish-language cinema was dead. On rare occasions, Yiddish-language films popped up: a 1968 comedy short, *The Cowboy*, which mixed the Old World with the Old West, and in large sections of dialogue in Joan Micklin Silver's 1975 feature *Hester Street*, which carefully recreated the Lower East Side Jewish neighborhoods of the early 20th century. *Yiddle with a Fiddle* returned in an English-dubbed version – if the new edition didn't capture the flavor of the Yiddish original, at least the film was being seen.

Unlike many of the race films, which were either lost or barely survived in cruddy prints, the Yiddish-language films were preserved and the vast majority of the genre is known to survive. Restoration work of these films has been intensive and very successful, with much credit going to the National Center for Yiddish Film at Brandeis University.

Today, the Yiddish-language films are finding new audiences in both retrospective theatrical screenings and through sales on video and DVD. Admittedly, they are being viewed through a bittersweet spectrum as the films (particularly those with a shtetl setting) can be seen to represent the shadow play of a lost culture. In some cases, they provide the only filmed record of many legendary works and artists of the Yiddish theater which itself is barely existing.

Even if the importance of the independently-produced Yiddish-language films is defined primarily through sociological and historic considerations rather than artistic or industry-shaking breakthroughs, they nonetheless deserve to be considered and sought out. After all, it was only in the world of independent filmmaking that the Yiddish language in America was able to put its voice on film.

Exploitation Cinema

In the 1934, the Motion Picture Production Code went into effect. Sometimes called the Hays Code after Will Hays, the head of the Motion Picture Producers and Distributors of America (MPPDA), this code drew the lines of industry self-censorship. Certain topics were considered taboo and were forbidden from being presented on screen. All Hollywood films had to be submitted for a Production Code Seal in order to be released in mainstream cinemas.

Beyond the studios, however, a small number of producers ignored the Hays Code and released films without the Production Code Seal. The MPPDA had no way to halt these efforts, and the theaters that showed these films were almost exclusively independently-owned venues specializing in less-than-prestigious entertainment (today they are called "grindhouses").

These films trafficked in exploitative subject matter banned by the Hayes Code. Although painfully tame by contemporary standards, they nonetheless dared to tempt audiences with presentations concerning nudism, drug addiction, teen pregnancy, prostitution, sexually-transmitted diseases, sadism and, in the case of the 1937 faux-documentary *Angkor*, bestiality. (That film allegedly showed Cambodians mating with gorillas, although it was never explained how the African primates wound up in Indochina.)

If these films lacked quality or even good taste, they were successful due to the ebullient marketing that went into their promotion. Carnival-style hucksterism was in full force here, with phony "experts" being hired to talk up the films as they were taken from city to city on road show distribution patterns. H. Kroger Babb, a producer-distributor, was particularly talented in perfecting the fine art of selling the sizzle and not the steak – which was fine, considering how anemic the fare really was.

It would be fun to devote time and attention to the exploitation films, but the cruel fact remains that almost none of them had any redeeming artistic, intellectual or social value, either in their day or in this day. A few titles, most notably *Reefer Madness* (1936) and *Mom and Dad*

(1944), achieved belated campy cult status based on their peculiar mix of naiveté and crassness.

But, on the whole, the genre was marked by amateurish production values and boring productions. In fact, the best thing about these films are their titles: *This Nude World* (1934), *Maniac* (1934), *Narcotic* (1934), *Marihuana: The Weed with Roots in Hell* (1936) are among the more titillating monikers. The films themselves, however, are grueling; bad acting, blatantly cheap production values, nonexistent direction and scripts that are too dumb to endure. These films don't even qualify as good camp.

Many of these films are in public domain and they are too easily available to access. Anyone coming to them will most likely be underwhelmed by what they discover. For the sake of saving people from wasted time, let's just acknowledge this genre exists and move on.

On the Fringes

On the outskirts of the indie world were the very-low-budget production companies that were commonly lumped together under the demeaning heading of "Poverty Row." Most of their output was undistinguished; too many cheapo Westerns, cheapo horror and sci-fi thrillers and cheapo melodramas. Although a couple of gems somehow emerged from this muck, they were only discovered many years after the fact. During their peak years, these companies were considered the barrel's bottom.

Nonetheless, they are ill-deserving of their obscurity. Whatever their deficiencies in regard to art, they offered some degree of entertainment to audiences in less-demanding times, and their efforts (if not requiring a full book of their own) deserve a moment of praise. Many of their films remained in circulation for years through re-releases from fly-by-night distributions that snagged the theatrical rights, from repeated broadcasts on television, and from VHS and DVD sales (many of these films are public-domain titles, so their proliferation is epic).

Here, in alphabetical order, were the most prominent of the Poverty Row crew:

Astor Pictures. This New York-based distributor initially specialized in the re-releases of older work, most notably a 1939 reprise of
William S. Hart's 1925 silent classic *Tumbleweeds*. The company briefly
flirted with the production of race films in the mid-1940s, but it later focused on offering theaters a choice of cheap and silly indie sci-fi/horror
(most infamously the 1953 stinkers *Robot Monster* and *Cat-Women of
the Moon*) or European art (most notably Federico Fellini's *La Dolce Vita*
and Alain Resnais' *Last Year at Marienbad*). The company's final release
was the 1963 presentation of Orson Welles' *The Trial*.

Educational Pictures. Also known as Educational Film Corporation
of America and arguably the most prominent company in this sector,
Educational began operations in 1915. Through the course of the silent
era they were a well-known producer of two-reel comedies starring Al
St. John, Lupino Lane, Lige Conley, *Monty* Collins, and the unjustly forgotten funnyman Lloyd Hamilton. Sadly, most of the silent output from
this company was lost in a 1937 laboratory fire.

Ironically, the inferior output of Educational Pictures, the company's
sound-era films, survived intact. During the early years after sound took
root, Educational took on a reputation for being a dumping ground for
has-been stars that were unable to make the successful transition into
talking pictures. Harry Langdon and Buster Keaton were the most notable names in the company's star roster, while Mack Sennett (far past
his prime) directed several shorts for the company. The company also
provided opportunities for many up-and-coming performers who were
new to films. Young unknowns such as Bing Crosby (who was directed
by Sennett), Bob Hope, Danny Kaye, the Ritz Brothers and Bert Lahr
appeared in Educational's films.

The Educational titles were distributed by Fox Film Corporation and
its successor, 20th Century-Fox, until 1937. The company attempted to
expand into feature films, but the effort was a failure. By 1940, Educational was out of business.

Grand National Pictures. This company's brief existence (1936-
1939) focused primarily on distributing and occasionally producing B-

level Westerns. Its main claim to fame was acquiring James Cagney's independently-produced *Great Guy* for a 1936 release. But most of the company's titles were along the lines of *Mr. Boggs Steps Out, Swing It, Sailor* and *Ride 'Em Cowgirl*. Needless to say, the company was barely missed when it went out of business.

Majestic Pictures. Active during the early 1930s, this low-rent production and distribution company is primarily recalled today for *The Vampire Bat* (1933), an off-beat horror/comedy starring Melvyn Douglas and Fay Wray (not exactly B-grade stars).

Mascot Pictures Corporation. The company was formed in 1927 and specialized in the production of serials. Its first hit was *The King of the Kongo*, a 1929 part-talking serial. In 1931, it produced its first all-sound effort, *The Phantom of the West*. The company is best remembered today for the 1935 sci-fi musical-western serial *The Phantom Empire*, a zany hodgepodge that somehow launched Gene Autry to stardom.

Mascot merged with Consolidated Film Corporation and Monogram Pictures in 1935 to become Republic Pictures, a minor but notable studio specializing in B-grade Westerns and occasional A-level productions. Monogram, itself the creation of merged production companies (Rayart, Sono-Art Pictures), was a minor studio prior to the merger. It withdrew from its union and re-established itself as a second-tier studio in 1937.

Producers Releasing Corporation (PRC). This company is better known today than it was during its prime, due primarily to the input of film scholars who rediscovered a trio of films directed by Edgar G. Ulmer (*Bluebeard, Strange Illusion* and *Detour*). For the most part, the company was somewhat less than classy, and they were known for some so-bad-they're-good chillers such as *The Devil Bat* (1940), starring Bela Lugosi, and *Gas House Kids in Hollywood* (1947), a Bowery Boys rip-off starring Carl Switzer in his awkward post-Alfalfa years. The company had two brief brushes with Hollywood's higher echelon: its 1943 *Hitler's Madman* was picked up for distribution by Metro-Goldwyn-Mayer and its 1944 *Minstrel Man* received Academy Award nominations for Best Score and Best Song ("Remember Me to Carolina"). PRC was absorbed by J. Arthur Rank's Eagle-Lion, which primarily functioned as a distributor of British releases but which occasionally produced their own B-level action offerings and some classic *noir* thrillers. To its credit, its movies had great titles: *Once to Every Bachelor*, *Two Heads on a Pillow*, *Sweepstakes Annie*, *Without Children*, *Dizzy Dames*, *Born to Gamble*, *The Crime of Dr. Crespi* and *The Spanish Cape Mystery*.

Tiffany Pictures. Also known Tiffany Productions and Tiffany-Stahl Productions, this entity offered low-budget features and shorts. It is best known for its popular *Voice of Hollywood* newsreel series, and for the 1930 Jack Benny feature *The Medicine Man*. The company's name created endless problems, particularly when the jewelers Tiffany & Co. sought litigation against the producers' marketing claims, "Another Gem from Tiffany." Created during the silent era, the company was unable to maintain profitability during the Great Depression and folded in 1932.

The 10 Most Important Independent Films of All Time:

Charles Pappas, film historian and author (*It's a Bitter Little World: The Smartest, Toughest, Nastiest Quotes from Film Noir*)

Q: If you were to look over the span of the history of U.S. independent cinema, from the silent era to today's output, what would you list as the 10 Most Important Independently-Produced Films of All Time ... and why?

1. *The Thing From Another World* (1951). Imagine Steven Spielberg chucking the whole Hollywood system to make Max Brooks' *World War Z*. You don't have to — because it wouldn't happen today, because science fiction is big bucks, because in 1951 Howard Hawks helped make it acceptable. Hawks bolted from the studio system where he had made *Scarface* and *To Have and Have Not* to craft the hard-bread science-fiction

movie Hollywood wouldn't have touched if you had offered it extra points off the gross. *The Thing* stands with *The Day the Earth Stood Still* (also 1951) as the movies that helped make science fiction respectable and, ultimately, remunerative.

2. *Easy Rider* (1969). Even though the American Film Institute ranked *Easy Rider* as the #84 Greatest Movie of All Time in 2007, like hip huggers, it didn't age well. But Dennis Hopper's movie was one of three pistols aimed at the head of mainstream movies that year: Along with Best Picture *Midnight Cowboy* and *Bob & Carol & Ted & Alice*, it Just Said No to the movie-America of *Hello, Dolly!* and *My Fair Lady*. After *Easy Rider*, counterculture was the new mainstream.

3. The *Night of the Hunter* (1955). All personal visions are by definition self-indulgent, and Charles Laughton's personal vision of a Davis Grubb redneck Gothic tale is no different. As coarse and cowardly as he was creepy, Robert Mitchum's Bible-toting, Bible-touting psychopath was a rare non-Hollywood portrait of a serial killer who isn't superhuman, but whose appetite for gullible female flesh is both his strength and self-destruction. Not until Brian Cox essayed the original Hannibal Lecktor (spelled Lecter in subsequent movies) in Michael Mann's *Manhunter* in 1986 was it done so well.

4. *Do the Right Thing* (1997). Quick, name two movies about race: Chances are you could remember only two immediately – *Guess Who's Coming to Dinner?* and *Do the Right Thing*, which could be renamed *Guess Who's Coming to Dinner?* and *Burning Down the House*. Where

Guess Who's Coming to Dinner? offered hope to America like candy to children, *Do the Right Thing* struck a match and held it next to a gasoline refinery. Shifting between its intermingling storylines felt like bubbles in a pot of water coming to boil. *Do the Right Thing* helped clear a path for movies like *American History X*, showing that race is the Rubik's Cube of human relations.

5. *Nanook of the North* (1922). Purists might sniff at Robert Flaherty's 1922 documentary because some scenes in the life of Nanook, an Inuit Eskimo, may have been partially staged. It doesn't matter: this is man with a primitive camera capturing the harsh life of a culture utterly alien, and its scenes of igloo-building and seal-hunting are real enough. The motivated-man-with-a-camera influenced the works of Frederick Wiseman, Errol Morris, Barbara Kopple, and even Michael Moore.

6. *Blood Simple* (1984). Joel and Ethan Coen's *film noir* built on a legacy left by another independently-made crime drama: Abraham Polonsky's *Force of Evil*. Here the Coens tell the tale with the familiar trope, what you need to live will kill you, and transfuse new life into it. It stamped out a template: ball-slapping meanness, the Greek-like implacability of fate, the lack of meaning in anything but grubby money and rancid sex, leaving meaty bones for their own *Fargo, No Country for Old Men* and *The Big Lebowski*.

7. *Harold and Maude* (1971). Like *The Rocky Horror Picture Show*, Hal Ashby's picture was a cult favorite, growing in popularity the way cults do – under the radar, by word-of-mouth. The film makes "inappropriate"

relationships seem happy and even healthy: morbidly depressed 20-year-old Harold hooks up with 80-year-old Maude and is the better for it. That's a feel-good movie – and buddy film – for the ages.

8. *A Woman Under the Influence* (1974). Movies are usually life with the dull, grating parts cut out. But John Cassavetes' *Woman* put them right back in. It's like a hidden webcam that's been left running nonstop for days, even weeks. Financed by Cassavetes and Peter Falk, the film's pacing isn't exactly Indiana Jones, and there are no MTV-inspired epileptic cuts between scenes. But watching Gena Rowlands' mental breakdown feels like having your most embarrassing/painful moments in high school drawn out in slo-mo. You can detect *Woman's* DNA in movies like Robert Duvall's *The Apostle*, which also takes the long way home to tell its story.

9. *Night of the Living Dead* (1968). George Romero made *Night of the Living Dead* for a paltry $114,000 and it grossed more than $50 million. Case closed. With a near 439-fold return like that there was no chance horror would disintegrate like a vampire under a sun lamp. Its influence would be felt for the next 40 years, including from the methamphetamine rush of *28 Days Later*, the faux-reality of *The Blair Witch Project*, and even the sweet satire of *Shaun of the Dead*.

10. *THX 1138* (1971). Without George Lucas' *THX 1138*, there would have been no *Star Wars*. That's good or bad depending on your point of view (and whether you've subjected yourself to the most recent three), but true all the same. Financed by American Zoetrope,

the studio Lucas co-founded with Francis Ford Coppola, the 1971 Orwell-topia was well received and created a platform for Lucas to pump out more, if not always as good, SF. But lurking inside it was a mind-borne virus that broke out not with the Flash Gordon-y science fiction of *Star Wars* but with the science friction of *Blade Runner*, *Terminator* (I and II), *Alien* and *Gattaca*.

CHAPTER THREE:
New Directions, New Horizons

"The only way to find the limits of the possible is by going beyond them to the impossible."
                                        – Arthur C. Clarke

A fter World War II concluded in 1945, the film industry underwent significant changes. Many of these changes were reactive to American society as a whole, which was in its own state of evolution on numerous levels.

Yet the independent cinema realm was not reactive to this changing environment. In many ways, it was aggressively proactive in agitating for a new playing field. Some aspects of what transpired – the rebirth of non-fiction filmmaking and the rise of underground cinema – will be addressed in separate chapters. For this part of the journey, we will focus on the core of the independent film world from the mid-1940s through the early 1980s.

SIMPP Goes to Court

In 1941, a group of independent producers came together to create the Society of Independent Motion Picture Producers (SIMPP). The original configuration included Charles Chaplin, Walt Disney, Samuel Goldwyn, Mary Pickford, David O. Selznick, Walter Wanger and Orson Welles; British producer Alexander Korda, who relocated to Hollywood during wartime, was also part of the mix. Other producers joined SIMPP later on, most notably William Cagney, Sol Lesser, and Hal Roach.

SIMPP had the purpose of standing up to the Hollywood studio system, particularly the studio control of theater chains. To achieve that goal, SIMPP filed a lawsuit in 1942 against the United Detroit Theatres chain that was owned and operated by Paramount Pictures. Why that chain was chosen is not clear, but SIMPP used it to file an antitrust suit as a means to dislodge the studios from controlling the exhibitor side of the business.

It took six years, but Society of Independent Motion Picture Producers v. United Detroit Theatres Corp. made it to the United States Supreme Court. SIMPP's argument against a monopoly by the studios resulted in a victory for the independents. As a result, the studios were ordered to sell their theater chains. Furthermore, they were also ordered by the court to cease and desist from certain anti-competitive practices that were designed to keep independent films from gaining wider exhibition.

Some people assumed this marked the end of the studio system, but that was hardly the case; the studios functioned for another decade, dominating the industry with the quantity of their output. As for SIMPP, it never quite found another battle to match its heady assault against the studios. And, for that matter, it never truly accomplished anything else that genuinely helped the cause of independent production. By 1958, with most of its original members no longer functioning as successful independent producers, SIMPP quietly dissolved.

Frank Capra at Liberty

The first major filmmaker to seek out a place in postwar independent filmmaking was Frank Capra. This was primarily by default rather than design; after distinguished service in World War II as a documentary filmmaker for the U.S. Army Signal Corps, Capra returned to Hollywood where he found relatively few worthwhile opportunities to pursue. Having tried independent production back in 1941 with *Meet John Doe*, he was willing to give it another shot.

Capra teamed with former Columbia executive Samuel Briskin and filmmakers George Stevens and William Wyler to form Liberty Films in April 1945. Since Stevens and Wyler had other contractual obligations, Capra opted to make the first production under the Liberty Films banner: *It's a Wonderful Life*, starring James Stewart, which was released by RKO.

By now, everyone knows what happened: Capra's film was not a box-office hit (its classic status would only come belatedly). Stevens and Wyler were suddenly less than eager to go out on a limb as their own independent producers. Capra struggled with Liberty Films for a second film, *State of the Union* (1948), for an MGM release. Capra then sold Liberty Films to Paramount Pictures. The operation was dissolved in 1951, having made no additional films. Capra's career never truly recovered; his remaining film output was spotty and undistinguished. As a result, relatively few prominent filmmakers were ready to take the indie plunge and remained in the safety of the studio system.

The Very Big Screen

During the late 1940s and early 1950s, movie attendance plummeted dramatically due to the popularity of television. Americans who spent their nights at the local theater were suddenly staying at home in droves to be entertained by the likes of Milton Berle and Sid Caesar. Despite the small, less-than-pristine monochrome visuals and frequent commercial interruptions, the new medium created unexpected problems for the big screen.

And how did the motion picture industry react? In a manner that, in retrospect, seemed fairly illogical: by making the big screen even bigger. There may have been a sense of déja vu in this approach, as Hollywood toyed with widescreen formats in 1930, right after the revolution brought by sound recording. But those early widescreen movies, *The Big Trail*, *Kismet* and *The Bat Whispers*, were box office duds. (French filmmaker Abel Gance experimented with a triptych widescreen in his

1927 epic *Napoleon*, but that version was never exported and Americans never saw Gance's challenge to the traditional 1:33:1 screen format until the film's 1981 restoration.)

Ignoring the 1930 failure, it was decided to give the widescreen format another chance. But the Hollywood studios were not behind the original attempts to expand the size and depth of the movie screen. Credit (or blame, if you will) belonged to independent producers and a pair of less-than-satisfactory features.

The first assault on screen dimensions was made by a man named Fred Waller, who had the funky notion of running multiple and overlapping film projectors in synchronization while aimed at a giant curved screen. He initially presented this concept at the 1939 World's Fair in New York, using an 11-projector system at the Petroleum Industry pavilion. Waller called his process Vitarama. Hollywood didn't call him.

Waller tinkered with his concept, dropping six of the projectors. By the time he was ready for a second chance, America was going into World War II. He offered this process to the Pentagon, which was impressed with the sense of dimension and scope available in the multiple projection process. The newly-christened Waller Gunnery Trainer was used to train pilots during wartime, but after the war ended there was no further use for the process.

But Waller was determined to make this system successful. Fortunately, he was also connected to several prominent and deep-pocketed individuals: film producer Merian C. Cooper, broadcaster Lowell Thomas, and Broadway showman Mike Todd. With their financial support, Waller made more adjustments to his process, losing two of the five projectors required for his system. The technological excellence, not to mention the commercial viability, of his tinkering reached the point that Waller and his team were ready to take the film world by storm. They called their venture Cinerama Productions and created an independently-financed feature film called *This is Cinerama*.

Waller's Cinerama process was somewhat complex: the film was shot with a large camera made up of three synchronized 35mm cameras sharing a single shutter. The film of each camera was projected from three synchronized projectors onto a curved screen subtending 146E of arc. There were also two curious aspects of the system. First, the running speed of the projectors required a speed of 26 frames per second, as opposed to the standard 24 frames per second. The extra two frames were needed to prevent screen flicker on the curved screen. Second, a seven-channel stereophonic sound system provided a fully audio component to match the majesty of the screen. Strereophonic sound was not common in movies at that period; Walt Disney presented a forerunner of the system in his original 1940 road show release of *Fantasia*, but the expensive technology didn't catch on with exhibitors and it remained half-forgotten until Waller came along.

This is Cinerama was a plotless travelogue designed to highlight the visual and aural power of Waller's invention. Some of the screen action was genuinely invigorating, particularly the opening sequence with the Cinerama camera perched at the front of a roller coaster. Most of the film, however, was fairly benign: views of Niagara Falls, Venice, a Spanish bullfight, a water skiing demonstration and scenes from a stage production of the opera *Aida*.

This is Cinerama premiered on September 30, 1952, at the Broadway Theatre in New York. The event was important enough to warrant front page coverage in the *New York Times*, and the guest list for the premiere included New York Governor Thomas E. Dewey. The film was a monster hit from the get-go, grossing more than $542,000 in three months from its single theater (its New York engagement lasted 122 weeks). The film's producers quickly made plans to bring it across the country.

However, there was a sticky problem in terms of distribution: Cinerama required refitting existing theaters to accommodate two more projection booths and a deeply curved screen. The installation price tag ran between $25,000 and $75,000, depending on the location, and, in terms of 1952 dollars, that was no small price. Thus, the film was dispatched on a road show basis, with single theater engagements per city that required advance ticket purchases. The second exhibition of *This is Cinerama* didn't happen until March 1953, when it opened in Detroit. Although it was successful – advance sales of 10,000 tickets – most of America only heard about Cinerama but could not get to see it.

Furthermore, Cinerama Productions opted not to license its technology to the Hollywood studios. Instead, it decided to produce its own feature films. This may have been a poor idea, as the output of Cinerama titles remained very limited. Keeping the format of *This is Cinerama* in place, the next round of films was little more than extended travelogues: *Cinerama Holiday* (1955), *Seven Wonders of the World* (1956), Search for Paradise (1957) and *South Seas Adventure* (1958).

Cinerama Productions toyed with the idea of remaking *King Kong* in the three-screen process, but that project was scrapped when problems arose in employing stop-motion animation with the three-camera system. Plans were also announced in 1955 to produce a film based on President Eisenhower's "Atoms for Peace" program, but nothing came of that. Cinerama eventually teamed with a Hollywood studio in 1962, when MGM used the process for its epic productions *How the West was Won* and *The Wonderful World of the Brothers Grimm*. Alas, MGM ran into problems when bringing the films into wide release; few theaters were willing to foot the costs of refitting their interiors to accommodate Cinerama. Thus, the two films went out in the CinemaScope widescreen format to most theaters, but those prints were marred with visible seams that separated the three overlapping images used in Cinerama.

Cinerama Productions scrapped the three-camera set-up in 1963, going instead for a single-camera 70mm solution. During the 1960s, several films that were billed as being shot in Cinerama were actually filmed in Ultra Panavision 70 or Super Panavision 70. In 1973, *This is Cinerama* was re-released in a reconfigured single 70mm film projection, but that version was a box-office failure.

Cinerama never completely disappeared: there are currently two theaters in America and one in England that continue to present the original three-camera Cinerama films. Two months after the premiere of *This is Cinerama*, another independent production that challenged the depth and scope of the big screen debuted. That film introduced most moviegoers to the concept of 3-D. As with Cinerama, 3-D was a long time in coming to the theaters.

Actually, 3-D predated Cinerama considerably. The first recorded attempt to exhibit 3-D movies took place on June 10, 1915. Edwin S. Porter, best known as the director of *The Great Train Robbery*, joined William E. Waddell to offer several test reels to an audience at New York's Astor Theater. The 3-D process involved an anaglyph process that created a stereoscopic effect when the viewer wore special glasses (one with a red lens, one with a green lens) to view a dual-layered image on the screen. The test screening did not result in the creation of additional 3-D films, and the reels that Porter and Waddell presented are now lost.

In 1922, the first 3-D film to be theatrically released premiered. It was called *The Power of Love* and it opened in Los Angeles. Independent producer Harry K. Fairall tried to get a theatrical distributor, but he was unsuccessful. Today, that film is also considered lost. Later in 1922 and into 1923, several would-be independent producers began shopping around short films shot in a variety of 3-D processes. Another 3-D feature, called *The Man from M.A.R.S.*, also turned up. None of these films resonated with audiences and, as with the earlier attempts at 3-D, they are all considered lost today.

More 3-D films were produced at various points in the 1930s, and at least one film was widely seen, *In Tune with Tomorrow*, a short produced for the Chrysler Motors Pavilion at the 1939 New York's World Fair. But it was not until 1952 that 3-D finally clicked with audiences. And for that achievement, we have to thank *Bwana Devil*.

Bwana Devil? Yes, one of the worst films of the 1950s, a by-the-numbers jungle adventure, captivated moviegoers with the sensationalist advertising promises of "A Lion in Your Lap A Lover in Your Arms " (Why anyone would want a lion in their lap was never explained.) It was written, directed and produced by Arch Oboler, an occasional movie producer who was primarily known for his innovative radio programming, most notably the horror show *Lights Out*. Oboler added two elements to *Bwana Devil* that helped bring audiences to 3-D: second-tier name actors in his cast (Robert Stack, Barbara Britton, Nigel Bruce) and lush color cinematography that brought out the fullest of the 3-D cinematography.

Bwana Devil premiered on November 26, 1952 at the Paramount Theatres in Hollywood and Los Angeles, self-released by the producer under the banner Arch Oboler Productions. Despite withering reviews, audiences packed the venues and Oboler quickly booked engagements in additional theaters around the country. United Artists later picked up the film for a general release.

Almost overnight, 3-D productions took root. Within two years of the *Bwana Devil* premiere, 3-D films were being made by nearly every studio. But also within two years, the 3-D craze came to an abrupt end.

What went wrong? For starters, 3-D exhibition was costly. The films required dual projectors to screen the stereoptical effect and a steady supply of annoying special glasses to catch the 3-D magic. Of course, wearing 3-D glasses were not enjoyed by moviegoers who already wore eyeglasses.

Furthermore, the bulk of the 3-D movies being made by the studios were junk; the majority of them were mediocre B-level fare that brought in 3-D to attract more attention. In reality, 3-D called attention to the weakness of the material. A few quality movies were produced in 3-D: *House of Wax, Kiss Me, Kate* and *Dial M for Murder*, but they weren't enough to warrant the continuation of 3-D production.

Oddly, very few genuine independent productions in 1953 and 1954 featured 3-D. And those films, the sci-fi turkeys *Robot Monster* and *Cat-Women of the Moon* and the Phil Silvers musical *Top Banana*, were just plain awful.

Over the years, 3-D kept popping up in independent productions, mostly horror and adventure films, although there was a brief spell of 3-D X-rated films in the early 1970s with *The Stewardesses* and *Andy Warhol's Frankenstein*. Hollywood, for the most part, stayed away from

3-D until the process was reconfigured so its effects could be presented without the annoying use of the dual-colored glasses. By that time, 3-D was reserved strictly for big-budget animated productions, including *Meet the Robinsons* and *Beowulf* (both 2007). But the 3-D screenings were in special theaters that included the large-screen IMAX process, not the local neighborhood venues. (IMAX is a Canadian operation, not a U.S. entity, hence its absence from these pages.)

In the wake of Cinerama and 3-D, a few Hollywood studios devised their own widescreen and deep-screen presentations: 20th Century-Fox's CinemaScope, Paramount's VistaVision and MGM's MGM 65 twisted and stretched the screen to greater lengths. A third independently-produced system, however, was also added to the mix, and in many ways it offered the best of all widescreen worlds.

Mike Todd, the Broadway producer who was part of the original Cinerama management team, split with his partners following a dispute and decided to offer his own widescreen process. He rounded up a new slew of financial partners and launched the Magna Corporation. Todd then hired the engineers at the American Optical Company in Rochester, N.Y., to create a new widescreen format. The result was Todd-AO.

Todd-AO offered films shot on 65mm negative and printed on 70mm film stock (the extra 5mm accommodated soundtracks blasted in stereophonic set-ups).The aspect ratio of this format was 2.20:1, and a large curved screen and (for its first two years in circulation) a special 30-frames-per-second projector was required to show films in Todd-AO.

But Todd was wise enough to avoid the early mistakes made by the push for Cinerama and 3-D films. Instead of creating pointless travelogues or mediocre movies, his Magna Corporation teamed with Richard Rodgers and Oscar Hammerstein II to shoot the 1955 film version of the Rodgers and Hammerstein Broadway musical *Oklahoma!* in Todd-AO. But since Todd-AO promised to be an expensive offering to theater exhibitors, *Oklahoma!* was simultaneously shot in the CinemaScope format that was more common among movie theaters of the 1950s.

Buoyed by the success of *Oklahoma!*, Todd then took the movie producing plunge, creating his first feature film with 1956's *Around the World in 80 Days*. This all-star Todd-AO production won the Academy Award for Best Picture in 1956 (making it the first widescreen movie to snag that honor).

Todd barely lived to enjoy the success of Todd-AO; he died in an airplane crash in 1958, with plans for a Todd-AO version of *Don Quixote* in the works. A few indie films, including Samuel Goldwyn's version of *Porgy and Bess* (1959) and John Wayne's *The Alamo* (1960), were shot in Todd-AO, but mostly the process was used by 20th Century-Fox for the road show version of its major productions, including *Cleopatra* (1963) and *The Sound of Music* (1965). By the early 1970s, the process was discontinued.

Widescreen cinema is now a common part of the filmmaking and film-viewing experience. But while independent cinema made the movies bigger (at least in regard to projection), the genre also made the context of the films deeper. For this accomplishment, several individual filmmakers deserve recognition.

Orson Welles in Exile

In the postwar years, several major Hollywood stars created their own production companies that independently financed feature films. But for the most part, these efforts were limited in the quantity of output. One Hollywood fixture, however, took self-financing to new horizons.

Had it not been for independent cinema, Orson Welles' career as a director may have ended when he was fired from RKO in 1942 following the problems involved in the post-production of *The Magnificent Ambersons* and the aborted production of his Brazilian-based documentary *It's All True*. (The problems that arose when the Hearst media empire interfered with the *Citizen Kane* release didn't help matters.)

While Welles was still accepted in Hollywood as an actor, his post-RKO attempts to secure studio backing for projected films went nowhere. Welles was certainly tireless in coming up with a variety of possible projects, most notably a film based on Dickens' *The Pickwick Papers* starring W.C. Fields. Alas, the studios were not eager to have Welles behind the camera.

In 1946, Welles was able to get a second chance from an independent outfit. Sam Spiegel, a Polish-born producer working (at the time) under the moniker S.P. Eagle, was seeking his own niche in films. He had produced one movie in the studio system, *Tales of Manhattan* for 20th Century-Fox in 1942, but he felt independent filmmaking would better suit his temperament.

Spiegel, aligned with the independent International Pictures, approached Welles to direct a post-World War II *noir*-style mystery that would tap into the American concerns about escaped Nazis settling on the U.S. mainland. Welles knew in advance he would not function as a producer, a role he played in his RKO films. Nonetheless, he accepted the assignment as well as Spiegel's insistence on casting Edward G. Robinson as the detective in search of a Nazi hiding on a New England boys' school campus and Loretta Young as the wife of the Nazi (a role that Welles took for himself, albeit with third billing).

The resulting film, *The Stranger*, is not considered by most Welles scholars as being among the director's finest. A great deal of blame from the Welles supporters goes to not having Welles as the producer, but that's hardly fair since Spiegel was not exactly a hack (his films included *The African Queen*, *On the Waterfront*, *The Bridge on the River Kwai* and *Lawrence of Arabia*). The problem is actually where *The Stranger* falls in the Welles canon. Coming after *Citizen Kane* and *The Magnificent Ambersons*, *The Stranger* pales in comparison; it is a perfectly fine little thriller, but it is not a grand artistic statement. As such, it has been dismissed for many years.

At the time, however, *The Stranger* worked wonders. Welles finished the film ahead of schedule and under budget, a much-publicized point designed to counter accusations of being careless and reckless with other people's money. And unlike the earlier classics, *The Stranger* was a box-office success; ironically, it was picked up for release by RKO.

The Stranger enabled Welles to return to the studio system. Unfortunately, that didn't last very long. His next two films, *The Lady from Shanghai* for Columbia Pictures and *Macbeth* for Republic Pictures (both released in 1948), ran into substantial post-production problems that reinforced concerns about Welles' ability to function as a responsible filmmaker. *The Lady from Shanghai* required an extensive, not to mention expensive, period of rewriting the script and shooting new footage when the original director's cut proved to be completely incoherent. *Macbeth* had to be entirely re-dubbed after complaints by critics and audiences that the Scottish brogues used by Welles' actors were impossible to understand. (Listening to the film today, however, that complaint seems curious; the film is very easy to follow and the brogues are not impenetrable.)

Realizing he was becoming persona non grata, Welles retreated to Europe in 1949 to begin a new film. This time around, Welles decided to put his own money into the production. The resulting *Othello* wasn't ready until 1952, and its creation is a film legend: Welles shooting on the fly across Italy and Morocco, shutting down the production so he could raise money by acting in other films (most notably *The Third Man*), and "borrowing" costumes and equipment from other movies for use in his work.

Whether you could call *Othello* an American independent film is open to debate. Welles himself didn't think of it as such, as he facetiously entered it in the 1952 Cannes Film Festival as a Moroccan creation. But as it was presented through his Mercury company, it was American in grounding if not in spirit.

Not that Americans shared much kinship with *Othello*; its very brief U.S. release in 1955 through United Artists was a flop, and it wasn't until the film's 1991 restoration that most Americans had access to this title.

After the U.S. release of *Othello*, Welles attempted to self-finance a modern update of *Don Quixote*. That project began in 1955 with a $15,000 gift from Frank Sinatra. It was filmed on-and-off until 1971, when it was left unfinished. An attempt by Spanish director Jess Franco to reconstruct Welles' plans for *Don Quixote* was released in Europe to 2001 to near-universal scorn; it was finally released in the US on DVD in 2008.

As a filmmaker, Welles used his European journeys to round up financing from a variety of sources. Not everyone was appreciative of his eccentric talents: the backers of his 1955 *Mr. Arkadin* took the film from him when he ran over budget and over schedule. In 1962, producer Alexander Salkind was supposed to offer Welles financing for his production of *The Trial*, based on the Franz Kafka novel. But Salkind was unable to provide the necessary funds and Welles, functioning as a de facto producer, wound up scrambling to secure locations based on his very limited funds (he used the abandoned Gare d'Orsay railroad station in Paris as the set for many of the film's sequences). He had more luck gaining a steadier sense of support from producer Harry Saltzman to produce *Chimes at Midnight* (1966) and French television for *The Immortal Story* (1968).

While recognized and celebrated for his artistic greatness, few filmmakers would seek to emulate Welles' erratic work habits and his endless problems in locating backers for projects. Indeed, many of his film projects were jettisoned due to lack of funds, and Welles left behind an extraordinary litter trail of unfinished work. His last work as a director was an incomplete, independent production, 20 minutes of test footage for a proposed adaptation of Isak Dinesen's *The Dreamers*, shot at his home between 1980 and 1982.

Stanley Kramer Raises the Bar

During the 1950s and early 1960s, Stanley Kramer occupied the role of the primary social agitator in American independent cinema. Yet most critics and film scholars have difficulty acknowledging Kramer's value as an artist.

Kramer had been involved in film production at lower assistant levels prior to World War II. After a wartime stint in the Army's film unit, but he opted to start his own company and focus on the creation of edgy, low-budget movies.

His initial presentation, *So This Is New York* (1948), was an undistinguished comedy that is primarily recalled for providing a rare leading role for radio comic Henry Morgan and an early directing gig for Richard Fleischer. Kramer had more luck with his next production, the boxing drama *Champion* (1949) starring Kirk Douglas.

Kramer's next two films established his reputation for creating films that dared to address troubling social issues, the so-called "message" films. *Home of the Brave* (1949) confronted racism in the World War II military, while *The Men* (1950) examined the problems facing disabled veterans who were unable to easily return to civilian life.

After an uncharacteristic excursion to costume drama with *Cyrano de Bergerac* (1950), Kramer began production on one of the most influential films of the 1950s: *High Noon* (1952), a Western that doubled as a thinly veiled swipe against McCarthyism. Kramer's exact role in the creation of the film has been called into question, particularly by screenwriter Carl Foreman, who was forced to relocate to England as a result of the McCarthy-era blacklisting. Foreman claimed producer credit for *High Noon* for himself, although no man has the producer credit on the release print while Foreman receives credit for his screenplay.

Kramer's box-office returns were erratic; *Champion* and *High Noon* were huge hits, but *The Men* and *Cyrano de Bergerac* were box-office flops despite Marlon Brando's debut film role in the former and Jose Ferrer's Oscar-winning performance in the latter.

Nonetheless, Kramer was recognized in Hollywood as someone who was a provocateur who was capable of creating quality films for relatively little money.

While *High Noon* was in production, Kramer was signed by Columbia Pictures to produce films for that studio. From an artistic standpoint, Kramer was responsible for producing a series of striking features: *Death of a Salesman* (1951), *Member of the Wedding* (1952), *The Four Poster* (1952), *The 5,000 Fingers of Dr. T* (1953) and the Marlon Brando biker flick *The Wild One* (1953). From a commercial standpoint, however, Kramer was the kiss of death: all of his films lost money for Columbia.

What went wrong? Reportedly, Kramer and studio head Harry Cohn never got along, with Cohn bemoaning Kramer's choices (particularly *Death of a Salesman*, which Cohn loathed). Furthermore, Kramer's films brought the studio the wrong type of publicity. In 1951, Red-baiting picketers disrupted the release of *Death of a Salesman* (which was ironic since Arthur Miller, the picketers' subject of scorn, had nothing to do with the movie and actually hated the film). In 1953, controversy arose over the sympathetic view of bikers in *The Wild One*; British censors banned the film's import for 14 years.

Kramer's losses were recouped entirely with his final Columbia production, a fairly workmanlike rendition of *The Caine Mutiny* (1954). After departing Columbia, Kramer decided to return to independent producing and also sought to take on the role of director. At this point, Kramer's limitations as a creative artist became fairly apparent. As the producer, he was able to coordinate the symphony of talents who were brought together in the creation of memorable and (for their time) daring productions. But as a director, Kramer was not a natural. His early work lacked the light touch, his initial visual style was often pedestrian and his films had a tendency to seem overlong and clumsy. Indeed, his first two efforts as producer-director, *Not As a Stranger* (1955) and *The Pride and the Passion* (1957), were fairly awful and are difficult to watch today.

Then, almost abruptly, something clicked and Kramer found the unique formula to mix two seeming disparate strategies, controversial "message" films with big-name star casts, into distinctive productions. Kramer drove brilliantly through the hot topic land mines of racial relations (*The Defiant Ones*, 1958), the threat of nuclear annihilation (*On the Beach*, 1959), the debate between evolution versus creationism (*Inherit the Wind*, 1960) and the Nazi atrocities in World War II (*Judgment at Nuremberg*, 1961). His films, while clearly liberal in their politics at a time when liberalism was not highly appreciated, were honored with awards and strong box-office returns, and Kramer seemed to have the golden touch.

But Kramer also weathered criticism from some corners that his films were too serious. Perhaps in response to such comments, or perhaps he felt like he wanted to try something different, he embarked on the independent production that has become a beloved favorite with many moviegoers: the 1963 all-star slapstick extravaganza *It's a Mad, Mad, Mad, Mad World*. The film was completely uncharacteristic of Kramer's previous work: loud, frantic, intentionally vulgar and exhaustively hilarious. It was also one of his most commercially successful productions.

But from that point, however, Kramer's career slowly began to fray. Hooking up with Columbia Pictures again, he produced and directed *Ship of Fools* (1965) and *Guess Who's Coming to Dinner?* (1967). While commercially successful, thanks mostly to their stellar casts, both films exposed the heavy-handedness that plagued his earlier films. Beyond those films, however, Kramer's later work was artistically undistinguished and commercially unsuccessful: under studio financing, he created *The Secret of Santa Vittoria* (1968), *R. P. M.* (1970), *Bless the Beasts and Children* (1971), *Oklahoma Crude* (1973), *The Domino Principle* (1977) and *The Runner Stumbles* (1979).

So why is Kramer so poorly considered today within the depth and scope of American independent film history? The distinguished critic David Walsh, writing for the World Socialist website, offers this perspective: "One might say that Kramer's great cinematic weaknesses, in so far as they were considered (his name hardly appears in film reference works), helped reinforce moods that valued ideas and causes less and less, that substituted formal play for serious thought and feeling, that made a fetish out of film style in an ultimately hollow and unproductive manner. Kramer's fatal flaws became part of the dishonest and essentially reactionary argument against making any films about social problems and 'great issues.' This is one reason why clarifying his career and legacy is useful and necessary. Kramer was a wholly inadequate artist and thinker; the pleasing moments he helped create were perhaps exceptional. If anything, his career is evidence of the inevitably artistically limiting character of not making a thoroughgoing break with the establishment, not of the supposed dangers of presenting social criticism in art."

As a compromise of sorts, moviegoers continue to seek out Kramer's classic films (both as a producer and producer-director) without giving direct credit to him for their greatness. If the man goes without tribute, at least his work continues to be appreciated, to the point that criticism of his shortcomings becomes tinny and meaningless.

The blacklisted creators of *Salt of the Earth*

Beginning in the late 1940s and running the course of the 1950s, an anti-Communist hysteria infected America. Hollywood became an attractive and convenient target for the self-righteous zealots who insisted (and, as it turned out, imagined) that the Commies were trying to subvert America through the movies. As a result of such shenanigans, scores of motion picture professionals with genuine or perceived left-wing political leanings found themselves forced out of their jobs as a result of blacklisting by the studios.

In retrospect, one might imagine that the blacklisted artists would've found haven in the independent cinema orbit. Alas, during that era a genuine sense of indie filmmaking (as defined in contemporary standards) did not exist. But that is not to say that an effort was not made by several blacklisted filmmakers to create their own parallel universe from the studio systems.

In 1950, a trio of blacklisted filmmakers – Paul Jarrico, Charles Katz and Adrian Scott – created a partnership to produce independent films based on relevant social issues (relevant to the left-wing sensibility, it should be said). Their initial project was to be a dramatization of the racially-charged Scottsboro Boys case, but prospective financial backers balked at putting money into a project that would clearly run into endless distribution obstacles.

Two additional blacklisted filmmakers, Herbert Biberman and Scott Lazarus, learned of this endeavor, however, and joined the partnership, which became known as Independent Productions Corporation (IPC). While the spirit was willing, the project was absent; repeated plans to push a Scottsboro Boys film ahead stalled while a proposed documentary on the life of Paul Robeson met the same fate.

Jarrico, vacationing in New Mexico in the summer of 1951, then found a story with greater potential: a strike by the predominantly Hispanic members of the International Union of Mine, Mill and Smelter Workers (IUMMSW) against the owners of a local zinc mining operation. Believing there was a story of racial and economic injustice that would inspire audiences, the IPC team began working to raise funds for this project.

The fundraising, however, took a bit longer than expected, from September 1951 to March 1953, to be precise, with hands outreached across the U.S. and Europe. With a $100,000 budget in the bank, the cooperation of the IUMMSW to provide some of its members as actors and extras, and Herbert Biberman serving as director, the first IPC film was ready to proceed under the title *Salt of the Earth*.

At this point, everything that could possibly go wrong went wrong with a vengeance. The producers wanted to use union crew members, but the production guilds refused to allow any of its members to be associated with this production. Word of the New Mexico-based production reached the Hollywood trade publications, bringing about local anti-Communist protestors and federal law enforcement surveillance of the *Salt of the Earth* set. In the middle of the production, Immigration and Naturalization Services officers arrested the film's leading actress, Mexican star Rosaura Revueltas, deporting her on a technicality (her passport was not stamped when she entered the U.S.). Her remaining scenes had to be shot surreptitiously in Mexico City under the guise of a screen test, while a double filled in for her in the remaining medium and long shots from the New Mexico set.

Post-production was even more harrowing. Editors who were hired for the project without knowing the film's history kept quitting when they discovered what they were working on. The music score was recorded with an orchestra that was duped into believing they were performing the soundtrack for a Mexican melodrama. One of the IPC partners, Scott Lazarus, and the film's composer, Sol Kaplan, were called before the House Un-American Activities Committee to explain their actions on *Salt of the Earth*. Union-run film laboratories were ordered by their management not to process the negative for this film.

Incredibly, *Salt of the Earth* was completed in December 1953. Into 1954, the IPC partners made a concentrated effort to get the film into theatrical release. No studio or independent distributor would touch *Salt of the Earth* because of the blacklist, so IPC was forced to self-re-lease its film. That was not the easiest task, since the theater projection-ist union forbade its members from handling this title. When IPC was able to find theaters, other film companies refused to provide short subjects and newsreels to play on the bill. In some cases, newspapers would not accept advertising for the film's theatrical engagements.

And adding the final insult to this skein of injuries, the reviews were overwhelming unsympathetic. Pauline Kael of *The New Yorker* led the charge, denouncing the film as "Communist propaganda" while *The Hollywood Reporter* sneered, charging that it was made "under direct orders of the Kremlin." Bosley Crowther, writing in the *New York Times*, gave the film its kindest review, calling it "a calculated social document."

Salt of the Earth played in ten theaters during its release; two of those cinemas were in New York. It was not a box-office hit, to put it mildly, and the repercussions from the film's failure were staggering. *Salt of the Earth* managed to play in foreign markets, but never made a profit (at least the producers claimed they never saw a cent from these screenings). IPC found itself deeply in debt and never produced an-other film. Other blacklisted filmmakers, scared off by what happened here, never attempted to create their own independent films. Rosaura Revueltas was blacklisted in her native Mexico and would not make an-other film until 1976, and years would pass before any of the IPC were able to shake the stigma of the blacklist and resume their respective Hollywood careers.

Strangely, *Salt of the Earth* took on a life of its own years after its failed release. In the 1960s, the film was discovered by film schools. The film's prescient advocacy of minority rights, coupled with its ex-traordinary back story, made it a cult favorite among moviegoers who were too young to know of its original release. Over the years, crit-ics began to reconsider the film in its own merits and *Salt of the Earth* gained classic status. In 1992, the U.S. Library of Congress added it to the National Film Registry, perhaps the ultimate irony, given the federal government's hysteria was behind the blacklisting that brought the film's creation.

Ida Lupino Stands Alone

By this point in the history of independent cinema, you may have noticed something was lacking: the presence of female directors. While some women were able to helm productions during the silent years (most notably Alice Guy Blanché and Lois Weber), there were no opportunities for women by the dawn of the sound era. Outside of Dorothy Arzner in the 1930s and early 1940s, no woman was directing films in Hollywood.

Ida Lupino broke the glass ceiling for women directors in the post-World War II film industry. Lupino, a popular actress under contract at Warner Bros. for most of the 1940s, formed her own production company in 1949 with then-husband Collier Young. Their first film, a drama about unwed mothers called *Not Wanted*, was supposed to be directed by Elmer Clifton. However, Clifton was sidelined by a heart attack three days into the production. Lupino abruptly stepped in to take up the reins. Lupino gave Clifton full screen credit for directing *Not Wanted*, but the experience convinced her that she had a new future behind the camera.

Lupino, serving as her own producer, turned out a series of low-budget dramas. Initially, she sought to portray social issues on the screen: *Never Fear* (1950) dealt with polio victims, *Outrage* (1950) focused on the aftermath of a sexual assault, *Hard, Fast and Beautiful* (1951) dissected the emotional pressure placed on a young female tennis star, and *The Bigamist* (1953) handled the thorny matter of one man with two wives. For the most part, Lupino's films were sincere but somewhat dull. To be blunt and perhaps a bit cruel, they are recalled today solely for the novelty of having a female director in the otherwise male-exclusive 1950s.

In fairness, Lupino did helm one genuinely notable independent production: *The Hitch-Hiker* (1953), a taut thriller about two men who make the mistake of picking up a ride-thumbing psychopath. As pure entertainment rather than limp social melodrama, *The Hitch-Hiker* is raw, diverting, pulse-driving endeavor.

Beyond her production company, however, Lupino found no offers to direct other films. However, she found steady work in television, directing episodes of many popular programs (most notably the eerie *Twilight Zone* presentation "The Masks"). Lupino directed one final film in 1966, Columbia Pictures' comedy *The Trouble with Angels*.

Lupino's presence behind the camera did not immediately open doors for women to become directors, although some women were able to gain a foothold via underground cinema, which will be explored later. However, her position in filmmaking deserves to be noted as a milestone in breaking down a significant barrier in the road to equal opportunity in the entertainment world.

Otto Preminger's Taboo Busting

Otto Preminger occupies a curious position in the history of independent cinema. For the most part, he was strictly a studio-bound producer/ director who did his best work at 20th Century-Fox (most notably the 1944 classic *Laura*). Yet, in a handful of independently-produced offerings, Preminger challenged the Hollywood status quo with full frontal assaults on taboo subjects and circumstances.

The first Preminger attack came in 1953 with *The Moon is Blue*, an adaptation of a popular Broadway comedy. The film was unremarkable in most ways, except that Preminger refused to have the dialogue censored to meet the requirements of the Hays Code. Three words that were considered verboten at the time – "virgin," "seduce" and "mistress" – were kept in the screenplay. The Catholic League of Decency condemned the film for its use of these words and the film was denied the Production Code Seal. Preminger, nonetheless, released it without the seal via United Artists. The controversy turned the release into a major box-office success.

Two years later, Preminger again faced the prospect of putting a film out without a Production Code Seal. In this case, the film was *The Man with the Golden Arm*, a stark adaptation of Nelson Algren's novel on a drug-addicted card dealer (played by Frank Sinatra in an uncommonly harrowing performance). Drug addiction was one of the taboo subjects as determined by the Production Code, but Preminger's success in getting the film into theaters (again via United Artists) helped score a blow against censorship.

Perhaps Preminger's most remarkable dare was to stand up to the Hollywood blacklist in openly hiring Dalton Trumbo to write the screenplay for the film version of Leon Uris' novel *Exodus*. Trumbo was among the Hollywood Ten of blacklisted film artists, but he was able to continue working (albeit under pseudonyms) via the intervention of Ingo Preminger, Otto's brother, who ran a talent agency. Preminger insisted on Trumbo receiving proper screen credit, which marked the first strike back against blacklisting.

Sadly, the remainder of Preminger's independent work was erratic and unsatisfactory, most notably his misguided *Saint Joan* (1957) and enervated *Porgy and Bess* (1959). Yet in the three aforementioned films, Preminger's willingness to take risks helped reshape the texture and character of film production.

Two Gritty New York Stories

In the mid-to-late 1950s, the combined efforts of writer James Hill, producer Harold Hecht and actor Burt Lancaster created a production entity that functioned under several names, but is primarily recalled as Hill-Hecht-Lancaster Productions.

This entity is primarily recalled for two landmark films. The first was *Marty*, produced in 1955, which was significant at several levels. *Marty* began its life as a television play that was broadcast live in 1953, with Rod Steiger in the lead role as a lonely butcher in the Bronx, N.Y., who is able to find true love, much to the chagrin of the less-than-helpful people around him. Taking a TV play to the big screen was a gamble;

would people pay admission in a cinema to see a production that was already available for free in their homes?

They did, in droves. Directed by Delbert Mann and written by Paddy Chayefsky, adapting his TV play, *Marty* also broke the rules of the era by keeping its production on the modest side. At a period when widescreen color films were the major screen offerings, *Marty* remained in black and white at the non-widescreen 1:37 ratio, with location photography in the Bronx that added a somewhat neorealist flavor to the film. In keeping with the original production's casting, a decidedly non-leading male actor played the title role (in this case it was Ernest Borgnine, a character actor whose previous screen work was primarily in supporting parts as venal heels).

The small, modest *Marty* created a sensation with its sincerity and simple charm. It was the first U.S. film to win the Palm d'Or at Cannes and it won four Academy Awards, including Best Picture.

The second Hill-Hecht-Lancaster classic was the 1957 *Sweet Smell of Success*. Lancaster cast himself as J.J. Hunsecker, the malicious New York gossip columnist who ruins lives and reputations with nary a quiver of remorse. The film offered a grim, scalding denouncement of the nastier underside of the entertainment world. Although considered a classic today, *Sweet Smell of Success* was a little too dark for the audiences of its time. Despite glowing reviews, it was not a box-office success.

Hill-Hecht-Lancaster turned out other films, most notably *Separate Tables* (1958) and *The Devil's Disciple* (1959); both starred Lancaster, who was admittedly miscast in each film. But the magic of *Marty* and *Sweet Smell of Success* was never recaptured and the partnership dissolved at the end of the 1950s.

Morris Engel's Single Lightning Strike

In 1953, a New York photographer named Morris Engel designed a lightweight 35mm camera that enabled him to employ handheld cinematography (a rarity for that time). Partnering with photographer Ruth Orkin and writer Ray Ashley, Engel created a low-budget ($30,000) neorealist-style film called *Little Fugitive*.

The film followed the misadventures of a seven-year-old New York City boy (played by nonprofessional Richie Andrusco) who mistakenly believes that he killed his brother during play. The boy runs away to Coney Island, where he spends the day absorbing the strange sights and sounds of the oceanfront amusement area.

Little Fugitive was remarkable in its documentary-style intimacy, a style that was achieved by Engel's special camera, which allowed him to work in a guerrilla style of direction. The film won the Silver Lion at the Venice Film Festival and earned an Oscar nomination for Best Original Screenplay. It also had a profound impact on Francois Truffaut, who cited *Little Fugitive* as the inspiration for his 1959 *The 400 Blows*, which, itself, was the catalyst for the French New Wave movement that followed.

Even more remarkable, *Little Fugitive* was a box-office success. Distributed by Joseph Burstyn Inc., a boutique company that specialized in European art house fare (most notably *Miracle in Milan* and *Umberto D.*), *Little Fugitive* was widely seen and appreciated.

Sadly, Engel never experienced a repeat of this success. Working as a solo director, his next two films failed to attract any degree of praise: *Lovers and Lollipops* (1956) and *Weddings and Babies* (1958) came and went with little notice. Engel returned to commercial photography. He made two attempts to return to film directing, *I Need a Ride to California* (1968) and *A Little Bit Pregnant* (1993), but neither production was released.

Engel's contribution to independent cinema was virtually ignored until a 2001 retrospective of his first three films was held in New York. His films were released on DVD shortly after, enabling new generations to appreciate his work. By the time of his death in 2005, Engel's place in the history of independent cinema was confirmed.

John Cassavetes Looks Inward

One of the most important forces within the independent cinema realm was John Cassavetes, who established himself as a major force with the 1960 production *Shadows*. While Cassavetes was not the first actor to direct films, he truly broke new ground at many levels.

Cassavetes was a rising actor in the mid-1950s who turned up on television and in films, most notably the TV series *Johnny Staccato*. Although he was not at A-list level, his name recognition nonetheless encouraged a degree of attention.

It is uncertain whether Cassavetes intentionally set out to become a filmmaker. We know that in the mid-1950s, he was hosting an actor's workshop in New York. While making a guest appearance on a late-night radio talk show called *Night People*, Cassavetes was there to plug the film *Edge of the City*, in which he had a starring role. Speaking freely, perhaps facetiously, he asked, "Wouldn't it be terrific if [ordinary] people could make movies?" When queried by the show's host, Jean Shepherd, about how he would finance such a film, Cassavetes replied: "If people really want to see a movie about people, they should contribute money."

What happened next cannot be independently verified. Cassavetes claimed that he received money from people who caught his comments on the radio show. He stated he received five dollars from a soldier who hiked 300 miles to make the presentation (why the soldier didn't just mail the money is not clear). How much was raised is also uncertain, with figures ranging from $2,500 to $20,000 finding their way into print. Cassavetes also stated he received an offer from the NAACP to help finance the film, which is curious since he didn't publicize any racial elements of *Shadows* at any time during its pre-production.

Cassavetes launched into *Shadows* with nonprofessional actors and no script. A basic premise emerged about a love affair between a light-skinned African American and a white man who is initially not aware of her race. The respective worlds of the young lovers spins out the remainder of the film; the woman's jazz musician brother and his struggles to launch a career, and the man's bohemian intellectual friends.

Shadows was originally shot in 16mm in 1957. Cassavetes recalled the production as chaotic, with many sequences filmed surreptitiously because he did not have municipal permits to shoot on the New York streets. In later years, he claimed inspiration from the Italian neo-realists for his production style, although it was more likely that he had no choice but to shoot it in a neo-realist manner due to his minuscule budget (which was later stated as $40,000).

Cassavetes was also quoted as claiming he was inspired by Jean-Luc Godard's *Breathless*, but that was obviously not possible since that film wasn't shown in America until after *Shadows* was finished.

Shadows was first screened in the fall of 1958 at New York's Paris Theater in an invitation-only presentation. Cassavetes claimed the audience reaction was unsatisfactory, with people walking out as early as 15 minutes into the film. Cassavetes reassembled his cast in 1959, jettisoned half of the footage from the film, and shot new scenes. The second version of *Shadows* was first shown in late 1959 at Cinema 16 in New York.

However, Jonas Merkas, writing in the *Village Voice*, questioned Cassavetes' claim that the first version of *Shadows* was inferior. "I have no further doubt that whereas the second version of 'Shadows' is just another Hollywood film–however inspired, at moments–the first version is the most frontier-breaking American feature film in at least a decade," he wrote. "Rightly understood and properly presented, it could influence and change the tone, subject matter, and style of the entire independent American cinema."

Cassavetes also confused matters further by claiming the entire film was improvised; even the film's closing credits stated this. In reality, the second version of *Shadows* was scripted by Cassavetes and Robert Alan Arthur. Clearly, Cassavetes decided not repeat the errors of the first version, which relied more on improvisational scenes, having a clear shooting script enabled the second go-round to flow with greater ease. (It is also unclear why Cassavetes did not cast himself in *Shadows*. It appears no one ever asked him that, at least not for any published interview.)

The first version of *Shadows* was never publicly shown and was considered lost for four decades. In 2004, Ray Carney, a professor at Boston University and a Cassavetes historian, announced he had located a pristine print of the first *Shadows*, although he added the discovery was "something of a letdown" and insisted the two versions were so different that they should be judged as separate entities rather than an evolutionary flow. To date, though, this version has not been made available to the general public due to a squabble between Carney and Gena Rowlands, Cassavetes' widow, over the ownership of the first *Shadows*.

The *Shadows* that came to establish Cassavetes, however, first gained attention at the Cannes Film Festival in 1960. The reaction at Cannes was strong enough to attract a British distribution deal. London critics praised the film and a British company that began to export films to the American market, Lion International, arranged for the U.S. commercial release of *Shadows* in 1961.

Shadows was a major hit with the American critics and, somewhat surprisingly (given its off-beat nature), a commercial success in art house release. Cassavetes found a new calling in Hollywood as a director.

However, Cassavetes did not fit comfortably into the studio orbit. He helmed two films that were released in 1962; *A Child is Waiting* and *Too Late Blues*. Both films were unsuccessful and Cassavetes was unhappy with the results. Yearning to duplicate the distinctive style of *Shadows*, Cassavetes saved up funds from his film acting gigs (most notably *The Killers* in 1964 and his Oscar-nominated role in 1967's *The Dirty Dozen*) to self-finance a new feature.

The resulting film was *Faces* and it broke new ground with its raw, aching consideration of human frailties and neuroses. Shot within his home, *Faces* examined a married couple's parallel infidelities in a cinema verité style that literally created an uncomfortable but emotionally supercharged in-your-face experience. The style was radically different from anything being produced in Hollywood – or, for that matter, by other independent filmmakers. Gena Rowlands, Cassavetes' wife, starred in the film; the filmmaker, however, did not appear on screen.

Cassavetes then did something that few independent filmmakers would dream of doing: he self-distributed *Faces*. It was a gamble that paid off, thanks to enthusiastic critical response that helped drive audiences to check out the film. *Faces* earned three Oscar nominations in major categories: Best Original Screenplay for Cassavetes, Best Supporting Actor for Seymour Cassel and Best Supporting Actress for Lynn

Carlin, and that was no mean feat for a small, no-budget, independent endeavor.

As with *Shadows*, Cassavetes was courted by the studios following the success of *Faces*. And, again, he created two films that did not find audiences: *Husbands* (1970) and *Minnie and Moskowitz* (1971). And, again, Cassavetes went back to his home to shoot another intensely personal film. And, again, he self-released the work – this time, *A Woman Under the Influence* (1974), gaining Oscar nominations for his direction and for Gena Rowlands' performance.

At this point, however, Cassavetes' experience took an unfortunate turn. His attempts to self-finance and self-distribute *The Killing of the Chinese Bookie* (1976) were a crashing failure, leaving him bankrupt. He was able to raise funds to create *Opening Night* (1979) and open it in Los Angeles, but no distributor wanted to bring it into national release; the film remained unseen until after his death in 1989. Cassavetes' final directing jobs were for-hire assignments: *Gloria* (1980), *Love Streams* (1985) and *Big Trouble* (1986, where he replaced Elaine May midway through a troubled production).

Over the years, Cassavetes' impact has grown substantially and many independent filmmakers cite him as a main influence on their work. Even the U.S. Postal Service recognized his influence: in 2003, a commemorative stamp series called *American Filmmaking: Behind the Scenes* was issued. For the stamp devoted to directing, the person chosen to represent film direction was Cassavetes.

New Blood in Horror Films

For most of the run of the independent filmmaking world, horror films were considered the poor relations of the genre. Most horror films were barely scary, due in large part to the acute lack of imagination behind the camera and shabby production values and poor acting on camera. Even amid the so-called exploitation filmmakers who operated beyond the reach of the Hays Office, the shock value offered in the films was barely visible. But even within the major, horror films were rarely a major focus. Universal Pictures had its run of monsters with *Dracula* and *Frankenstein* (both in 1931), *The Mummy* (1932), *Bride of Frankenstein* (1935) and *The Wolf Man* (1941). But the unwise decision to milk these films in seemingly endless sequels only diluted whatever chill factor they may have originally created. By 1948, Universal could only make fun of what was originally considered frightening when the studio played its monster characters for laughs in *Abbott and Costello Meet Frankenstein*.

Over at RKO, producer Val Lewton enjoyed unusual free reign in creating a series of low-budget/high-imagination chillers such as *Cat People* (1942) and *I Walked with a Zombie* (1943). While celebrated today for their bold use of suggestive horror (as opposed to actually showing the carnage and terror), Lewton's output was actually fairly limited and his influence was not acknowledged until many years after his 1951 death.

During the 1950s and 1960s, horror was primarily the realm of the no-budget indie filmmakers and the ebullient mini-studio American International Pictures. These films gained audiences primarily through their overbearing marketing hucksterism, not by means of quality filmmaking. While a couple of genuinely striking horror films did turn up in this time, most notably Herk Harvey's 1962 Kansas-based *Carnival of Souls*, for the most part there was little of value to shake up audiences or critics.

Two films, however, created a seismic shift in how horror films were made and judged. The first was *Blood Feast*, made in Florida in 1963 by Herschell Gordon Lewis. The film focused on an Egyptian caterer who opted to use human parts in his culinary offerings. Shot in color, the film has widely been acknowledged as painfully inept at too many levels. Yet *Blood Feast* broke new ground for daring to show raw, bloody, gory sequences in unapologetic violence, most notably the sequence where a woman's tongue is ripped from her body (a lamb's tongue coated in cranberry sauce was the crude special effects ploy). *Blood Feast* created a minor sensation and enabled Lewis to turn out a series of horror films where the violence quotient increased dramatically as the artistic value of the productions dropped substantially.

In 1968, a far more sophisticated horror film had a more dramatic effect on the genre. The grim, dark story of a group of people trapped in an isolated farmhouse surrounded by flesh eating zombies, George Romero's *Night of the Living Dead* had everything going against it: it was shot in black and white (at a time when monochrome was no longer being used in Hollywood) for $114,000 in the Pittsburgh area with mostly amateur actors (and it looked it). Romero had problems getting quality distribution; Columbia rejected the film because it was not in color while American International Pictures abhorred its downbeat ending. Oddly, the art house Continental Releasing, a division of the Walter Reade theater chain, acquired the film; this was not something that was typical for its theatrical offerings. Incredibly, a very bad programming decision helped secure the film's reputation for pure horror. For reasons that still remain unexplained, *Night of the Living Dead* was booked for a Chicago-area kiddie matinee. Even more peculiar was the presence of Roger Ebert, film critic for the *Chicago Sun-Times*, at the show. Ebert reviewed the film and the screening, noting how the nine-year-olds in the audience were either stunned into silence or left crying at what they witnessed on screen. Other critics began to weigh in on the film, and the reaction was polarizing. *Variety* condemned its "unrelieved orgy of sadism" and openly challenged the "integrity and social responsibility" of its creators. Vincent Canby of the *New York Times* dismissed it as a "junk movie." But Pauline Kael of *The New Yorker* called it "one of the most gruesomely terrifying movies ever made – and when you leave the theatre you may wish you could forget the whole horrible experience." Rex Reed, with the *New York Daily News*, proclaimed it was "unthinkable for anyone seriously interested in horror movies not to see it."

Night of the Living Dead, not unlike its zombie characters, never truly died. The film's mainstream theatrical release was followed by a second life on the midnight movie circuit, where it remained a staple of the late night crowd for years. And due to an accident by Continental Releasing where the film's copyright was left off the finished print, *Night of the Living Dead* fell into the public domain, allowing an endless number of bootleggers to sell cheap dupes of the film, thus spreading its availability far and wide while denying Romero any profits from these sales.

By this period, the film industry's self-censorship efforts had pretty much collapsed into failure. Violence and bloodshed were no longer kept off the screen, and a new ratings system created by the Motion Picture Association of America simply alerted audiences to what was in a film; it became impossible to prevent filmmakers from putting questionable content in their productions. Partly as s a result of this new environment, horror films became more violent and filmmakers were not shy about depicting excessive scenes where blood and gore filled the screen with often-reckless abandon.

In the 1970s, horror films began to grow in popularity as audiences were bombarded with a level of cinematic terror that never existed before. Wes Craven's *Last House on the Left* (1972), with its presentation of torture and castration, Tobe Hooper's *The Texas Chainsaw Massacre* (1974), Craven's *The Hills Have Eyes* (1977), Romero's *Dawn of the Dead* (1978) and John Carpenter's *Halloween* (1978) brought a new wave of gruesome yet compelling horror to the big screen. These films, all independently produced, redefined what audiences came to expect from the horror genre.

Sadly, these films represented the peak of the output. For every *Last House on the Left* and *Dawn of the Dead*, there were (and continue to be) a seemingly endless number of cheaply made horror flicks that mistake the blatant display of blood and guts with genuinely terrifying storytelling. As time progressed, the quantity of independent horror films increased dramatically. The quality of these films, for the most part, has often been lacking. Nonetheless, audiences have yet to become bored with the genre, and indie horror continues to thrive.

A Brief Fling with the Anti-Establishment

One of the most profitable independent films of the 1960s was *Easy Rider*. Shot on 16mm with a $400,000 budget, the film epitomized its era with the celebration of the drug-fueled, motorcycle-riding anti-heroes (Peter Fonda, the film's producer, and Dennis Hopper, who directed the film). A great deal has been written about the film's contents and its raucous creation, but what is often overlooked is that *Easy Rider* was an independently-produced film. Both Fonda and Hopper had worked at American Independent Pictures and felt the small studio, which had no qualms in thumbing its nose at polite society, would be interested in this anti-establishment film.

Remarkably, American International rejected the proposal. Hopper and Fonda then approached producer Bert Schneider, who was best known for *The Monkees* TV series. Schneider bankrolled most of the film, which was picked up by Columbia Pictures. The rest, as they say, is history.

Also in 1969 was Haskell Wexler's *Medium Cool*. A disturbing drama about a reporter being drawn into the violent environment surrounding the violent protests around the 1968 Democratic National Convention in Chicago, the film echoed *Easy Rider* with its direct assault on the establishment and its beatification of the enigmatic anti-hero as the new celluloid icon. Paramount Pictures acquired the film and successfully distributed it. Strangely, neither film sparked a flurry of anti-establishment filmmaking; they remain anomalies that defined a point in time but did not change the face of film world in a truly significant manner. Even more peculiar, both films marked the directing peaks of their respective creators. Wexler helmed several documentaries, but focused the bulk of his career as a cinematographer, most notably *Days of Heaven* (1978) and *Blade Runner* (1982). Hopper followed *Easy Rider* with the catastrophically awful *The Last Movie* (1971). He would not be able to direct another film until *Out of the Blue* in 1980; his subsequent directing work was relatively undistinguished, although he still remains in popular demand as an actor.

The African American Experience

The question of civil rights baffled the film industry for years. The post-World War II agitation for racial equality created a sense of confusion. Independently-produced films that attempted to address issues of racism, *Home of the Brave* and *Lost Boundaries*, both made in 1949, and the 1951 French-financed adaptation of Richard Wright's *Native Son*, starring the author as the maladjusted central character, came across as unsubtle and often strident. Race was such a touchy issue that even something as relatively benign as *The Jackie Robinson Story* (1949) carefully omitted several thorny incidents in the baseball player's life, including the blatantly racist court martial that he faced during his wartime service.

During the 1950s, occasional attempts were made by isolated independent producers to offer the African-American experience on screen. *Go, Man, Go!* (1954) presented a highly-fictionalized presentation on the creation of the Harlem Globetrotters basketball team (the film also broke another racial barrier by having Chinese-American cinematographer James Wong Howe as its director). The 1958 *Anna Lucasta* adapted the popular all-black Broadway show to the screen, providing a rare opportunity for musical stars Eartha Kitt and Sammy Davis Jr. to enjoy serious dramatic starring roles.

It wasn't until the early 1960s, at the peak of the civil rights movement, that independent filmmakers began to feel comfortable in returning to black-themed films. Nicholas Webster's *Gone Are the Days* (1963), a film version of Ossie Davis' play *Purlie Victorious*, took a sharp satirical view of racial attitudes in the Old South. Larry Peerce's *One Potato, Two Potato* (1964) confronted the taboo of interracial marriage with a frank, unapologetic and genuinely heartbreaking presentation. Michael Roemer's *Nothing but a Man* addressed issues of class division within the African-American community, with its story of a railroad worker's love for a preacher's daughter. Both films were lavishly praised by critics, but neither black nor white audiences were eager to seek them out.

Why did these films fail to find an audience? One cannot blame it on racism. At the time, Sidney Poitier was rising as Hollywood's first black superstar; in fact, his Oscar-winning performance came in the independently-produced 1963 United Artists release *Lillies of the Field*. Yet that film gingerly touched on racial issues, instead offering a feel-good tale involving a mix of racial, ethnic and religious differences.

Perhaps audiences were just not in the mood for a message film – or at least not messages that pushed the sense of guilt. Contrary to contemporary belief, a great many white Americans of the early and mid-1960s were vehemently opposed to the progress being sought by the civil rights leadership. Films that drove across points of racial equality, let alone interracial marriage, may have been too heavy for the time.

On the fringe of this environment, however, came Melvin Van Peebles, an African American writer who relocated to Europe in order to create *The Story of a Three Day Pass* (1967), based on his novel. As with *One Potato, Two Potato*, Van Peebles' film also had an interracial love story. However, the difference of three years saw a distinctive change in audience attitudes. Whereas moviegoers stayed away from *One Potato, Two Potato*, they sought out Van Peebles' film.

Van Peebles returned to America and broke the color bar in Hollywood as the first African American to direct a studio film. Alas, *Watermelon Man* (1970) was a shrill, lame comedy that was only made passable by the over-the-top performance of Godfrey Cambridge as a white bigot who wakes up one morning to discover he has become black.

Van Peebles was unhappy with his Hollywood experience and sought to create a new feature on his own terms. He successfully raised the $500,000 budget ($50,000 reportedly came from comic Bill Cosby) and created a somewhat bizarre story about a male hustler who is on a seemingly endless run from the police after he kills two white cops that brutalized a young Black Panther. The film was given the somewhat unwieldy name *Sweet Sweetback's Baadasssss Song*.

While not a great film, by any stretch, it benefited from Van Peebles' marketing genius. The MPAA gave it an X-rating for its sexual content, so Van Peebles advertised it as being "Rated X by an all-white jury." A small independent distributor called Cinemation, which previously specialized in horror flicks such as *Teenage Mother* and *I Drink Your Blood*, picked up the film for release. An aggressive distribution strategy brought in $15 million at the box office, which was phenomenal for 1971 (especially for a low-budget, black-oriented, no-star film). Both black and white audiences came out for this unusual production, and the notion of sexually-charged violent films centered around a black anti-hero was born. With *Sweet Sweetback's Baadasssss Song* came the birth of Blaxploitation.

As luck would have it, Hollywood grabbed the idea of having a tough, no-nonsense black protagonist and ran with it. Or actually, the studios ran it into the ground. During the early 1970s, a sudden and startling glut of Blaxploitation flicks was churned out by the studios. MGM got there first in 1971 with *Shaft* (released several months after *Sweet Sweetback's Baadasssss Song*), and Warner Bros. followed suit in 1972 with *Super Fly*. Other studios quickly followed, particularly American International Pictures with the outlandishly campy *Blacula* (1972).

The independent producers found themselves struggling for audience attention amid the new wave of Blaxploitation flicks. Many independent films got overlooked in the shuffle during that time, but were able to emerge years later as cult favorites: Bill Gunn's *Ganga & Hess* (1973) provided a trippy mix of vampirism, eroticism and interesting comments on class divisions. *Dolemite* (1975), despite painfully egregious production values, provided a wacky vehicle to highlight the distinctive talents of funnyman Rudy Ray Moore, who also turned up as the star of *Petey Wheatstraw* (1977).

Even worse were independent films with black themes that did not fall into the realm of Blaxploitation. Two 1972 releases, *Georgia, Georgia* (starring Diana Sands) and *Man and Boy* (starring Bill Cosby) were barely acknowledged when they were released and are obscure today. Charles Burnett's *Killer of Sheep* (1977), made while the director was a student at UCLA, managed to find non-theatrical and festival play dates over the years, but problems in clearing music rights prevented it from having a proper theatrical distribution until 2007.

A Curious Hybrid

It is no secret that many independent filmmakers feel their work lacks prestige. Considering that many of these films suffer from the absence of budgets and star power, these feelings can be justified. But during the 1970s, an attempt to import prestige to independent filmmaking tried to take root. It was a fascinating but doomed experiment.

Ely Landau was an independent producer best known for his 1962 presentation of *Long Day's Journey Into Night*, the 1965 film *The Pawnbroker*, and the 1972 Oscar-nominated documentary *King: A Filmed Record ... Montgomery to Memphis*. Landau, working with his wife Edie, came up with an idea that he called the American Film Theatre, where he conceived the production and release of a series of feature films based on well-regarded stage plays.

Adapting a play into a movie was not unusual by itself, but Landau's distribution model was peculiar: the films would be presented once a month in a select number of venues across the U.S. and Canada. Admission to the films could only be purchased on a seasonal subscription basis, with the season lasting eight months. Those who did not have subscriptions to the series were not allowed to see the individual films being presented.

There was no precedent for Landau's distribution model, yet the producer had no problem finding exhibitors who were willing to try it out. In its first season, 1973-74, Landau built a network of more than 500 theaters in 400 cities across North America. But in order to sell the American Film Theatre to audiences, Landau needed to turn up the star wattage to a blinding brightness.

To his credit, Landau succeeded brilliantly in gathering the finest talent available for this endeavor. The opening presentation, a film based on Eugene O'Neill's *The Iceman Cometh*, was directed by John Frankenheimer and starred Lee Marvin, Fredric March, Robert Ryan and Jeff Bridges. Other stellar attractions included Edward Albee's Pulitzer-winning *A Delicate Balance*, directed by Tony Richardson and starring Katharine Hepburn, Paul Scofield, Joseph Cotten and Lee Remick; John Osborne's *Luther*, directed by Guy Green and starring Stacy Keach, Judi Dench, Hugh Griffith and Patrick Magee; and Bertolt Brecht's *Galileo*, directed Joseph Losey and starring Topol, John Gielgud, Edward Fox, Tom Conti and Georgia Brown.

Landau also imported a pair of previously unreleased films with theatrical foundations: Anton Chekhov's *Three Sisters*, directed by and starring Laurence Olivier, and an Irish production of Brian Friel's *Phila-*

delphia, Here I Come, starring Donal McCann and Siobhan McKenna.

But the films in the series were not well received by the critics, particularly the New York reviewers. John Simon was dismissive of the endeavor, claiming the productions "are sorry halfway houses in which neither theater nor cinema can feel at home." (Considering what John Simon was capable of saying, that's a fairly light slam.) Actually, Vincent Canby of the *New York Times* took up the acidic insults, dismissing Landau for "manufacturing the Coffee Table Movie, something that is supposed to establish one's intellectual credentials by physical association. Purchase tickets but give them to your friends."

Landau, in a printed rebuttal, criticized Canby as being a snob. But at day's end, it didn't matter: the first season of the American Film Theatre was a commercial success for Landau, who harvested 500,000 subscribers and was emboldened to launch a second season for 1974-75.

But as meteorologists and would-be aphorism spouters are prone to pronounce, lightning did not strike twice. The second season's returns were not strong (the reviews certainly didn't get better). Although one production in the series did get the notice of Academy voters (Maximilian Schell's performance earned an Oscar nomination as Best Actor), Landau closed down the endeavor.

The American Film Theatre series was unseen until 1979 when Landau, reversing an original desire not to televise his productions, syndicated all of the films for a one-shot package on independent stations across the U.S. In the early 1980s, the Magnetic label briefly offered the titles for the nascent home video market. But after that, the American Film Theatre productions disappeared for nearly two decades, until Kino on Video presented them in 2003 on DVD.

Viewed in retrospect, the American Film Theatre was striking primarily for its inconsistency. The finest offerings of the series – *The Man in the Glass Booth, The Iceman Cometh, Luther, Galileo* (even with Topol playing the astronomer like he was Tevye with a telescope) and musicals *Jacques Brel is Alive and Well and Living in Paris* and *Lost in the Stars* – were invigorating and powerfully made works of art. *Jacques Brel is Alive and*

Well and Living in Paris is particularly remarkable, as it predated the MTV techniques with its whirling, surreal interpretations of the Belgian balladeer's classic songs.

But that's when the series worked. Among the problem efforts were the aforementioned *A Delicate Balance*, Jean Genet's *The Maids* (with Glenda Jackson and Susannah York), Eugene Ionesco's *Rhinoceros* (with Zero Mostel, Gene Wilder and Karen Black) and Simon Gray's *Butley* (starring Alan Bates and Jessica Tandy and directed by Harold Pinter, working for the first and last time behind the camera). These works did not lend themselves well to cinematic adaptation, and the resulting movies were basically filmed plays whose claustrophobic and unimaginative stagings magnified the stridency of their texts and the low budgets of their celluloid interpretations.

Landau's distribution pattern vaguely inspired the Shooting Gallery series, which began in the late 1990s as a means to distribute a collection of films (in that case, U.S. and international titles, six films per season) in block form. Shooting Gallery differed in it was far more limited in scope (15 theaters, versus the American Film Theatre's 500). But as we will discover later, that outing was also unsuccessful. In reel life as in real life, people have a way of repeating past mistakes.

The Cult of the Indie Filmmaker

One of the greatest influences to affect the depth and scope of independent cinema did not occur on the screen. Instead, it occurred in a magazine, when Andrew Sarris published the essay "Notes on the Auteur Theory in 1962" in the magazine *Film Culture*. Auteur is the French word for author, and Sarris assigned the creative authorship of motion pictures solely exclusively to the director.

For the era, this was a revolutionary notion. Although American cinema (both the Hollywood and independent variety) had its share of larger-than-life directors, these individuals were rarely seen as the driving force behind the distinctive personalities of movies. For every Alfred Hitchcock or John Ford whose name and style were immediately recognizable to the general public, there were a countless number of seemingly anonymous directors whose names barely registered with audiences.

But to Sarris, the director was the primary creative force behind the creation of films. It didn't matter if the director was a household name, as in the case of Hitchcock or Ford, or if he labored in near-anonymity amid the chaos of B-level Westerns or cheapo horror flicks. In the auteur theory, the finished film was a reflection of the director's personality and distinctive vision. Indeed, the credit for the film was given solely to the director.

Contrary to popular belief, Sarris was not the creator of the auteur theory. In fact, he was responsible for bringing it across the Atlantic; it was first argued in France in the film magazine *Cahiers du cinéma* in the early 1950s, via the passionate writings of André Bazin, Alexandre Astruc and an aspiring filmmaker named François Truffaut (who first used the word "auteur" in connection with film authorship). Sarris, who was the editor and translator for the English-language edition of *Cahiers du cinéma*, expanded on these notions and introduced them to an American perspective.

The theory, as framed by its original French authors, insisted that directors work with a particular style and recognizable themes to their work. In practice, this may have been more obvious in the French cinema, where eccentric styles were more appreciated. The American cinema of that era (at least the Hollywood output) barely tolerated individual style flourishes. For every Hitchcock, there were dozens of directors along the lines of, say, Walter Lang or Richard Thorpe, competent helmsmen who could ferry a movie along on its schedule and budget without burdening the final work in artistic barnacles.

Sarris' presentation initially received little attention. The celebrated writer William Goldman, speaking years after hearing about Sarris' views, stated his initial reaction to the auteur theory was the statement: "What's the punch line?"

Actually, Goldman's putdown was thoroughly benign compared to the volley presented by Pauline Kael. Writing in *Film Quarterly's* spring

1963 edition, her essay "Circles and Squares" not only eviscerated the auteur theory as rubbish, but clearly belittled both its French fathers and Sarris for their take on film appreciation, which she dismissed as "intellectual diddling."

It is not certain if the French were aware of Kael's volley, but Sarris was obviously cognizant of the intellectual assault. For years to follows, Sarris and Kael engaged in a rough war of words that often took deep personal slices. Both critics would later publish books that held up their views on who deserved primary credit for film authorship.

Sarris, in 1968, expanded on the auteur theory with his highly acclaimed *The American Cinema: Directors and Directions, 1929–1968*. This book detailed the output of the major American directors. In 1971, Kael published *Raising Kane*, which took a grand slam against the ultimate icon of the auteur theorists, Orson Welles, by daring to suggest that Herman J. Mankiewicz, the co-author of the *Citizen Kane* screenplay, deserved equal credit with Welles for the 1941 masterpiece. Welles reportedly considered suing Kael, and many critics faulted her for the lapses in her research surrounding the genesis of the landmark film.

In the end, however, the game went to Sarris. While Kael is, arguably, considered the most influential and articulate film critic of the 20th century, Sarris nonetheless reshaped the perception of films. The auteur theory had an especially profound effect on the manner in which films and directors were perceived, both by the moviegoing public and the industry. This was especially profound in relation to independent cinema, where the director often served double- or triple-duty as producer and writer. All of a sudden, the director became the focal point of the attention regarding the film's creation. Compared to the 1930s through the 1950s, when producers were generally considered the force behind a movie, the notion that the director was the true author of the film's style and substance created a seismic shift in both the artistic and production power that went into movies.

Of course, there were independent film directors who were able to gain recognition for themselves; the aforementioned examples of Maya

Deren in the late 1940s and John Cassavetes following the 1960 premiere of *Shadows* put the independent film director in the proverbial spotlight. But after Sarris expounded on the importance of the director, a new age in film appreciation was created. In retrospect, it was a blessing and a curse.

The blessing of the wide-scale embrace of the auteur theory came in the rediscovery of many filmmakers who had toiled with little or no recognition during the course of their careers. Into the 1970s and beyond, the proliferation of film studies at American colleges and universities, coupled with a wider focus on the history of filmmaking through books and documentaries on the subject (the latter launched, in large part, by Peter Bogdanovich's 1971 independently-produced *Directed by John Ford*) enabled the opportunity to revisit the output of forgotten filmmakers.

But at the same time, it was also a curse because the new focus concentrated heavily on artists and productions that the public initially chose to ignore. When the general public took notice, it was usually for the wrong reasons. Most notably, the 1980 publication of Harry and Michael Medved's book *The Golden Turkey Awards*, a parody of movie industry tributes that honored the worst achievements in cinema history, brought the hitherto-unknown Edward D. Wood Jr. into the center of popular culture. Wood, who was obscure to everyone except a small number of horror film writers, suddenly became synonymous with so-bad-they're-good cinema, and his 1959 magnum opus, *Plan 9 from Outer Space*, became something of an anti-classic.

The Golden Turkey Awards and a 1986 sequel text also called attention to other independent filmmakers who specialized in so-bad-they're-good movies; Phil Tucker, Herschell Gordon Lewis, William Beaudine, Larry Buchanan, Al Adamson, Art J. Nelson, Arch Hall Sr., Ray Dennis Steckler and Bert I. Gordon were held up to comic scorn by the Medveds for their perceived ineptitude. As a result of such attention, a new appreciation of bad movies as unintentionally amusing entertainment became a fixture in popular culture. Video releases and film festivals devoted to the "best of the worst" became commonplace. The popular TV show *Mystery Science Theater 3000* offered the apotheosis of this school of film appreciation: wild and snarky commentary that ran parallel to the weird flicks featured each week.

Of course, none of the filmmakers highlighted in the so-bad-they're-good category intentionally set out to make inane films. In fact, the online indie entity seeking deliberate camp has been Troma, the New York-based producer and distributor of no-budget, high-camp titles such as *The Toxic Avenger, Class of Nuke 'Em High, Chopper Chicks in Zombietown, Sgt. Kabukiman NYPD, Surf Nazis Must Die* and *Poultrygeist: Night of the Dead Chicken.*

But, on occasion, overlooked serious talents were able to gain a belated recognition based on the auteur theory's insistence of the director's vision as the driving force in filmmaking. In many instances, this helped to rescue the reputations of independently-financed filmmakers whose output was extremely limited, often to a single film. Among the one-hit directors who gained late recognition were blacklisted filmmaker Abraham Polonsky and his 1948 *Force of Evil*; actor Charles Laughton, who directed the 1955 thriller *Night of the Hunter*; industrial filmmaker Herk Harvey and his sole narrative feature, 1962's *Carnival of Souls*; Leonard Kastle and the offbeat 1970 *The Honeymoon Killers*; actress Barbara Loden and her sole directing effort, the 1971 *Wanda*; Richard Blackburn's 1972 horror film *Lemora: A Child's Tale of the Supernatural*; and Douglas Bourla's experimental offering *The Noah*, which was shot in 1968, not completed until 1975, and unseen by audiences until a 2006 DVD release.

Somewhat more prolific artists also gained recognition through auteur-inspired scholarship and celebration. Edgar G. Ulmer, whose three-decade career pinballed wildly between studio and independent films (including the helming of Yiddish- and Ukrainian-language features and race films), was discovered years after his peak period. While the bulk of his work is, admittedly, forgettable, a handful of his titles, most notably *The Light Ahead* (1939) and *Detour* (1945), were brought to wider attention and a long-overdue classic status.

Samuel Fuller also received belated recognition in this manner. Barely acknowledged by the public and the industry during his peak years of the 1950s and early 1960s, the after-the-fact overview of his output brought classic status to his independently-produced films that were initially either overlooked or panned: *The Baron of Arizona* (1950), *The Steel Helmet* (1951), *The Crimson Kimono* (1961), *Shock Corridor* (1963) and *The Naked Kiss* (1964). The rediscovery of Fuller's work helped him gain a new slot in Hollywood in the early 1980s, but the commercial failure of *The Big Red One* (1980) and the problems regarding the Paramount Pictures production of *White Dog* (which was made in 1982 but not theatrically released) put a permanent end to his U.S. filmmaking career.

Roger Corman, whose career took off at mini-studio American International Pictures during the 1960s with a colorful series of Vincent Price-starring horror flicks inspired by the works of Edgar Allan Poe, also saw a new appreciation of his pre-Price/Poe work when he was an independent filmmaker in the 1950s, including *It Conquered the World* (1956), *A Bucket of Blood* (1959) and *The Little Shop of Horrors* (1960). One could make an argument these films are recalled solely because of Corman's name attachment and the publicity surrounding their rapid productions on tiny budgets (*A Bucket of Blood* was made in five days for $50,000, while *The Little Shop of Horrors* was made in two days for $30,000); the artistic value of these little films could charitably be considered as charming.

Other directors who received after-the-fact cult movie recognition have included Russ Meyer (whose films include the 1959 *The Immoral Mr. Teas* and the 1965 *Faster, Pussycat! Kill! Kill!*). Curtis Harrington (best known for his 1961 *Night Tide*), Jack Hill (best known for 1968's *Spider Baby*) and Monte Hellman (best known for his 1965 Westerns *Ride in the Whirlwind* and *The Shooting*).

The Indie-to-Hollywood Train

Beginning in the 1960s, a seemingly endless skein of filmmakers who cut their teeth in independent films were noted and appreciated by the Hollywood studios and quickly absorbed into their orbit. Some filmmakers rose to the highest ranks of the industry and became the most prominent creative forces in the industry. Others got stuck in mediocre projects, or wound up doing made-for-television products. And others never quite found their Hollywood niche and came back to the indie world, but were unable to recapture the magic that first sparked interest in their works. All of them shared the history of being quickly hailed by the media and the industry as the next big thing, at which point they departed the indie platform for the studios and wider audience releases.

In chronological order of their breakthrough films, these indie-to-Hollywood artists include:

Francis Ford Coppola. His career began in the direction of so-called "nudie" features *The Bellboy and the Playgirls* and *Tonight for Sure* (both 1962) and the Irish-based slasher flick *Dementia 13* (1963). Coppola moved into the studio system in 1966 with *You're a Big Boy Now* (1966) and remained a fixture therein afterwards.

Martin Scorsese. The New York filmmaker graduated from short subjects to the 1967 feature *Who's That Knocking at My Door* in 1967, which first attracted attention via a rave review by Roger Ebert following a screening at the Chicago Film Festival. Success was slow in coming; an assistant director job on *Woodstock* (1970), an unreleased documentary called *Street Scenes* (1970) and an assignment for American International Pictures with *Boxcar Bertha* (1972) followed. In 1973, the independently-financed *Mean Streets* brought Scorsese into the world of Italian-American New York tough guys (including a little-known actor named Robert De Niro). De Niro was tapped for Hollywood after *Mean Streets* was released (ironically, for a decidedly non-Scorsese project, the feminist drama *Alice Doesn't Live Here Anymore* in 1974).

John Waters. The Baltimore-based free spirit worked in 16mm with his off-kilter comedies *Mondo Trasho* (1969), *Multiple Maniacs* (1970), *Pink Flamingos* (1972), *Female Trouble* (1974) and *Desperate Living* (1977). Waters' outrageous and scatological humor was hugely popular on the cult-friendly midnight-movie circuit, but mainstream audiences rarely had the chance to experience his gross-out brand of comedy.

Waters went Hollywood in 1981 via New Line Cinema, which originally functioned as his distributor before becoming a production entity.
While his seriously toned-down films *Polyester* (1981), *Hairspray* (1988)
and *Cry-Baby* (1990) found appreciative audiences, the anarchic spark of
his original work was extinguished.

Ralph Bakshi. One of the relatively few creators of independent
animated features, Bakshi scores a major cultural coup with the first-
ever X-rated feature in 1971's *Fritz the Cat*. His follow-up feature, *Heavy
Traffic* (1973), also received an X rating and it created a sensation with
its raw content and biting style. But lightning did not strike three times;
Coonskin (1975) failed to generate the same level of excitement and ran
into controversy over allegations by several civil rights groups of racist
content. Bakshi went Hollywood, but his later work – *Wizards* (1977),
The Lord of the Rings (1978), *American Pop* (1981), *Hey Good Lookin'*
(1982), *Fire and Ice* (1983) and *Cool World* (1992) – never generated
the same level of excitement as his first two works.

George Lucas. In 1971, Lucas was pegged by Francis Ford Coppola
to direct a feature version of a student film that Lucas shot in 1967 at
the University of Southern California.   The resulting film, *THX 1138*,
offered a disturbing view of a dystopian future where human emotions
were suppressed by medications and law enforcement. The film was not
a commercial hit, but Lucas managed to move into Universal Studios in
1973 for *American Graffiti* and then to 20th Century-Fox for a 1977 sci-
fi adventure that took place long ago in a galaxy far, far away.

Terrence Malick. In 1973, Malick created a sensation with critics
(but not audiences) by offering the independently-produced *Badlands*, a
stylish crime spree drama starring Martin Sheen and Sissy Spacek. Malick never went back to the indie world. His later work – *Days of Heaven*
(1978), *The Thin Red Line* (1988), *The New World* (2005) and *The Tree of
Life* (2009) – were studio-financed productions.

Tobe Hooper. The 1974 horror film *The Texas Chainsaw Massacre*
broke new ground for sheer gore and violence. Hooper went Hollywood with *Salem's Lot* (1977), *Poltergeist* (1982) and *Invaders from Mars*

(1986), but never quite found a niche in the studios and subsequently returned to independent productions.

John Carpenter. Hollywood was slow to recognize the creator of the sci-fi comedy *Dark Star* (1974), the action/adventure *Assault on Precinct 13* (1977) and the slasher landmark *Halloween* (1978). Needless to say, the unexpected success of *Halloween* kicked open the studio doors and Carpenter became a studio fixture ever since.

Joan Micklin Silver. The director's black-and-white feature, *Hester Street* (1975), earned critical acclaim for its sensitive depiction of Jewish immigrants to New York's Lower East Side in the early 20th century; leading lady Carol Kane received an Oscar nomination for her performance. Silver's later work in Hollywood never quite resonated with the same level of appeal, although *Crossing Delancey* (1989) offered a warm celebration of contemporary Jewish New York culture.

David Lynch. The off-beat, disturbing experimental feature *Eraserhead* (1977) became a staple on the midnight movie circuit. Lynch was tapped for Hollywood work with *The Elephant Man* (1980) and remained an iconoclastic studio fixture ever since.

Joe Dante. The low-budget *Piranha* (1978) found an audience that didn't mind the obvious *Jaws* rip-off. Dante quickly went Hollywood and never looked back.

Susan Seidelman. Her debut feature, the $60,000 *Smithereens* (1982), received positive notice at the Cannes Film Festival and a much-hyped release via New Line. Hollywood called and Seidelman established her career with *Desperately Seeking Susan* (1985), which had the fortuitous luck of casting a hitherto-unknown pop singer named Madonna as one of the leads.

Joel and Ethan Coen. This sibling team hit the ground running with *Blood Simple* (1984), which won the Grand Jury Prize at the U.S. Film Festival (the forerunner of Sundance). Hollywood called and the Coens took off on a long and successful ride, peaking with the 2007 Best Picture Oscar for *No Country for Old Men*.

Gus Van Sant. The low budget, unapologetically queer *Mala Noche*

(1985) showed the filmmaker's willingness to take chances on supposedly non-commercial subject matter. While occasionally returning to the indie fold with *Gerry* (2002), Van Sant has brought indie-style daring and attitude to studio-financed productions.

Spike Lee. The $80,000 feature *She's Gotta Have It* (1986) established Lee's career, and he quickly went to Hollywood. The film's critical and commercial success helped to reinvigorate interest in independent films dealing with African-American subject matter (the death of the Blaxploitation genre a decade earlier gave the impression this subject no longer possessed commercial value). Lee's success also helped pave the way for other African-American filmmakers, including Robert Townsend with *Hollywood Shuffle* (1987), Charles Lane with *Sidewalk Stories* (1989) and Julie Dash with *Daughters in the Dust* (1992).

Steven Soderbergh. The 1989 Sundance screening of *sex, lies and videotape* and the subsequent Miramax acquisition of the film helped elevate Soderbergh to the position of a major film talent. Although Soderbergh flirted with indie productions, including *Gray's Anatomy* and *Schizopolis* (both 1996), his career focus remained in the Hollywood system.

Richard Linklater. The 1991 loose-limbed *Slacker* offered a diverting approach at free-form, almost plotless filmmaking. Shot in Austin, Texas, the film's breezy style had its admirers, and Linklater was able to leave Texas for the proverbial bigger and better horizons.

Quentin Tarantino. Tarantino was widely credited for reviving the popular concept of independent cinema with the wildly successful *Pulp Fiction* (1994), but that technically wasn't an independent film (Miramax's financing put that across). Tarantino's earlier *Reservoir Dogs* (1992) was a genuine independent production, but it was a commercial disappointment during its U.S. theatrical release. It wasn't until after the success of *Pulp Fiction* that people rediscovered *Reservoir Dogs* on video – at which point it earned a belated cult classic following. Tarantino's post-*Pulp Fiction* career has nothing to do with traditional indie cinema.

Kevin Smith. Another Miramax discovery, the New Jersey-based Smith connected with moviegoers with his $27,000 black-and-white comedy *Clerks* (1994). While the filmmaking style admittedly left a lot to be desired, Smith's brilliantly funny screenplay and the rich ensemble performance (including Smith as the mute hanger-on "Silent Bob") resonated. Smith also followed the career train to the Hollywood system.

Robert Rodriguez. In one of the classic flukes of the film industry, Rodriguez's 1992 $7,000 Spanish-language *El Mariachi*, which was originally produced as a direct-to-video release solely for the Hispanic market, was picked up by Columbia Pictures for $150,000.

Edward Burns. The 1995 feature *The Brothers McMullen* put actor-director Burns on the map, thanks to the efforts of Fox Searchlight, which presented the film as its first title. Burns' subsequent film output as a director pinballed between studio and indie productions, but none of his later films ever generated the level of interest as his first   effort.

Darren Aronofsky. Mathematics is rarely the subject of films, but *Pi* (1998), with its distinctive monochromatic cinematography and aggressive storytelling style, proved to be an offbeat hit that launched the filmmaker's career forward, including the indies *Requiem for a Dream* (2000) and *The Wrestler* (2008) and the studio-financed *The Fountain* (2006).

But this is not to say that every indie filmmaker jumps into Hollywood once receiving recognition. Among the number of filmmakers who have remained firm and fast in the indie orbit are the following:

Henry Jaglom. Self-financing and self-releasing his films since the 1970s, Jaglom has enjoyed longevity within the indie world. Despite criticism of excess verbosity and chronic navel-gazing, Jaglom has been able to score with critics and art house audiences with titles such as *Eating* (1990), *Babyfever* (1994) and *Last Summer in the Hamptons* (1995).

John Sayles. Having scored a critical home run with *Return of the Secaucus 7* (1980), Sayles has offered a diverse and unpredictable canon that includes *Brother from Another Planet* (1984), *Matewan* (1987), *Passion Fish* (1992), and the Spanish-language *Men with Guns* (1997) and *Casa de los Babys* (2003). Sayles' occasional forays into studio-financed films include *Eight Men Out* (1988) and *Lone Star* (1996).

Abel Ferrara. The New York-based filmmaker with a talent for violent action flicks has been directing since the early 1970s, but didn't click with audiences until the rise of home video enabled cult followings for his previously-overlooked features *The Driller Killer* (1979), *Ms. 45* (1981) and *Fear City* (1984); *Bad Lieutenant* (1992) is, arguably, his best-regarded work.

Wayne Wang. The Chinese-American experience has been captured by Wang through *Chan is Missing* (1982), *Dim Sum: A Little Bit of Heart* (1985) and *Eat a Bowl of Tea* (1989). Following a Hollywood-financed adaptation of Amy Tan's *The Joy Luck Club* (1993), Wang branched out beyond the borders of Chinese-American storytelling with films such as *Smoke* and *Blue in the Face* (both 1995).

Jim Jarmusch. The deadpan, cult-friendly style of films such as *Stranger Than Paradise* (1982), *Down by Law* (1986), *Mystery Train* (1989) and *Dead Man* (1995) have confirmed Jarmusch as one of the most popular independent filmmakers of modern times.

Hal Hartley. Hartley's off-beat storytelling has also found a cult following, as witnessed by the success of *The Unbelievable Truth* (1989), *Trust* (1990), *Simple Men* (1992) and *Henry Fool* (1997).

Bill Plympton. The creator of acclaimed animated shorts, Plympton has directed the feature-length animated productions *The Tune* (1992), *Mondo Plympton* (1997), *I Married a Strange Person* (1997) and *Mutant Aliens* (2001). He also directed the live-action features *J. Lyle* (1994) and *Guns on the Clackamas* (1995).

Larry Clark. Inviting controversy with his harsh view of contemporary youth, Clark has helmed *Kids* (1995), *Another Day in Paradise* (1997), *Ken Park* (2002) and *Wassup Rockers* (2005).

The 10 Most Important Independent Films of All Time:
Dennis Schwartz, editor, Ozus' World Movie Reviews

Q: If you were to look over the span of the history of U.S. independent cinema, from the silent era to today's output, what would you list as the 10 Most Important Independently-Produced Films of All Time ... and why?

1. *The Birth of a Nation* (D.W. Griffith, 1915, silent). One of the most influential and controversial films in the history of American cinema. It's important in film history for its innovative technical and narrative achievements, and that it was Hollywood's initial blockbuster. The controversy arose because it promoted white supremacism and the glorification of the Ku Klux Klan as an organization whites needed for protection, and brought that out in the open so America had to face up to its racist past. A film that is outdated by today's filming standards, but is still a must-see for its bitter history lesson.

2. *The General* (Buster Keaton, 1927, silent). It was a box-office disaster and received extremely poor reviews upon its release. Today, most critics accept it as a masterpiece, and it is arguably the greatest comedy ever made. Keaton, known as the Great Stone Face, gave voice to film as art and spared no expenses while filming, even laying down 19th-century tracks for the signature train chase sequence. The film plays a pivotal role in how comedy evolved from the more primitive times of Keystone Kop flicks.

3. *Meshes of the Afternoon* (Maya Deren, 1943). Maya Deren, from 1943 until her death in 1961, led the

avant-garde movement in cinema. In this 18-minute short she disregards traditional linear narrative structure and instead employs powerful dreamlike images that manipulate time and space to achieve a twilight zone between fiction and reality. Deren has made the following comment: "This film is concerned with the interior experiences of an individual. It does not record an event which could be witnessed by other persons. Rather, it reproduces the way in which the subconscious of an individual will develop, interpret and elaborate an apparently simple and casual incident into a critical emotional experience." The dreamlike *Meshes* has influenced many subsequent outstanding films, such as David Lynch's *Lost Highway* (1997).

4. *Detour* (Edgar G. Ulmer, 1945). Although this *film noir* was made on a small budget and contains only rudimentary sets and camera work, the film has amassed substantial praise over the years and is held in high regard as a way to make on the cheap an outstanding idea film that can embrace a subversive stance without the need to be itself a subversive film. It's the kind of shoestring film made in six days using a back projection and made entirely in the studio on three minimal sets (the sole exterior is a used-car lot to represent Los Angeles) and with a cast of unknowns. It retains the art of shooting in the studio, a lost art as modern films insist on location shots. It's a throwback film that is still talked about for the passionate emotional level it reached and for the haunting dreamlike pulp fiction world it created, and how it still outranks most, more distinguished, productions as a film of great merit despite all its technical flaws. Every time I see this film

about doomed lovers it brings out in me a moment of deep reflection, as the final words of the protagonist are that "Fate or some mysterious force can put the finger on you or me for no good reason at all."

5. *Killer's Kiss* (Stanley Kubrick, 1955). Kubrick's second feature was a successful experimental low-budget, independently-produced film. He used obtuse flashbacks, had surreal nightmare sequences and an eye-popping imaginative climactic fight in a factory of mannequins. It catches the seedy side of life around Times Square. Kubrick has created a sinister *noir* film, employing dark angle shots from a hand-held camera which he used effectively in the street scenes, where he probably didn't have official permission to be filming and shot it guerrilla-style. It's a way of filming that has not been lost on many modern filmmakers—a reason I believe this to be an important film, far beyond its modest critical acclaim or modest box-office appeal.

6. *Blow Job* (Andy Warhol, 1963). Andy Warhol's underground classic, one of the last films he actually directed himself. He uses a 16-millimeter Bolex camera to shoot this 35-minute short film featuring the visually static close-up of a young man's facial expressions as he receives a b-j from the unseen giver. It's timed to simulate the actual fellatio act and meant to shock with its expressions of raw reality, as the actor on the receiving end is placed in the ludicrous position of doing nothing but experiencing the sex act and after orgasm lighting up a cigarette. This is Warhol's artful way of redefining reality and having both a laugh at the thriving porn movie industry and Hollywood's compromised version of sex. Though the film elicited no excitement, it re-

moves the sex from the sex act and the actor is viewed without an identity, who is neither homosexual nor heterosexual (though in the film credits we learn the b-j giver was a man). It's a personal and very human film that mirrors the way the male viewer might look if he can see himself in such a position getting pleasured. The Warhol film literally goes along with Marshall McLuhan's concept that the medium is the message and does nothing further to intellectualize what is seen visually. It was this kind of raw film that caught on with select filmmakers, who changed forever the notion that film must have a narrative and must only cater to heterosexual audiences.

7. *Night of the Living Dead* (George Romero, 1968). This crude film revolutionized the way gory horror films are made and made it possible for the radical visions of directors like David Cronenberg to emerge. It's shot by a hand-held camera in grainy black and white that resembles a documentary, and was made for peanuts. It was filmed in the surrounding confines of Pittsburgh by a cast of nonprofessionals, and gives off a mock *cinéma vérité* look to its nightmarish tale that threatens Middle America. Its story about flesh-eating zombies becoming activated by radiation from a space rocket and these silent ghouls, the unburied dead, still in human form, are seen ravaging the countryside as cannibals. This popular midnight event film soon became part of America's pop culture scene and still is often imitated and fondly remembered.

8. *Husbands* (John Cassavetes, 1970). It's a seriocomic lengthy improv piece about loneliness in the suburbs and tells about three men who go on a wild binge after

the unexpected death of one of their friends. The influential experimental film promoted *cinéma vérité* and that a film didn't need much of a plot to succeed, and influenced directors from all over the world to not be afraid to make personal films.

9. *Eraserhead* (David Lynch, 1977). It's perhaps the most famous cult film of all time. The strange tale about urban angst was shot in a unique dreamy way and filmed entirely in a deserted Beverly Hills garage, usually from one a.m. until dawn. It's even hard to pin down if the film is an industrial nightmare or perhaps a post-holocaust science-fiction tale. Because the film was so odd, impenetrable, touching and funny, it had a great impact on the underground film scene.

10. *Pi* (Darren Aronofsky, 1998). A truly original story about math crossing with millennial doom. The title refers to the mathematical constant called Pi. This intellectual film, with a nerdy loner math genius as the protagonist, strangely enough proved popular with selected audiences and gave renewed hope for other indie filmmakers to do their thing and not worry about satisfying studio moguls. It kicks around such odd subjects for a film as the Hebrew Kabbala, the Japanese game Go, the Dow Jones industrial average, and a supercomputer named Euclid that analyzes mathematical patterns in the Torah. It adds up to being a film that reached out to an audience that has been mostly neglected by Hollywood and because of its success spawned a rash of Hollywood films aimed at the film's targeted more daring youth market, though none has so far captured this film's funkiness or the genuine freakiness portrayed by its hero.

Miriam Makeba (right) performs for South-African miners in Lionel Rogosin's *Come Back, Africa* (1959), part of the non-fiction film movement that blurred the line between documentaries and scripted narratives. (Photo courtesy of Milestone Film & Video)

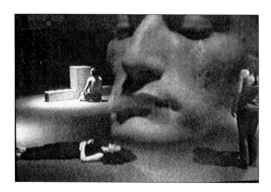

A moment of surreal contemplation from underground filmmaker Antero Alli's experimental documentary *Crux* (1999). (Photo courtesy of ParaTheatrical ReSearch)

Dennis Hopper, Peter Fonda and Jack Nicholson hit the open roads in the
groundbreaking *Easy Rider* (1969), an independently-produced feature.
(Photo courtesy of Columbia Pictures)

The Kwakiutl Indians paddle out to sea in Edward S. Curtis' pioneering 1914 feature *In
the Land of the War Canoes.* (Photo courtesy of Milstone Film & Video)

Mountain Girl (Constance Talmadge) warns Belshazzar (Alfred Paget) that Babylon is going to fall in a scene from D.W. Griffith's 1916 epic *Intolerance*. (Photo courtesy of Movie Star News)

Russ Russo, Margaret Rose Champagne and Thomas Edward Seymour enjoy a horizontal respite in London Betty (2009). (Photo courtesy of Hale Manor Productions)

A group of inner city children watch the world go by in Charles Burnett's 1977 *Killer of Sheep*. (Photo courtesy of Milestone Film & Video)

Little Richie Andrusco soaks in the Coney Island wonderland in *Little Fugitive* (1953). (Photo courtesy of Kino International)

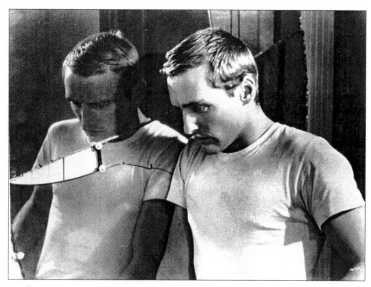

Dennis Hopper experiences a moment of angst in Curtis Harrington's 1961
Night Tide, an underappreciated film that received a belated cult following.
(Photo courtesy Milestone Film & Video)

Steve Buscemi and Harvey Keitel shoot it out in Quentin Tarantino's
1992 Reservoir Dogs. (Photo courtesy of Miramax)

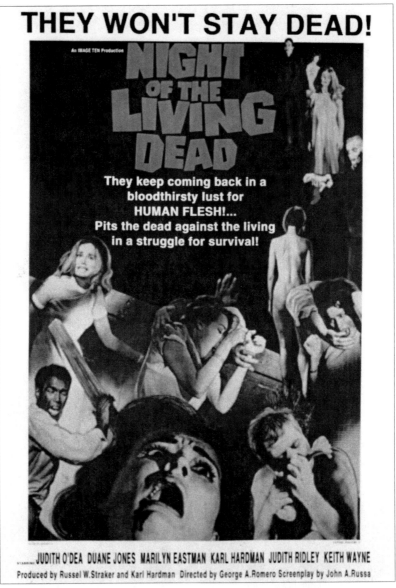

The provocative poster art for the original theatrical release of George Romero's 1968 horror classic Night of the Living Dead. (Photo courtesy of Movie Star News)

Filmmaker Ryan Dacko sizes up the road for his cross-country marathon trek in his 2008 documentary Plan 9 from Syracuse. (Photo courtesy of Ascension 3 Studios)

Henry B. Walthall leads the Confederate charge in D.W. Griffith's 1915 The Birth of a Nation. (Photo courtesy of Movie Star News)

Buster Keaton tends to his beloved locomotive in The General (1927), a film that was a commercial dud in its day but is considered a classic today. (Photo courtesy of Movie Star News)

Paul Robeson contemplates his newfound power in The Emperor Jones (1933).
(Photo courtesy of Movie Star News)

Charlie Chaplin faces a bleak Arctic winter in The Gold Rush *(1925), his first feature under the United Artists banner. (Photo courtesy of Movie Star News)*

*Jane Russell luxuriates in a haystack in this famous publicity still for Howard Hughes'
controversial 1943 Western The Outlaw. (Photo courtesy of Movie Star News)*

Orson Welles dominates Anthony Perkins in The Trial (1962), one of Welles' European-based independent productions (Photo courtesy of Milestone Film & Video).

Robert Strauss surveys a post-apocalyptic isolation in Daniel Bourla's The Noah, an experimental feature shot in 1968, completed in 1975, but not released until a 2006 DVD presentation. (Photo courtesy of Pathfinder Pictures)

T.D. Jakes confronts Kimberly Elise in a tense moment from Woman, Thou Art Loosed *(2004), one of the new wave of independently-produced films focusing on the African-American community. (Photo courtesy of Magnolia Pictures)*

Chapter Four:
The Underground Film Movement

"I get a kick out of being an outsider constantly. It allows me to be creative. I don't like anything in the mainstream and they don't like me."

– Bill Hicks

Running parallel to independent cinema, but only rarely overlapping it, is the realm of underground cinema. In many ways, it provides a more invigorating and challenging story than the traditional independent cinema that we've seen up to this point.

Underground cinema has mostly existed as a fringe territory to independent cinema. Indeed, an argument can be made that underground films are true independent cinema, since they exist in total independence of the mainstream movie model from both a production and distribution viewpoint. The name "underground" may not be the best moniker, since it suggests a cred that many films within this genre lack. The titles "avant-garde" and "experimental" are often used in its place, but for lack of a better substitute, we'll refer to this school of cinema as underground.

Yet charting underground cinema is tricky. For most of its history, the depth and scope of its artistic importance has been acknowledged in something of a time-delay method; specific titles are discovered years, sometimes decades, after their creation. Sometimes the underground classics barely register a blip on the radar of mainstream moviegoers – and, for that matter, with self-proclaimed film experts. That also represents the downside of the genre; the films are so far underground that no one knows of their existence.

Even today, underground filmmaking is barely acknowledged outside of the very tight circles where such artistic rebellion is appreciation. In many ways, it might be the very best kept secret in the motion picture world.

And, yes, it is artistic rebellion. Underground filmmaking represents a radically different approach to how films are produced and appreciated. Often, this approach is the only way to go: imagination compensates for a lack of funds.

But, for the most part, underground filmmaking dares to be different by consciously avoiding the protocol of Hollywood-style notions of what a film should look and sound like. From its nascent era in the 1920s through today's digital endeavors, underground films represent the ultimate in celluloid nonconformity. And for an industry where nonconformists are rarely rewarded with lucrative offers of fame and fortune, the willingness to stand out and be different gives the underground filmmakers a sense of boldness and daring that few of their prestige-chasing peers could ever aspire to possess.

In the Underground Beginning

It would be lovely to claim underground cinema as an American art form, but it actually originated across the Atlantic with the German feature *The Cabinet of Dr. Caligari*. That 1920 film, directed by Robert Wiene (who earned the job after Fritz Lang rejected the assignment), sped miles from traditional filmmaking with a striking Expressionist style that had no precedent in motion pictures at that point. Blessed with a wildly distorted set design, make-up that emphasized the inner turmoil of its characters, off-beat camera angles that emphasized the demented aspects of the storyline, the film was an extraordinary departure from the school of conventional filmmaking that sought to mirror the protocol of daily reality.

While the emotional and intellectual impact of *The Cabinet of Dr. Caligari* does not hold up particularly well by contemporary standards (particularly with its disappointing twist ending), the artistic value of *The Cabinet of Dr. Caligari* cannot be underestimated. Even today, its deep, dark style can be traced through horror, sci-fi, *film noir* and even action/adventure genres.

Of course, everyone knows about *The Cabinet of Dr. Caligari*. But where did American underground cinema begin? It actually had its roots in 1921, the same year that the German film was presented in U.S. theaters. But unlike *The Cabinet of Dr. Caligari*, the first American underground offering was barely acknowledged in its day. Even at this late date, many people are not aware of its existence. The film is a 10-minute creation called *Manhatta*.

Manhatta was a collaboration of two acclaimed visual artists with no previous filmmaking experience and no connections to the film industry: painter-photographer Charles Sheeler and photographer Paul Strand. The circumstances surrounding this collaboration were never recorded, so it is unclear why Sheeler and Strand decided to try their hand at motion pictures.

Manhatta was a very curious film for its time, since it didn't fit into any established genre. It has no plot, but it is not a documentary in the true sense of the word. It is a non-fiction film in presenting a day in the life of lower Manhattan, but there's no particular storyline that takes the viewer from Point A to Point B. One could imagine it as the cinematic equivalent of an abstract poem; the film's images are linked with passages from Walt Whitman's *Leaves of Grass*, albeit with no attribution to Whitman's authorship, but in 1921, no such genre existed.

As far as anyone can determine, neither Sheeler nor Strand openly stated their desire to purposely create a new school of cinema.

Manhatta consists of 65 different shots that highlight the physical majesty of New York City, as seen from the peaks of its skyscrapers and the harbor that connects the city to the ocean. The film is a celebration of architecture and transportation, not human achievement. At no time does *Manhatta* look at the New Yorkers directly from street level. Instead, the camera's strange perspective does everything possible to de-emphasize the human elements to an extreme degree.

Sheeler and Strand aimed their camera from great heights in the city's office towers, thus making the New Yorkers look like ants. In their film, the city's architecture repeatedly minimizes its inhabitants: the soaring arches on the Brooklyn Bridge create a huge void above the pedestrian traffic that travel across its span, while the huge windows of a Wall Street corporate fortress seem more appropriate for fairytale giants than ordinary wage slaves.

Even the construction of these mighty edifices is not a celebration of human greatness. In one scene focusing on the construction of a new office tower, Sheeler and Strand shoot from the ground level upwards, capturing the construction workers in silhouette as they labor furiously amid the massive steel beams that will form the shell of their building.

Camera movement in *Manhatta* is also curious: there is very little of it. Occasionally, there is a slight horizontal pan. But for the most part, the camera stays stationary to capture the images of the extraordinary cityscape. Yet that is not to say the film is stagnant. When there is movement, it mostly involves the transportation vehicles that move people and commerce to and fro: the ferry that disgorges passengers onto a terminal ramp, the trains that chug along railroad lines with their cars full of passengers and cargo, the rectangular freighters gliding in quiet majesty across the choppy waves of New York harbor, and a massive cruise ship slicing its way across the harbor after a journey from across the sea.

Manhatta also fills its screen with swirls of smoke from chimneys and smokestacks. It is visually striking to behold, with the thick white curls of smoke dancing across the skyline. Needless to say, air pollution wasn't much of a concern back in 1921.

But what does it all mean? For the most part, *Manhatta* had no specific meaning. It didn't say anything that wasn't already obvious – New
York is a very big city. And the stillness of the motion picture camera
aimed at buildings and skylines clearly suggests Sheeler and Strand were
attempting to create the cinematic equivalent of still photography (mercifully, their visual artistry prevented the film from being a monotonous
montage of static shots). Yet in its quiet, abstract and often disturbing
glimpse across a city that seems too large for its people, *Manhatta* is a
powerful celebration of how man's creations overwhelmed its creator.

So why isn't *Manhatta* more famous? Sadly, Sheeler and Strand
didn't give much effort to getting their film widely seen. The film debuted in New York in 1921 under the title *New York the Magnificent*. It
turned up in Paris a year later as *La Fumee de New York*. It was shown
again in New York 1926, and then the London Film Society screened it
in 1927 as *Manhatta*. And as far as anyone can determine, those were
the only public screenings for *Manhatta*.

Sheeler never worked in films again, although he made prints from
some of the *Manhatta* shots for display in photographic galleries. Strand
made a few additional independent films, but he showed little pride in
creating *Manhatta* and never spoke of the film, which vanished after its
1927 London screening. During the 1920s, several filmmakers sought
to make similar motion pictures celebrating a city in motion; Walter
Ruttmann's *Berlin: Symphony of a Big City* (1927), Joris Ivens' Amster-
dam-based *Rain* (1929) and Dziga Vertov's Moscow-based *Man with the
Movie Camera* (1929) were hailed in their time for their avant-garde artistry. But it is unlikely that Ruttman, Ivens or Vertov knew of *Manhatta*.

In 1950, a 16mm print of *Manhatta* was located in the British Film
Industry vaults. Over the years, *Manhatta* belatedly began to receive
recognition as being the first U.S. avant-garde movie. As a public domain
film, it has been duped endlessly and can be found on numerous websites, in museum exhibits and in DVD anthologies – which is ironic, considering at the time of its creation it was barely seen and acknowledged.

The 1920s also saw a radical change in the concept of film creation thanks to outside forces. A stream of films imported from Germany, France and the Soviet Union presented a new concept to U.S. audiences of how films could be made. Innovations in cinematography, editing, art direction and set design (not to mention different approaches to coaxing performances from actors) twisted and turned the language of cinema in directions that many people of the era could barely comprehend.

This created positive and negative reactions. The positive, of course, was the exhilaration of the sheer newness of the style; here was something very different and daring, and the European imports made the U.S. movies seem pale and quotidian in comparison. But the negative was the opposite reaction – a newness that baffled and confused moviegoers who had no complaints with the American output and were not impressed with attempts to tinker (or, in many cases, completely reinvent) the medium they came to embrace.

The Hollywood system's first venture into daring to try something even vaguely avant-garde came in 1925 when first-time filmmaker Josef von Sternberg scrapped together $4,900 to shoot a feature film called *The Salvation Hunters*. The concept of the film was very simple: a poor young couple and their child live in the California mud flats, where they face a life of dire monotony. The wife tries to raise money for them by selling herself out to a brutish character, but her husband inevitably saves her honor.

Where von Sternberg sought to differentiate himself from other filmmakers was in his approach to the film's ebb and flow. Rather than create a movie that was rich with action, he slowed down the pace and visuals to a point that *The Salvation Hunters* seemed like a near-motionless motion picture. Indeed, there were many shots where the characters sat around morosely, with only blinks of their eyelids to signal they were alive and functioning.

To drive home the dreariness of the film's symbolism, there were repeated (some have suggested endless) cutaway shots to a steam dredger scooping up great heaps of mud and depositing them in hideous clumps.

Although the film's style was clearly outside of the mainstream, von

Sternberg realized he needed mainstream distribution in order to earn back his costs and advance his career. Thus, von Sternberg started a routine that many others would follow; the underground filmmaker trying to get into the mainstream.

According to legend, the film's leading man, George K. Arthur, bribed a projectionist at United Artists to show the film's first reel "by mistake" for a screening by the studio's star-moguls: Mary Pickford, Douglas Fairbanks and Charlie Chaplin. The trio were impressed enough to request a viewing of the full feature. Fairbanks secured the rights to the film and Chaplin lent his clout to the publicity efforts by declaring the film to be a masterpiece.

However, the United Artists team was stung by the reaction to *The Salvation Hunters*. Critics loathed the film; the *New York Times* dismissed it as "that disagreeable production," and audiences were bored and angered by what they perceived as its meandering presentation and sour view of life. Chaplin, unaccustomed to such harsh criticism, found himself questioned on his lofty pronouncement of the film's merits. He defended his comments by stating, "Well, you know, I was only kidding. They all take everything I say so seriously. I thought I'd praise a bad picture and see what happened." (It was never asked why Chaplin would commit his studio's finances to distribute a "bad picture.")

The lesson learned from the critical and commercial failure of *The Salvation Hunters* resonated far and wide, particularly with von Sternberg, who took his artistic output in the opposite direction by helming a series of highly entertaining vehicles designed to accentuate the otherworldly glamour of his protégé Marlene Dietrich. The studios were not eager to gamble their resources on a film that deviated from the accepted norms of storytelling.

But two years later, another independently-produced avant-garde endeavor made its way into the mainstream. Paul Fejos, a Hungarian-born bacteriologist and anthropologist, decided to switch careers and pursue filmmaking. Fejos made some films in Hungary and helmed *The Last Performance* in 1927, which was released by Universal Pictures. But his decision to create a feature that followed an unconventional story-telling design prompted him to go independent.

Working on a tiny $13,000 budget, he created *The Last Moment*, an odd feature film about a drowning man whose life flashes through his memory during his final descent into a watery grave. The film did not use intertitles, but instead offered a wild kaleidoscope of artistic imagery to signal the riot of emotions that ultimately led to his suicide (train whistles blowing, candles burning, caged birds fighting, etc.).

Ironically, *The Last Moment* was picked up for release by United Artists. It is not clear if this was because Fejos' leading lady was Georgia Hale, the star of Chaplin's *The Gold Rush* – and, maybe not coincidentally, she was also the star of *The Salvation Hunters*.

The Last Moment received wary reviews. *Variety* dubbed it an "interesting, freaky, and slightly morbid arty picture" while the *New York Times* stated it was a film "for the Greenwich Village faddists to chew over." Alas, the film's release came at the tail end of the silent era and it was overlooked by audiences that were eager for sound films. The film's unsuccessful release did not hurt Fejos' career; he went on to direct the highly-regarded features *Lonesome* and *Broadway* (1929) before returning to Europe in the 1930s to continue filmmaking there until the start of World War II.

Sadly, neither *The Salvation Hunters* nor *The Last Moment* has received any degree of serious recognition. Prints of *The Salvation Hunters* survive, but the film is very rarely screened in public and there has never been a home video release. *The Last Moment* is considered to be a lost movie, though one could hope that it may be recovered in the near future. (Fejos' *Broadway* was also considered lost for 75 years before it turned up in a Hungarian archive.)

Short Films, Big Ideas

Outside of these two features, avant-garde cinema in the U.S. existed on the fringes of the film world via independently-produced shorts. The fact these films existed was something of a minor miracle, given that they literally had everything going against them.

For starters, these films were either self-financed or relied on ex-tensive private fundraising. Working without studio support, the exper-imental filmmakers served as a combination of artist and entrepreneur (no mean feat, particularly during the Great Depression). Not surpris-ingly, many of the classics of the genre were created by filmmakers who only made one or two shorts before abandoning the process due to its lack of financial returns. Recognition of their artistic greatness came be-latedly, with after-the-fact rediscoveries by film scholars trying to piece together cinematic evolution.

The tightness of money created technical limitations. Many of the avant-garde films had to be shot on 16mm, as it was too expensive to cre-ate films in 35mm. Sound recording was also an expense that many film-makers could not overcome, so a high number of avant-garde films were shot as silent movies, even as late as the 1940s. These problems limited the commercial viability of the films, since few theaters screened 16mm films and audiences had long since turned their backs on silent movies.

Of course, commercial viability was never ensured in the first place. The Hollywood studios had their own divisions that churned out short subjects, so there was no reason for them to seek out and acquire inde-pendently-produced shorts, especially shorts that carried a visual style and an intellectual subject matter that deviated from the mass-produced entertainment one expected from Hollywood.

However, some independent art house exhibitors located in major cities occasionally gave screen time to avant-garde works. New York's Museum of Modern Art also provided screen time for such films, while smaller art galleries in New York and other cities were also known to set up screens and projectors. The American branch of the Communist Party, strangely enough (since it never considered itself artistically pro-gressive), encouraged such works through screenings organized by its Workers Film and Photo League. The results of such endeavors remain unclear, since political messages, particularly of a red hue, rarely perme-ated these films.

There was also something called Amateur Cinema League, which was created in New York in 1926. This organization helped distribute avant-garde films and worked to call attention to the genre via its magazine *Amateur Movie Makers*. In 1940, the organization published its own book, *Amateur Cinema League Movie Book: A Guide to Making Better Movies*, which offered a how-to guide for would-be filmmakers.

But calling avant-garde films "amateur" was actually a slap in the face to many creative artists who were striving to expand the style and substance of filmmaking. If anything, many of these films enjoy a level of sophistication and prescience that suggests they were many years ahead of their time.

Yet in that distant era, many of these films were seen as amateurish, particularly those that strived to emulate the surrealism and expressionistic schools of cinema emerging from Europe. And there are at least two avant-garde films that exist solely as parodies of the most excessive and outlandish elements of the genre: *The Hearts of Age*, a 1934 riff co-directed by a 19-year-old Orson Welles in his first venture behind the camera, and the 1937 *Even–As You and I*, about a trio of would-be filmmakers who opt to create a clumsy experimental movie after reading about surrealism in *Time Magazine*.

But, nonetheless, several films and their creators were able to generate works that received a modicum of praise at the time of their release and continue to be celebrated by contemporary film scholars. For the most part, their output was severely limited and they are recalled for a very small canon of work. Among those who were the pioneers in the avant-garde area were the following:

Dudley Murphy (1897-1968). A journalist who turned to filmmaking, Murphy's first production was the short *Soul of the Cypress* in 1920. His reputation was secured in 1924 with *Ballet Mecanique*, a French production that he co-directed with Fernand Leger (although in the years that followed, Leger's role in the film's creation received more praise than Murphy's). Back in the U.S., Murphy helmed three early sound classics of African American cinema: *St. Louis Blues* (1929) starring Bessie Smith in her only film appearance, *Black and Tan Fan-*

tasy (1929) starring Duke Ellington and His Orchestra, and *The Emperor Jones* (1933), starring Paul Robeson. Murphy's subsequent screen work was not particularly distinguished; his best-known mainstream film is the 1939 adaptation of *One Third of the Nation*, and he ended his career directing two features in Mexico before retiring to take over operations of an exclusive hotel in Malibu.

Robert Florey (1900-1979). The French-born Florey's major contribution to avant-garde cinema was the extraordinary 1927 short *The Life and Death of 9413–A Hollywood Extra*. Co-directed with Slavko Vorkapich (who later went on to become a major Hollywood art director) and filmed by Gregg Toland (who later became, arguably, Hollywood's greatest cinematographer), this strange little film follows the disastrous adventure of a movie extra whose dreams of achieving stardom results in his untimely death.

The title refers to a number stamped on the extra's forehead, suggesting the lack of personal identity among the many faces in the movie crowds. Florey is credited with the direction of three other experimental shorts (*The Loves of Zero*, *Skyscraper Symphony* and *Johann the Coffin Maker*), but he is perhaps best known today for co-directing (with Joseph Santley) the Marx Brothers in their first feature, *The Cocoanuts* (1929) and for guiding Bela Lugosi through *Murders in the Rue Morgue* (1932).

Dr. James Sibley Watson, Jr. (1894-1982) and Melville Webber (1871-1942). Based in Rochester, N.Y., this team's creative output was financed by Watson, the heir to the Western Union fortune. Their first collaboration, *The Fall of the House of Usher* (1927), retold the Poe story with an Art Deco design motif and a German expressionist visual style. Sadly, the film was eclipsed in its day by a feature-length version of the same material by French filmmaker Jean Epstein. Watson teamed with composer Alec Wilder for an undistinguished one-reel comedy, *Tomatoes Another Day* (1930), and then reteamed with Webber for *Lot in Sodom* (1933). That film retold the Biblical tale using blatantly sexual imagery (both heterosexual and homosexual) and was listed by the National Board of Review as being among the Best American Films of 1934. But after *Lot in Sodom*, Watson took no further interest in filmmaking and found other career pursuits (medicine, philanthropy, writing) to keep him occupied. Webber was cited as a co-director on the 1934 *Rhythm in Light*, but made no additional films afterwards.

Ralph Steiner (1899-1986). A photographer by training, Steiner created lyrical film essays depicting the natural and man-made world. His first work is perhaps his best, *H2O* (1929), which celebrated water in its many different forms. Other films include *Mechanical Principles* (1930), *Surf and Seaweed* (1931), *Hands* (1934) and *The City* (1939), the latter two films co-directed with Willard Van Dyke. Most moviegoers know his cinematography in the landmark documentary *The Plow That Broke the Plains* (1937). Steiner quit filmmaking after *The City* to concentrate on commercial photography and media, most notably in his stint as photo editor for *PM Magazine*.

Willard Van Dyke (1906-1986). Steiner's collaborator on *Hands* and *The City* also helmed *Valley Town* (1940), *To Hear Your Banjo Play* (1947, co-directed with Irving Lerner) and *American Frontier* (1953). He was also director of the film department at the Museum of Modern Art from 1965 to 1974.

Joseph Cornell (1903-1972). A surrealist artist and sculptor, Cornell's first film is also his most famous: *Rose Hobart* (1936), a pioneering work of "found footage." In this case, Cornell snipped up a 1931 B-movie called *East of Borneo* until all that remained was about 20 minutes of footage featuring the starlet Rose Hobart, with whom Cornell had an unrequited obsession. Cornell also removed the film's soundtrack, replacing it with a recording of two songs from Nestor Amaral's record "Holiday in Brazil" (which he reportedly found in a New York junk store). The film was meant to be projected at 18 fps, the speed for silent films, through a blue tint. However, the film's premiere at Julian Levy's New York gallery in December 1936 was marred by Salvador Dali, who was in the audience and became infuriated by what he saw. Dali knocked over the projector halfway through the film and supposedly declared: "My idea for a film is exactly that, and I was going to propose it to someone who would pay to have it made. I never wrote it down or told anyone, but it is as if he had stolen it." Cornell withdrew *Rose Hobart* from public exhibition for three decades, and in the following years made a number of avant-garde shorts. However, none of his later film work enjoyed the reputation of *Rose Hobart* (and it is not certain if the real Rose Hobart ever saw the film or even knew about it).

Rudy Burckhardt (1914-1999). The Swiss-born artist and photographer began shooting experimental short films in New York in the mid-1930s and continued making a combination of short documentaries, cinematic poems and an occasionally goofy satire for the next five decades. His best-known work includes *Seeing the World* (1937), *Pursuit of Happiness* (1940) and *Up and Down the Waterfront* (1946).

Jay Leyda (1910-1988). Leyda's name appears as director on a single film, but it turned out to be among the most influential avant-garde shorts of its time: *A Bronx Morning*, a 1931 "city symphony" of a working-class New York street. Leyda was invited to work with Sergei Eisenstein in the Soviet Union on the ill-fated 1935 feature *Bezhin Meadow*, and later wrote two biographies on Eisenstein. He also co-directed the pro-labor propaganda short *People of the Cumberland* (1937), but chose to identify himself with a pseudonym for the screen credits.

Mary Ellen Bute (1906-1983). One of the few independent filmmakers who worked exclusively in animation, Bute's abstract and surreal imagery was often paired with iconic works of classical music. Her most notable films include *Synchromy No. 2* (1935, paired with "O Evening Star" from Wagner's *Tannhäuser*), *Escape* (1937, paired with Bach's "Toccata in D Minor") and *Polka Graph* (1947, paired with Shostakovich's Polka from *The Age of Gold*).

Willard Maas (1906-1971) and Marie Menken (1909-1970). The husband-and-wife team were New York writers and socialites who collaborated on the 1943 *Geography of the Body*. Maas later teamed with Ben Moore on *The Mechanics of Love* (1950) and *Narcissus* (1956), while Menken created *Glimpse of the Garden* (1957) and *Moonplay* (1962). Actually, their contribution to culture was not based on what they created but who they were; their raucous and barbed personalities reportedly inspired Edward Albee's creation of George and Martha for his 1962 play *Who's Afraid of Virginia Woolf?*

David Bradley (1920-1997). At the age of 21, Chicago-based Bradley shot a feature-length silent 16mm film of *Peer Gynt*. After serving in the U.S. Army Signal Corps in World War II, Bradley returned to Chicago and created another 16mm feature, based on Shakespeare's *Julius Caesar* (1950). Neither film would be recalled today had Bradley not had the good luck of casting a handsome young local actor as the lead in both productions: an unknown named Charlton Heston. Bradley was recruited by MGM after *Julius Caesar*, but his studio time was limited to directing the undistinguished 1952 feature *Talk About a Stranger*. He is best known for his 1963 atrocity *They Saved Hitler's Brain*. He regained some degree of respect in later years as a film historian and archivist.

Up until the mid-1940s, avant-garde cinema flourished on the fringes of the film world. For the most part, no one objected; outside of Dudley Murphy and Robert Florey, none of the major figures of the genre seemed dissatisfied to be working with relatively little recognition (or at least no serious effort was made by them to gain fame and fortune from their work). But due to the creative output and the indefatigable personality of an unlikely artist, the genre suddenly took on a new importance. That person was the Ukrainian-born Eleanor Derenkowsky, who later rechristened herself as Maya Deren and took avant-garde/experimental filmmaking into a new realm.

The Mother of the Genre

Maya Deren (1917-1961) had no experience in filmmaking before arriving in Los Angeles in 1941 as the secretary to the celebrated choreographer Katherine Dunham. Already married and divorced, her flirtations with socialist politics and academia did not amount to anything truly satisfying.

While in Los Angeles, she met Austrian filmmaker Alexander Hammid, and they wed after a brief courtship. Settling in Los Angeles, Deren purchased a used 16mm Bolex camera. Using their home as set, Hammid and Deren created the 1943 short *Meshes of the Afternoon.*

There has been much controversy over the creative division behind *Meshes of the Afternoon.* Filmmaker Stan Brakhage claimed that film was primarily Hammid's design, and that the couple's marriage failed when Deren began receiving sole credit for the work. It is difficult to ignore Hammid's background: he directed five films prior to *Meshes of the Afternoon,* including the 1941 Mexican-based documentary *The Forgotten Village.* Clearly, he was the influence on steering Deren into cinema.

In truth, there is nothing in *Meshes of the Afternoon* that corresponds with Hammid's work before or after the film's creation (his credits included the patriotic *Hymn of the Nations* in 1944 and the Oscar-winning *To Be Alive* in 1964). His knowledge of classic European avant-garde film may have been brought to this production, particularly the great close-up of Deren's eye (obviously an homage to the Buzuel-Dali collaboration *Un Chien Andalou*).

But Deren's contributions and influences are evident; the film's focus on a woman (played by Deren) in the midst of an emotional war with herself plumbs the depths of psychoanalysis to create a work that is both strikingly artistic and deeply intellectual. With its disturbing imagery (Deren's knife clutching, her multiple reflections in mirrors, her balletic descent down the stairs), the film presents issues of violence and identity that are questioned with a raw, visceral energy.

Even more striking was the decision to present the film as completely silent. Whereas other avant-garde films of the time relied on synchronized musical scores, *Meshes of the Afternoon* was originally meant to be seen without any supporting soundtrack.

Deren, emboldened by *Meshes of the Afternoon,* set out to explore her own style as a solo filmmaker, without relying on Hammid as a collaborative partner. After a false start with an aborted production with Marcel Duchamp called *The Witches' Cradle,* she turned out *At Land* (1944), *A Study in Choreography for the Camera* (1945) and *Ritual in Transfigured Time* (1946). These three films focused on movement, ritual, expression and the unleashing of emotions. Their mix of unsettling imagery and bold physicality created works of art that challenged and provoked the viewer with uncommon strength. And as with *Meshes of the Afternoon*, none of these short 16mm films carried musical soundtracks or dialogue.

But Deren went in a different direction from her peers in avant-garde cinema: she pushed for mainstream recognition. And this was not just a mere push, but a dramatic attention-grabbing assault that took the genre into new territory.

In 1946, she became the first filmmaker to be awarded a Guggenheim Fellowship. The following year, she took *Meshes of the Afternoon* across the Atlantic to the Cannes Film Festival, where it won the Grand Prix Internationale. For a relatively obscure filmmaker creating independently-produced experimental films (let alone being the rare female filmmaker), these achievements were without precedent.

What was also unprecedented was Deren's pursuit of an audience. Clearly, her films were not going to be picked up for theatrical release by a Hollywood studio. Thus, Deren took the initiative of self-distributing her work in a city-by-city journey where the screening of her shorts was accompanied by a lecture discussion on their creation and her views of the filmmaking process.

Some venues were open to this presentation: colleges and universities were open to Deren's bohemian personality and unusual film line-up, while edgy venues such as Cinema 16 and the Provincetown Playhouse in New York and the Art in Cinema film series at the San Francisco Museum of Modern Art gave Deren the platform she needed.

But in cities where she was unable to find a venue that would invite her, she opened her purse and paid to four-wall theaters. For an independent filmmaker, this was a highly unusual course of action. She traveled across the U.S., and even went to Canada and Cuba to connect with audiences.

Through this strategy, Deren presented herself as an independent alternative to the studio system. The appeal of her approach was obvious: a single woman going up against a male-dominated industry, a lone voice of eclectic creativity challenging mass-produced entertainment, and a vocal critic of the direction that American popular culture was taking in the post-war environment.

Furthermore, she defined herself exclusive through her work. Whereas other filmmakers on the avant-garde fringes disappeared from their craft after a small number of shorts and sought new careers in other fields, Deren squarely identified herself as a full-time filmmaker who could survive and flourish outside of Tinseltown.

For its part, Hollywood couldn't have cared less; Deren posed no financial impediment to the growth of the film industry. And when Deren openly pegged Hollywood as "a major obstacle to the definition and development of motion pictures as a creative fine art form," she did not strike a nerve with the vast population of moviegoers who still trekked to their local cinemas in search of their favorite stars.

But for those who heard her, Deren established a parallel universe to the defined standard of what filmmaking was supposed to be about. In retrospect, Deren's emergence signaled a dramatic change. The notion of experimental, avant-garde or (dare we say) amateur filmmaking as a fringe pursuit was out of date. A new genre of filmmaking was emerging, where distinctive voices, working on edges of popular culture in risky low-budget endeavors, repeatedly made themselves heard and did not vanish after one or two barely-seen productions. At the time, the genre had no official name. Today, though, we know it as underground filmmaking.

Ironically, the rise of the modern underground movement dovetailed with Deren's decline as a filmmaker. Following *Meditation on Violence* in 1948, her filmmaking output abruptly stopped. She did not offer another film to audiences until 1958, when she collaborated with choreographer Antony Tudor on *The Very Eye of Night*. During most of the 1950s, Deren found herself trying but failing to launch several projects. Films bearing the tentative titles of *Medusa, Ensemble for Somnabulists* and *Haiku* never traveled beyond the drawing board.

So what became of the Guggenheim Fellowship that was supposed to enable her to continue her filmmaking? The Guggenheim funds enabled her to visit Haiti on four occasions during 1951 and 1952, where she hoped to create a documentary on the island's culture, particularly the voodoo religious practices. Her Haitian journey produced a remarkable book, *Divine Horsemen: The Living Gods of Haiti*, which was published in 1953 and was widely hailed as a major work of anthropological research and literary grace.

But Deren's filmed record of the Haitian customs and protocol, which totaled hours of remarkable footage, was never assembled in her lifetime. Her third husband, Teiji Ito, edited the hours of footage into a 1985 documentary that carried the same title as her book. Alas, the film was barely seen.

However, this is not to say that Deren was completely absent from view. She revamped her earlier work, replacing the original silence of the shorts with a new (and, admittedly, imperfect) selection of Japanese classical music composed and performed by Ito.

Deren also worked hard to create two influential organizations – the Film Artists Society in 1953 and the Creative Film Foundation in 1955 – that were designed to encourage new underground filmmakers to seek out their destinies. This was an act of uncommon generosity, considering her filmmaking brought her prestige but not significant profits. Financial support, however, came thanks to the new audiences who found her work as a writer and public speaker. Reportedly, she even snagged a guest spot on NBC's *Today Show* to discuss her theories of filmmaking (though no kinescope of that appearance is known to exist).

Deren died in 1961 from a cerebral hemorrhage, brought about through a combination of an amphetamine addiction and severe malnutrition. She was 44 years old. At the time of her passing, underground cinema was on the verge of blending into the cultural mainstream, with new techniques challenging the traditions of filmmaking and new talents who were becoming household names thanks to their aggressive and innovative talents. Without Deren, however, this may not have taken place; at the very least, it would have been delayed for a long time.

Curiously, Deren's influence waned almost immediately after her death. For years, her films and writing were unavailable, making it impossible to appreciate what she offered. Time, however, was Deren's ally. In 1990, the Library of Congress named *Meshes of the Afternoon* to the National Film Registry, making it the first avant-garde film to be so honored. In recent Deren has became the subject of countless essays, while biographical celebrations, including Bill Nichols' book *Maya Deren and the American Avant-Garde* (2001) and Martina Kudlacek's documentary *In the Mirror of Maya Deren* (2002) provided a much-needed review of Deren's impact on American culture.

Even better, Deren's films have been made available for wide viewing, both officially on commercial video and DVD releases and unofficially in unauthorized presentations via popular online video sites (while a violation of copyright laws, we have to acknowledge these are clearly acts of adoration and not malice).

Film historian Annette Michelson offered a fine elegy to this creative force of nature: "Maya Deren stands as an especially salient figure, the pioneer who located and defined the issues, options and contradictions of filmmaking as an artistic practice."

And critic Gerald Peary summed up Deren most succinctly, dubbing her "the mother of underground cinema."

Maya Deren's Children

Deren's influence, both as a filmmaker and a film personality, enabled a new wave of creative talent to seek out a niche in the underground cinema genre.

Kenneth Anger was the first major underground filmmaker to emerge in this period. As a youth growing up in Beverly Hills, California, Anger shot several short films in the early and mid-1940s; sadly, none are known to survive and it is not certain if they were ever publicly screened. However, Anger made himself more than conspicuous in 1947 with the unveiling of his groundbreaking film, *Fireworks*.

Shot when he was 17 (reportedly over a weekend when his parents were away), Anger cast himself as a youth whose homoerotic obsession with sailors results in both violence and ecstasy. The film's most celebrated image, of a handsome sailor sporting a Roman candle in his fly, was a bold and (for its time) shocking vision.

Not that many Americans were able to experience Anger's work. Since homosexuality was still a taboo subject in mainstream movies, *Fireworks* could only be screened in non-theatrical settings. Trying to find receptive audiences outside of the parochial settings of post-war America, Anger submitted the film to European festivals, where the subject matter restrictions were more liberal, and in 1949 it won an award at a festival in Biarrritz, France. Inspired by the reaction in France, particularly from Jean Cocteau (who was on the festival jury that honored *Fireworks*), Anger relocated to Paris and combined his film work with duties as an assistant to Henri Langlois, the founder of the Cinematheque Francais.

The relocation to Paris was not problem-free, and Anger attempted suicide in 1950. That same year, he began work on the commedia dell arte-inspired *Rabbit's Moon*, but the work remained unfinished until 1970. He relocated again, this time to Italy, and created the lyrically amusing *Eaux d'Artifice* in 1953, where a woman flits in and out of a fountain before disappearing beneath its watery surface. He then came back to Hollywood and made the Dionysian romp *The Inauguration of the Pleasure Dome* in 1954.

For the remainder of the 1950s and the early 1960s, Anger attempted to start several self-financed works. Most of these projects came to naught. Then, after years of misfires, Anger struck gold in 1964 with a short called *Scorpio Rising*.

A wild mix of biker and leather subculture imagery (with bits of Nazi ideology, Hollywood rebel worship and warped religious icons thrown in), the film provided a startling yet campy dissection of masculinity taken to extreme degrees. The film blurred the lines of manly behavior to the point that an argument could be made of whether this was supposed to be gay fantasy or a comment on American manhood in general. Audiences were amazed by Anger's sweep of imagery, which was accompanied by thirteen pop music tunes (none of which were properly licensed, which gave the film a distinctively rebellious personality, and a choppy release due to problems with music clearance issues).

The popularity of *Scorpio Rising* enabled Anger to find new audiences for his older films, and he followed in Maya Deren's path by presenting programs of his shorts to enthusiastic audiences in non-theatrical venues. Time was also on his side in connecting with the audiences that once eluded him: the nascent gay rights movement embraced *Fireworks* as an early classic of homoerotic cinema, and *The Inauguration of the Pleasure Dome* was re-released as the *Sacred Mushroom Collection* in 1966, to cash in on the rising drug culture.

Anger then embarked on what he called his "Magic Lantern" cycle, with the films *Kustom Kar Kommandos* (1965) and *Invocation of My Demon Brother* (1969). For the late 1960s, Anger was the bad boy darling of the underground scene thanks to the psychedelic and sexual nature of his counterculture work.

Anger's films, however, seemed suddenly outdated as the 1970s progressed, and over the years his output became far more limited and less interesting. The Egyptology-inspired *Lucifer Rising* began production in 1970, but by the time it was completed in 1980 it seemed more like a curio. It appeared that inspiration abandoned him: Anger occasionally turned out a new short, but nothing resonated with any degree of importance.

However, during this time he found new audiences with his juicy *Hollywood Babylon* book series, which revisited half-forgotten Tinseltown scandals.

If Anger's output was relatively limited, his influence remains strong. It is not difficult to detect the MTV style of editing and image selection from *Scorpio Rising*, while his unapologetic celebration of the gay lifestyle took the hinges off the cinematic closet door and gave queer cinema a respectable cred. Anger also enjoyed (and continues to maintain) a distinctive celebrity status that was uncommon for filmmakers in underground cinema.

Outside of Kenneth Anger, the most significant creative force to emerge from underground cinema was arguably Andy Warhol. A brilliantly self-promoting painter, Warhol gave the impression that he came to filmmaking in a nonchalant manner; a well-circulated story, most likely apocryphal, found Warhol purchasing a 16mm camera in 1963 and declaring: "I'm going to make bad films."

Whether Warhol's films were genuinely bad has been open to debate ever since. To his credit, Warhol attempted to deconstruct the filmmaking process by focusing his 16mm camera on seemingly mundane situations, as if to glorify the ordinary aspects of quotidian life.

To be charitable, he was too successful: silent and black-and-white films like *Sleep* (1963), which kept a stationary camera on poet John Giordano's six hours in slumberland, and *Empire* (1964), which kept the same stationary camera aimed at the Empire State Building for eight hours at a deliberately slowed-down 16 fps, tested the patience of the relatively few who willingly subjected themselves to their marathon running lengths. Oddly enough, the Library of Congress considered *Sleep* artistically worthy for inclusion on the National Film Registry, but it is not certain if anyone connected with that decision actually ever sat through the entire eight-hour offering in one sitting; even New York's Museum of Modern Art spared its patrons by presenting a mere two-and-a-half-hour condensed version for its 2007 Warhol retrospective. (Of course, there is also Warhol's 24-hour film **** from 1966, which may be the longest movie ever made – and the longest movie *no one* ever sat through from start to finish.)

Warhol mercifully reined in his other slice-of-dull-life films with such productions as the 35-minute *Blow Job* (1963, which, thankfully, focused solely on the face of the recipient of the oral sex and not the practitioner) and the 45-minute *Eat* (1965).

Warhol, who made his first great public impact with paintings of Campbell Soup cans, apparently felt he could appropriate popular culture icons into his films. Two early films, *Batman Dracula* (1964) and *Vinyl* (1965), misappropriated well-known intellectual properties: the DC Comics superhero for the former film and the plot of Anthony Burgess'

A Clockwork Orange for the latter. Neither film was shown outside of Warhol's art exhibitions, and the intellectual property problems surrounding *Batman Dracula* drove it so far out of circulation that it was considered lost for four decades.

If Warhol's films were peculiar, his reasoning was not. He understood that his seemingly absurd experiments worked in violent antithesis to the basic concepts of filmmaking. He further solidified this alternative cinematic universe by creating his own version of the old-fashioned studio system: The Factory, his New York creative and administrative headquarters, became his studio lot and a line-up of bizarre performers, dubbed "superstars," became his exclusive talent. Even today, references to the likes of Edie Sedgwick, Nico, Ondine, Viva, Paul America and Joe Dallesandro inevitably identify them as Warhol superstars (though what they ever did to deserve superstar status was never clear).

For better or worse, Warhol's strategy paid off. In 1964, he received an Independent Film Award from *Film Culture* magazine. The following year, he formed his own distribution company, Andy Warhol Films, which began booking commercial engagements. Warhol began creating edgier films, most notably the 1965 *My Hustler*, with its frank and unapologetic view of the Fire Island gay subculture. This feature film found its way into art house release, and its daring to explore the taboo subject of homosexuality without recriminations also attracted enough moviegoers to earn a small profit (no mean feat for 1965).

In 1966, Warhol achieved a breakthrough with his challenging (some say maddening) feature *Chelsea Girls*. The film offered a unique novelty by presenting its story by running two 16mm films in simultaneous projection. *Chelsea Girls* created a minor sensation, particularly when some critics went into full-throttle attack. Roger Ebert, writing in the *Chicago Sun-Times*, did not seek a diplomatic explanation of his disappointment: "For what we have here is 3½ hours of split-screen improvisation poorly photographed, hardly edited at all, employing perversion and sensation like chili sauce to disguise the aroma of the meal. Warhol has nothing to say and no technique to say it with."

Chelsea Girls was also a commercial success. While Warhol's previous films were limited to non-theatrical venues and tiny art house cinemas that sought out off-beat movies, *Chelsea Girls* found its way into mainstream theaters. Warhol the underground filmmaker was now a serious commercial force in movies.

But just as abruptly as Warhol became a mainstream fixture, he suddenly withdrew from the limelight. Films such as *I, a Man* (1967) and *Lonesome Cowboys* (1968) did not resonate with audiences in the manner of *Chelsea Girls*. In 1968, Warhol survived an attempted assassination by Valeria Solanas, a would-be writer who appeared in *I, a Man* – and the shooting seemed to have killed whatever interest he had in making movies. *Blue Movie*, made in October 1968, marked the end of Warhol's concentration on filmmaking.

Warhol turned over the filmmaking reins at The Factory to Paul Morrissey, who collaborated without credit as co-director on several of Warhol's films. Morrissey's films, under the Warhol aegis, became more mainstream and polished than Warhol's offerings, and few people considered them as genuine underground work. Ironically, Morrissey's films are the productions that many people associate with the Warhol name: *Flesh* (1968), *Trash* (1969), *Heat* (1970), the X-rated 3-D *Andy Warhol's Frankenstein* (a.k.a. *Flesh for Frankenstein*, 1973) and *Andy Warhol's Dracula* (a.k.a. *Blood of Dracula*, 1974).

Warhol and Morrissey co-directed *L'Amour* in 1973, but the film made no commercial impact. By that late date, however, underground cinema had drifted into very different directions and Warhol's contributions were strictly viewed as historic curios.

For years, Warhol's reputation has relied mostly on reputation rather than retrospective screenings; most of his films remain out of circulation, and the ardent film buff would need to locate bootleg copies to get an idea of what he created. Nonetheless, his importance to the underground genre cannot be understated.

Another influential underground filmmaker, at least for a period of time during the 1960s, was Stan Brakhage, who made his first film,

Interim (1952), at the age of 19, and went on to create more than 300 films (most which were shorts).

Brakhage's use of non-linear storytelling and experimental visual effects made his work stand out significantly. Films such as *Wonder Ring* (1955) and *In Anticipation of the Night* (1958) showed Brakhage opening new dimensions for filmmaking as an expressive medium, as opposed to an entertainment or information vehicle; his work offered the cinema technology as an extension of avant-garde art. *Window, Water, Baby, Moving* (1959) and *Thigh, Line, Lyre, Triangular* (1961) placed the camera on Brakhage's wife during her pregnancies, offering a raw and compelling personal diary that predated the self-focused videographers of the YouTube generation by four decades.

Brakhage is best known today for his project *Dog Star Man* (1961-64), which collected a series of shorts into a feature-length presentation. *Dog Star Man* broke ground through its innovative layering of imagery (some benign, some erotic, some indescribable). Brakhage would later reincorporate the *Dog Star Man* into a different line-up with another presentation, *The Art of Vision*. Jonas Mekas would comment on these films by proclaiming: "The images become like words: they come back again, in little bursts, and disappear, and come back again – like in sentences – creating visual and mental impressions, experiences."

Brakhage would continue redefining the style of filmmaking with abstract works such as *The Text of Light* (1974), where illumination is filmed through a green ashtray. At the time of his death in 2003, he was at work on *The Chinese Series*, which was composed of 35mm black leader scratched up with his fingernails.

Other underground filmmakers who gained some degree attention in the 1960s included Robert Downey Sr., whose underground features *Babo 73* (1964), *Chafed Elbows* (1966) and *No More Excuses* (1968) paved the way for a brief flurry of mainstream recognition with *Putney Swope* (1969) and *Greaser's Palace* (1972) plus the controversial made-for-television film *Sticks and Bones*. Also emerging from the underground were George and Mike Kuchar, whose no-budget 8mm camp exercises, such as *I Was a Teenage Rumpot* (1960), *Night of the Bomb* (1962), *Lovers of Eternity* and *Sins of the Fleshapoids* (1965), enjoyed a cult following among many underground film devotees.

There was also Shirley Clarke who succeeded Maya Deren as the most prominent women in underground cinema. She came to filmmaking following work as a dancer and choreographer. Actually, dance and choreographed movement were the subjects of her first short films: *Dance in the Sun* (1953), *In Paris Parks* (1954), *Bullfight* (1955) and *A Moment in Love* (1957).

In 1959, Clarke switched her focus and aimed her camera at the construction of a high-rise New York office building. *Skyscraper* offered Clarke her first major exposure as director, winning prizes at several festivals and an Academy Award nomination for Best Live Action Short Subject. Clarke later won the Oscar for another short film, the 1963 documentary *Robert Frost: A Lover's Quarrel with the World*.

But Clarke's reputation as a filmmaker is recalled today in three underground feature films: *The Connection* (1962), *The Cool World* (1964) and *Portrait of Jason* (1967). All three films took what was perceived as an outsider view of the polite society of the era. *The Connection* found a group of heroin addicts in search of a fix; *The Cool World* followed the lives of a Harlem street gang, while *Portrait of Jason* was a lengthy (105 minutes, from 12 hours of footage) movie about a gay black male hustler.

Clarke's films created a minor sensation in their time, and she was even recruited to play herself in Agnes Varda's 1969 *Lion's Love*. But afterwards, lightning struck again. She began work in 1968 on a documentary about jazz musician Ornette Coleman. The resulting film, *Ornette: Made in America*, would not be completed until 1985. During that period, her focus shifted to teaching at UCLA and experimenting with video production technology.

Clarke may not have been totally satisfied as an underground artist. In the late 1960s and early 1970s, she made unsuccessful attempts to get a foothold in Hollywood, but her proposed projects never received the green light from the studio executives. It is sad to recall that even in the midst of the so-called women's lib movement, when Hollywood has no qualm having strong women on camera, there was resistance to having a strong woman behind the camera as director.

While Clarke was able to secure recognition on a handful of films, other underground filmmakers found immortality with just one production. *Pull My Daisy* (1959) has earned underground cred over the years, although it actually generated little attention in its day (even though its initial New York run came on a double bill with John Cassavetes *Shadows*). Co-directed by Robert Frank and Alfred Leslie, this short film was rooted in Jack Kerouac's unfinished play *The Beat Generation*. Kerouac offers a running narration – the film was shot without sound and Kerouac reportedly improvised his wordplay while watching an early screening – and fellow Beat writers Allen Ginsburg, Gregory Corso and Peter Orlovsky provide genial on-screen hamming as variations of themselves. The mild plot involves the Beat writers crashing the New York apartment of an artist, her railroad breakman husband, and their young son.

Frank, Leslie and Kerouac would never make any significant contributions to filmmaking (Frank came closest with his 1972 Rolling Stones documentary, *Cocksucker Blues*, but that was also barely released). Yet *Pull My Daisy* continues to be praised, and it was included on the Library of Congress' National Film Registry.

Another single film that gained attention over the years was Jack Smith's *Flaming Creatures* (1963). A plotless, dialogue-free exaggerated orgy of cross dressers, it is primarily recalled today because the film was seized by New York police during its premiere screening and was later judged as obscene by a New York Criminal Court. But time has not been the film's ally. Nora Sayre, reviewing the film for the *New York Times* in 1975, said it best: "This lighthearted pantomime of a group-grope seems almost as genteel as your in-laws' home movies. Since many of the participants are male transvestites, some in quasi-Victorian costume, it's occasionally startling to see a real breast. Though the turn-ons are elderly, they're still amusing, and the film has acquired a historical interest."

Smith's other films, including *Buzzards Over Baghdad* (1951) and

Normal Love (1963), never generated the same interest that *Flaming Creatures* briefly stirred.

While Frank and Leslie and Smith secured a spot in film history for a single film, the more prolific filmmakers James Broughton (who directed 20 films between 1946 and 1988) and Lawrence Jordan (who created 40 films ranging from animation to live action from 1952 through 2008) are barely known beyond the circle of the most dedicated film scholars who have access to underground cinema. However, Brought's and Jordan's films have recently been gathered for DVD release, so it is possible that wider recognition may come about in the near future.

No discussion of underground cinema would be complete without mentioning Jonas and Adolfas Mekas. The Lithuanian-born brothers created a stir in the film world during the early 1960s with films like *Hallelujah the Hills* (1963 directed by Adolfas) and *The Brig* (1964, directed by Jonas). Jonas was also an influential figure in raising awareness for independent and underground cinema through the media and distribution channels. He became editor-in-chief of *Film Culture* magazine in 1954 and the Movie Journal columnist for the *Village Voice*, a New York weekly newspaper, in 1958. In 1962, he co-founded the Filmmakers Co-operative, a non-profit distributor of avant-garde and experimental films. (Mekas' co-founders were Shirley Clarke, Stan Brakhage, and filmmaker Gregory Markopoulos.) In 1964, Mekas opened the Filmmakers' Cinematheque in 1964, which later evolved into Anthology Film Archives, a New York cultural center for the preservation and presentation of films.

In the 1970s and 1980s, underground cinema saw its cred fade. Changing audience tastes shifted away from the style and substance of productions that reigned in the 1950s and 1960s and mainstream films became edgier and more daring in their context. An occasional underground effort would gain attention, most notably David Lynch's 1977 feature debut *Eraserhead*, which found cult classic status on the midnight movie circuit, which took the once-fatal 12:00am time slots for Friday and Saturdays and turned them into festivals of subversive screenings for both indie titles (most notably *Night of the Living Dead* and *Pink Fla-*

mingos), studio oddities (*The Rocky Horror Picture Show*) and assorted miscellany (the Mexican import *El Topo* and revivals of 1930s mayhem *Reefer Madness* and unedited shorts from the Three Stooges and Our Gang series).

Today's 20 Top Underground Filmmakers

With the dawn of the new video production technology and the Internet in the 1990s, coupled with the expansion of the film festival circuit and do-it-yourself DVD distribution channels, underground cinema saw a renaissance that enabled the genre to thrive, perhaps with greater passion than ever before. The persistence of many talented artists to push ahead and present what they see is a much-needed alternative to the studio and so-called "Indiewood" brand of filmmaking.

Within this sphere, there are some creative artists who have brought forth works that earned them praise and respect from the critics and audiences who seek out this genre. Some of these filmmakers have been able to occasionally break through the underground barrier and share their productions with wider audiences. But for the most part, they are appreciated primarily by those who are plugged into the underground channels. At this point in time, we can offer a tribute to the Top 20 underground filmmakers who have proven their worth in both the quantity and quality of their work.

Antero Alli. The Finnish-born, Berkeley-based filmmaker has explored the complexities of societal interactions in diverse varieties: through the breakdown and reconstruction of protocols and customs, the redefining of religious traditions to meet changing needs, the rise of telecommunications as the substitute for human interactions, and the demands in bringing the notions of artistic and literary perfection into the decidedly less-than-perfect real world. Working in narrative features, documentaries and experimental shorts, Alli's films have raised questions relating to isolation, love, memory and community. Wisely, he realizes there is no be-all/end-all solution to the world's thorniest matters, and thus he leaves the answers for his viewers to decipher and determine.

Notable films: *Requiem for a Friend* (1991), *Archaic Community* (1992), *The Drivetime* (1995), *Lily in Limbo* (1996), *Crux* (1999), *Tragos* (2000), *Road Kill* (2001), *Hysteria* (2002), *Orphans of Delirium* (2004), *The Greater Circulation* (2005), *The Invisible Forest* (2008).

Craig Baldwin. The Bay Area filmmaker took the concept of found footage to new heights, using innovative editing and a wickedly off-center sense of humor to provide cutting commentaries on how America perceives itself. Baldwin's work blurs the lines between documentaries and mockumentaries, creating remarkable hybrids that simultaneously question, mock, celebrate and baffle the American experience. If Baldwin's output has been somewhat spotty, with long breaks between films, the power and fury of his work more than compensates for his absence from the screen.

Notable films: *Wild Gunman* (1978), *RocketKitKongoKit* (1986), *Tribulation 99: Alien Anomalies Under America* (1991), *O No Coronado* (1992), *Sonic Outlaws* (1995), *Spectres of the Spectrum* (1999), *Mock Up On Mu* (2008).

Jacob Burckhardt. A second-generation New York-based underground artist (his father was Rudy Burckhardt), the filmmaker began making films in the 1970s. Comfortable in traditional narrative features and experimental shorts, his work has explored the various enigmas, indignities and frustrations of quotidian existence. Whether his subjects are aggravated souls trying to resolve a crime, live-wire personalities taking in too much of a wildly hedonistic existence, or vast cities ebbing and flowing in distinctive rhythms, Burckhardt provides a mature yet playful observation at the daily drama.

Notable films: *Yaknetuma from the Lower East* (1974), *The Girl Can't Help It* (1997), *This Object* (1982), *It Don't Pay to Be an Honest Citizen* (1984), *Landlord Blues* (1988), *The Frankie Lymon's Nephew Story Or, Why Do Fools Fall in Love* (1990), *The Monkey and the Engineer* (1995), *Black and White* (2001), *Roma* (2004); *The Surface v.3* (2007).

A.D. Calvo. The Argentine-born, Connecticut-based filmmaker made his initial reputation by helming a series of offbeat documentary shorts that explored the creepier aspects of fine art. Whether focusing on the unlikely artistic presentation of polarizing political figures or ruminating on the unlikely fixation on items with grisly backstories, Calvo's work provides a compelling debate on what art is truly all about. The filmmaker has since graduated into feature-length narrative productions, choosing a romantic fantasy as his first endeavor here, which would suggest he is ready to expand his outlook to wider horizons.

Notable films: *Sitter* (2004), *Hypnogothic* (2005), *The Several Severed Heads of Daniel Edwards* (2005), *Hillary's Bust* (2006), *Castro in Central Park* (2006), *La Danse Macabre: Portrait of a Serial Sculptor* (2007), *The Other Side of the Tracks* (2008).

Martha Colburn. A leader in underground animation, the Pennsylvania native (who now divides her time between New York and Amsterdam) creates striking shorts in a variety of styles (collage, paint on glass, hand coloring of frames, manipulating found footage). Her work can be surreal and biting, with sharp observations mixed in the fanciful swirl of images. At home in both a cinematic and gallery setting, Colburn's animation is both a timely commentary on today's world and a timeless celebration of deep talent.

Notable films: *Acrophobic Babies* (1994), *Killer Tunes* (1996), *Persecution in Paradise* (1997), *There's a Pervert in Our Pool* (1998), *Cats Amore* (2002), *Destiny Manifesto* (2006), *Don't Kill the Weatherman* (2008).

James Fotopoulos. The Chicago-based filmmaker has worked in both the traditional cinematic format and in gallery installations. He made his first short film at age 15 and his first feature (clocking in at 142 minutes) while a student at Columbia College (he dropped out of school after making the film, which he dubbed *Zero*). His films mix a wealth of emotional imagery that speaks volumes on issues relating to love, death, self-identity, and isolation. While he prefers working in lower-budget production values, his visual artistry and emotional depth provides uncommon wealth for those who find his work.

Notable films: *Zero* (1997), *Migrating Forms* (2000), *Back Against the Wall* (2002), *Christabel* (2002), *The* Nest (2003).

Erica Jordan. The San Francisco-based director has already earned a spot in independent film history when her 1994 feature *Walls of Sand* became the first contemporary feature film to be presented for Internet viewing. Beyond that digital achievement, Jordan has earned a reputation for creating sensitive dramatic films about women in various stages of self-discovery. Her lead characters are flawed but determined women who slowly learn valuable lessons regarding their sense of worth and value. Jordan's films inspire without veering into sentiment, their messages of gaining independent strength resonates with a gentle but firm power.

Notable films: *A Different Shade of Blue* (1993), *Walls of Sand* (1994), *Tales from the Heart* (1998), *In the Wake* (2001), *On tha Wise* (2005).

Jon Jost. One of the veterans of underground cinema, the self-taught filmmaker created his first short in 1963 and his feature in 1974. He continues to produce compelling works covering a wide variety of subjects. While his 1990 feature *All the Vermeers in New York* earned him a degree of recognition due to its successful art house commercial release, the bulk of his work has remained far outside mainstream audience consideration. The lack of wider recognition has taken its toll on Jost; a 2006 profile in the *New York Times* found him "sitting in a borrowed New York apartment in hand-me-down clothes" and that he "doesn't have a place to live and has no visible means of support, other than a coming arts residency at the University of Nebraska." Currently living in Seoul, South Korea, Jost still pushes ahead in creating his films to suit his artistic vision. It is not hard to believe that the rest of the world will catch up to him.

Notable films: *Last Chants for a Slow Dance* (1977), *Chameleon* (1978), *Slow Moves* (1983), *Sure Fire* (1990), *All the Vermeers in New York* (1990), *Frame-up* (1993), *The Bed You Sleep In* (1993), *Oui non* (2002), *La Lunga Ombra* (2005), *Over Here* (2007).

Young Man Kang. The Korean-born, Los Angeles-based filmmaker has been at home in romantic comedy, action/adventure and non-fiction filmmaking. Kang has brought forth polished and professional work on the smallest of budgets, even gaining praise from the *Guinness Book of World Records* for presenting *Cupid's Mistake* for theatrical release on a $980 budget. His films are noteworthy for presenting Asian-American women outside of the mainstream cinema stereotypes; his leading ladies are tough, funny, independent, take-charge ladies who can command situations with either a casual glance or a well-swung frying pan.

Notable films: *Cupid's Mistake* (2000), *1st Testament: CIA Vengeance* (2001), *Haitian Slave Children* (2002), *Soap Girl* (2003), *The Last Eve* (2005), *Kimchi Warrior* (2009).

Josh Koury. Brooklyn-based Koury was among the first wave of young filmmakers to gain recognition via the Internet-based presentation of short video productions; in his case, Koury's first work appeared at www.StudentFilms.com during his studies at Pratt Art Institute. After dabbling in experimental and comedy motifs, he found his groove in non-fiction filmmaking. Placing his camera's viewfinder within his own home, Koury's work offers a stark, often harsh view of a family struggling against serious physical and emotional challenges. Critical acclaim for his breakthrough feature, the 2002 release *Standing By Yourself*, pegged Koury as a talent to watch, but his focus changed from directing to festival programming (including the Brooklyn Underground Film Festival, which he co-founded). He has since returned behind the camera, expanding his focus into wider subject matter with the 2008 commercial release *We Are Wizards*.

Notable films: *Whores Are Expensive* (2000), *Bullethead* (2001), *Richard Shakes* (2001), *Standing By Yourself* (2002), *We Are Wizards* (2008).

Michael Legge. The Massachusetts filmmaker takes a very different approach to the horror and sci-fi genres by emphasizing their comic elements. One could consider his work as satirical, unless you consider horror and sci-fi to be grisly satires of reality. In Legge's universe, it is not uncommon to find zombies being employed to fill gaps in corporate personnel or malcontent mad professors being recruited to host television horror movie shows. His films are cheerful and wry in their approach; the humor arises from gently holding a light to the absurdity of life, while posing situations where witches, monsters, aliens and the like suddenly find themselves facing the same glaring stupidity and societal confusion that their mortal opponents need to challenge on a daily basis.

Notable films: *Working Stiffs* (1989), *Loons* (1991), *Cutthroats* (1994), *Sick Time* (1995), *Braindrainer* (1999), *Honey Glaze* (2003), *The Dungeon of Dr. Dreck* (2007).

Matt McCormick. The Oregon-based filmmaker defines his work (via his website) as work that blurs the lines between documentary and experimental filmmaking to fashion witty and abstract observations of contemporary culture and the urban landscape. At home in microcinemas and MTV, he has also promoted underground film via his Peripheral Produce video distribution label, thus spreading the underground cred to a wider audience.

Notable films: *Sincerely, Joe P. Bear* (1999), *The Vyrotonin Decision* (1999), *Going to the Ocean* (2001), *The Subconscious Art of Graffiti Removal* (2001), *American Nutria* (2003), *Towlines* (2004).

Andrew Repasky McElhinney. The Philadelphia-based filmmaker has sought to bend and mold traditional concepts of filmmaking into daring new configurations. In his canon, it is not unusual for the genteel aristocracy of the costume drama to come face-to-face with serial killing, or deep philosophy to rest alongside provocative eroticism. McElhinney's works have polarized critics, with some championing his daring and others wondering if he went too far in the wrong direction. If there is agreement on his work, it would come in admiring his ability to present a vibrant and unique artistic vision.

Notable films: *Magdalen* (1998), *A Chronicle of Corpses* (2001), *Georges Bataille's Story of the Eye* (2003), *Animal Husbandry* (2009).

John Orrichio. The New Jersey-based underground horror filmmaker has taken the staples of the genre – demon-infiltrated priests, vampires with a hunger for a Type O chaser, haunted houses and lethal objects with deadly histories – and successfully breathed new life into their protocol with unconventional casting, decidedly warped story twists and a brazen refusal to surrender to genre clichés. His films recall the early, uncluttered work of Roger Corman: low in budgets, high in spirit, energetic and unapologetic in their pursuit of bump-in-the-night shocks.

Notable films: *The Possession of Father Thomas* (2004), *Requiem for a Vampire* (2006), *The Haunting of Danbury House* (2007, co-directed with Karl Petry), *Black Ribbon* (2007), *Process* (2009).

Tim Ritter. The Kentucky-based filmmaker entered the film world as a high school student by shooting the feature *Day of the Reaper* (1984) in Super 8mm and then selling it via the then-nascent direct-to-video market as a self-distributed title. Ritter's horror films have focused on psychological imbalances; his villains (or anti-heroes, to some viewers) are sad, twisted individuals who lost their connection to their surroundings and function in their own bizarre spheres, crashing occasionally into the real world with grisly results. His films are not for the weak-stomached, but those with a taste for the genre's edgier elements can enjoy the zeal and passion of his high-octane offerings.

Notable films: *Twisted Illusions* (1985), *Truth or Dare? A Critical Madness* (1986), *Killing Spree* (1987), *Wicked Games* (1994), *Creep* (1995), *Dirty Cop No Donut* (1999), *Reconciled* (2004).

Thomas Edward Seymour. Working both as a solo artist and in collaboration with two sets of partners – Mike Aransky and Philip Guerette in the Hale Manor Collective and Jonathan Gorman for the *Bikini Bloodbath* series – the Connecticut native has brought a raucous view of life to his comedy film output. Whether skewering comic book action/adventure or sending up cheesy slasher flicks, Seymour's films (both feature-length narratives and Internet shorts) take an in-your-face rude-boy approach that insists life's ephemeral nature can only be conquered without the burdens of seriousness or self-importance.

Notable films: *Thrill Kill Jack in Hale Manor* (2000), *Everything Moves Alone* (2001), *Land of College Prophets* (2005), *Bikini Bloodbath* (2007), *300 PG Version* (2007), *Bikini Bloodbath Car Wash* (2008), *Tetris: The Movie* (2008), *Marv's Psychic Shop* (2008), *Bikini Bloodbath Christmas* (2009), *London Betty* (2009).

Eric Stanze. The St. Louis-based Stanze completed his first feature,

The Scare Game (1980), at the age of 18. Focused in the horror genre, Stanze's films provide a disturbing blending of physical violence and cerebral sadism. In Stanze's work, torture runs deep in numerous directions: the assault on the body, the battering of religious faith, and the attack on basic dignity – yet the trials endured by his characters can be seen as the preservation of self-esteem in the midst of a world that has twisted seriously out of control. Some critics have complained of excessive gore in his work, but Stanze knows well enough to keep gore as an aspect of his work. The greater goal, in his consideration, comes in putting ordinary people up to extraordinary circumstances and watching how they either rise or fall.

Notable films: *The Scare Game* (1980), *The Fine Art* (1994), *Savage Harvest* (1995), *Ice From the Sun* (1999), *Scrapbook* (2000), *I Spit on Your Corpse, I Piss on Your Grave* (2001), *China White Serpentine* (2003), *Deadwood Park* (2007).

Jimmy Traynor. Arguably the most indefatigable personality in contemporary underground cinema, the Baltimore-based director/producer/writer/actor/editor has turned out over 100 films since 1994. The majority of his work is shorts, though he has also created narrative features, and he often casts himself as the conflicted anti-hero struggling against a myriad of emotional and physical upheavals. Comfortable in all genres (though off-beat comedy seems to be his forte), Traynor's work has a rough and raw vitality that takes cinema verité to a new edge, and his willingness to experiment in fully improvised productions offers a sense of daring that few focused filmmakers are willing to pursue.

Notable films: *Billy Saves Christmas* (1994), *The Weird Thing* (1996), *Jealousy* (2002), *Game Plan* (2003), *Jimmy's Devils* (2003), *Bear Movement* (2004), *Home Made Dad* (2005), *Beat the Bastard Down* (2006).

Caveh Zahedi. The San Francisco-based director and actor has taken a deeply personal approach to his films – to the point that he is the focus of his work, consisting of both documentaries and narrative recreations of his life. Whether exposing family struggles, reliving (or, perhaps, rehashing) once-buried heartaches, or detailing issues relating to drug usage and sexual peccadilloes, Zahedi's films can often be un-comfortable due to his willingness to offer a shocking depth and scope to his various anxieties and obsessions. While some may consider this to be self-indulgence, Zahedi's ability to speak openly and honestly about what shapes his personality enables him to stand apart as a cinematic equivalent of the graphic memoirist.

Notable films: *A Little Stiff* (1990, co-directed by Greg Watkins), *I Don't Hate Las Vegas Anymore* (1994), *I Was Possessed by God* (2000), *Worm* (2001), *In the Bathtub of the World* (2001), *Tripping with Caveh* (2004), *I Am a Sex Addict* (2005).

Nick Zedd. The New York filmmaker can claim a place in the mo-tion picture lexicon by coining the term Cinema of Transgression to de-fine underground filmmakers who use shock value and black humor in their productions. Active since 1979, Zedd's work mixes punk outrage with perverse humor, creating a seemingly perpetual state of agitation where outrageous behavior barely raises a peep of concern. Zedd's universe mixes violence, eroticism, agitprop and insouciant absurdity into a glaring, glowing style. To many, he personifies the best of the underground cinema.

Notable films: *They Eat Scum* (1979), *The Wild World of Lydia Lunch* (1983), *Geek Maggot Bingo* (1985), *Thrust In Me* (1985), *War is Men-strual Envy* (1992), *Tom Thumb in the Land of the Giants* (1999), *Lord of the Cockrings* (2002), *Electra Elf: The Beginning Parts One & Two* (2005).

The 10 Most Important Independent Films of All Time:
Matthew Sorrento, film editor, Identity Theory

Q: If you were to look over the span of the history of U.S. indepen-dent cinema, from the silent era to today's output, what would you list as the 10 Most Important Independently-Produced Films of All Time ... and why?

1. *Nanook of the North* (1922). While historians have noted its lack of veracity – director Robert J. Flaherty staged many of the scenes – *Nanook of the North* virtually constructed the feature-length documentary. True, the earliest films were in themselves documentaries (going all the way back to Lumiere's "actualities"). However, Flaherty's arctic landscapes coupled with the routines and folkways of the Intuit people (nearly died out) realized the extent to which cinema could detail life, with the extraordinary situated alongside the everyday.

2. *Meshes of the Afternoon* (1942). This short film brought surrealism from Europe into the American cinema. The film's psychoanalytic tendencies – to lay bare the psyche of a woman (director Maya Deren) chased by a cloaked figure in a dreamlike, mobius-strip narrative – arguably should be the goal of surrealism, more so than the random mental play of Bunuel and Dali's *Un Chien Andalou*. Freud mused that, by depicting the unconscious, Dali's paintings made us wonder about the conscious of the artist and his work. Deren's nightmarish short immerses us in the depths of the mind, while shedding light on her character's anxiety and sexual tension, even if the filmmaker exploits trademark Freudian images (a knife and a key). This early underground film tested the boundaries of narrative, and thus inspired many experimental films after it.

3. *Scorpio Rising* (1962). In this short, Kenneth Anger looked back to Deren's surrealism, infused it with pop sensibility and fetishism, and thus took one of the first steps toward a queer cinema. With Top 40 hits on his soundtrack, Anger found visual rhythms that realized

a homoerotic gang of bikers in a vivid color scheme and a very different male gaze. He never sought permission for the songs, which resulted in legal action(s) that made the film hard to see for decades. Ironically enough, *Scorpio Rising* became cinema's first effective use of pop, especially "Blue Velvet" ironically crooning over a newly leather-clad biker. The film laid the path for the rock soundtracks of the New Hollywood movement (especially in *Easy Rider* and Scorsese), with the "Blue Velvet" scene directly inspiring Kubrick's trademark ironic use of sound and image.

4. *Who's That Knocking At My Door* (1968). A life of crime meets Catholic guilt for a New York youth trying to make it with a girl. Can a filmmaker's debut foresee a decade's worth of personal themes? Well, Martin Scorsese's did, in this film starring Harvey Keitel that the director cobbled together on his own time and dollar. The film may occasionally slip into self-conscious artiness and was overshadowed by the similarly-themed *Mean Streets* (1973), yet the New York film would never be the same after it. While many would look past this to Cassavetes, *Knocking* channeled such inspiration into an American tradition.

5. *Night of the Living Dead* (1968). Along with *Psycho*, this independently-produced cult classic re-conceived the horror genre, with its humans becoming the true monsters, to its oppressive, downbeat ending. Romero's film is a cinematic exercise in which tension never subsides within a confined setting; the pressure of death knocking turns the prisoners of a graveyard house against one another. With all its narrative inventiveness – which, unlike the classic horror formula, creates ten-

sion right away – the film also delivered ghoulish gore from the underground cinema into the mainstream consciousness. Many fans want to keep this a pure horror film, but as its opening image of a black-and-white, bleached-out American flag attests, this a story of American anxieties, then and now.

6. *Easy Rider* (1969). This trademark piece of the New Hollywood movement (which even earned a place in the title of a trademark book about the era) may seem like an obvious, perhaps overrated choice. But did any other film *by* outsiders, *for* outsiders, *about* outsiders capture the dropout mood of the late 1960s? Occasional trippy editing of two bikers on the road doesn't dilute from some fresh tastes of the American landscape in what helped make the road movie a dominate genre for independent filmmakers. Much of the acting is hammy; filmmakers Dennis Hopper and Peter Fonda reportedly went for verité during drug-taking scenes, but Oscar-nominee Jack Nicholson, as a bottomed-out lawyer who goes for a ride, proved he was one to look out for.

7. *Sweet Sweetback's Baadasssss Song* (1971). Often cited for launching the 1970s "Blaxploitation" movement, this self-produced piece channels the collective rage of a race, stemming from its lack of civil and artistic freedom. After a debut in France and helming one American studio project, Melvin Van Peebles wrote, directed, produced, and starred as Sweetback, who resists and runs from white authority. This rag-tag narrative, which was "rated X by an all-white jury," undermines the mainstream (read: White) cinema by focusing on an extended flight lacking a resolution. The film may veer toward hyperbole, with a cop screaming at a deafened

black man and Sweetback performing sex for whites. And its theme may also feel as heavy-handed as its thick Earth, Wind and Fire score. But by sporting a "by any means necessary" tone reflective of the times, the film helped to articulate a cinematic voice for the oppressed, and in turn helped establish black filmmaking.

8. *Evil Dead* (1981). Horror filmmakers have made us laugh at least since James Whale. And when the '60s and '70s called for a new taste of horror in the form of psycho-killers, some gags were thrown in. But the age of horror comedies wouldn't come until the 1980s. Perhaps it was the Reagan era and its threat of sheer annihilation that called for us to laugh at the gruesome. Whatever the reason may be, it was started by Sam Raimi's *Evil Dead*, a project that cleverly uses an omnipresent ancient curse in a remote woodland setting. Seemingly more than ever in horror films, the possibilities were endless, as the curse could jump into a host at any time. Thus, Raimi and his band of mavericks brought much suspense and gore, but threw in laughs when we'd least expect them. A number of successful horror comedies followed suit, including Stuart Gordon's *Re-Animator* and *Return of the Living Dead*, an offshoot of Romero's classic series. Raimi's sequel, *Evil Dead II: Dead by Dawn*, made comedy a priority and lost all the horror. Thus signaled the end of a revolutionary take on a steady genre.

9. *Stranger Than Paradise* (1984). Although *sex, lies and videotape* takes credit for bringing independents into high profile, this personal piece of the early 1980s showed viewers how fresh and original a film narrative could be from an underground voice. In long, black-and-white

shots, Jim Jarmusch's *Stranger Than Paradise*, a new take on disaffected youth, at first seems like pretension on high order, like a student film gone way too far. Yet it settles into a lethargic, revealing narrative style that winks to Wenders and reminds American filmmakers that the classic structure is just convention.

10. *Blood Simple* (1984). The Coen Brothers made the *film noir* into a reflexive playground. The destructive passions of James M. Cain's *The Postman Always Rings Twice* became very modern in this film, in which layers of evil appear and the hunted proves to be not much better. The twists and turns throughout the story of lovers sought by a vengeful husband, which cumulate in an infamous, quirky finale, expand the possibilities within a contained narrative that is self-aware of its *no-irish* traits. It was a bold debut for a bright new talent that would continue to re-imagine the classic genres for aware modern audiences.

CHAPTER FIVE:
In the Realm of the Non-Theatrical

"Cinema is the most beautiful fraud in the world"

– Jean-Luc Godard

Running parallel to the world of independent cinema is the non-theatrical film industry. As its name would suggest, these are productions that were never meant to be seen within the comforts of a cinema (or, for that matter, in the comfort of a home for television or video viewing).

Non-theatrical films can roughly be divided into two sectors: industrial films designed to celebrate a particular line of work and educational films designed to speed up the learning process for tomorrow's leaders or bring today's workforce up-to-speed. On the whole, this sector is dominated by short films. As they are produced by low-budget independent entities for exhibition during the course of the work or school day, the notion of feature-length films rarely found their way into this genre.

Non-theatrical film production is not to be confused with the concept of non-theatrical distribution, which involves the release of films to schools, trade groups, libraries, community organizations and government agencies. This distribution channel often incorporates feature-length films (mostly documentaries), but these films were clearly not meant to be seen exclusively beyond the cinema. Indeed, many of these films have active histories on the festival circuit and some turned up on television and even in a few theaters. In this chapter, we are discussing the section of the independent film world where movies were not meant for general release, but were aimed at specific target audiences.

Prior to the dawning of the 1980s video age, non-theatrical films were long seen in 16mm formats, although there have been some notable exceptions involving 35mm and even 70mm presentations. The rise of the VHS video format killed off the 16mm market – and, of course, the rise of the DVD format effectively killed off the VHS video market. (Whether Blu-Ray will speed DVD to a high-tech grave remains to be seen.)

Non-theatrical films have traditionally been viewed negatively by those within the film industry; the snob appeal here has long dictated that any production that was not meant to be seen in a theater is just not good enough. They have also been largely taken for granted by their intended audiences. In some ways, the scorn showed to them is understandable; many of these films are unremarkable, and there are more than a few (mostly produced in the 1940s through the 1960s) that have become unintentionally funny due to changes in viewer sophistication.

But, for the most part, this poor perception is grossly unfair. Non-theatrical films have always served an important purpose through their use of the cinematic medium to relay messages – health, education, military readiness, vocational proficiency; even driver awareness comes into play here. Admittedly, these messages could be considered self-serving to an outsider, particularly if they involve commercial enterprise or government propaganda.

Any consideration of non-theatrical films needs to be prefixed with an acknowledgment that rarely gets made in public: there is no accurate way to keep track of the exact number of non-theatrical films that have been produced. Corporate-sponsored films, the first subsection within this genre, date back into the very early years of the silent cinema, and many of these films from the pre-sound era are considered lost. Furthermore, a large number of surviving non-theatrical films from the first six decades of the 20th century did not have copyright registrations with the Library of Congress. Thus, it is easy to assume that there are other copyright-free films that may exist but remain unaccounted for.

Additionally, the vast majority of the surviving and acknowledged non-theatrical are not easily accessible for review. Unless one is willing to go through great lengths to secure screenings at archives or with private collections, these films remain out of sight. This is a shame, since more than a few of these titles have achieved a substantial degree of recognition, and a handful managed to go beyond the limits of the genre to snag Academy Award recognition.

In a sick irony, many of the films that are easily accessible (either in video anthology collections or through online video sites) are often the worst of the genre: films made decades ago that have aged so badly that they come to today's viewers as little more than vintage nonsense of low-camp value. Having the weakest and dumbest films available inevitably suggests that they are representative of the genre as a whole.

While some archivists and film scholars have made an effort to keep track of this genre, particularly the indefatigable Rick Prelinger, this sector of the independent film world still contains vast stretches of uncharted and unknown territories.

Yet if an effort is made to review these films (admittedly, this is no mean feat), one can find something fairly remarkable. In many ways, non-theatrical films took a bold and daring initiative to challenge notions of what is expected from American society. The Hollywood fare of the Golden Era provided an idealized view of American society (either as a satisfied middle-class suburban fantasy or a savvy, edgy upper-class urban adventure). This is not to say that Hollywood only created rose-colored fantasies. But for every hard-hitting social drama like *The Grapes of Wrath* or *The Ox-Bow Incident*, there were tons of celluloid confectionary designed solely to distract and entertain.

The non-theatrical films, however, enjoyed the liberty to venture into areas that were off-limits due to the restrictions of the Production Code and the timidity and indifference of the studio chieftains. These films questioned issues relating to tolerance, socio-economic imbalances, health care crises, and the challenge of maintaining individual responsibility without losing self-identity.

While a high number of the non-theatrical films may have answered these questions in a manner that could be seen by today's standards as either self-serving (for the corporate-sponsored films) or out of step with contemporary considerations (for the educational films), the fact they even bothered to initially raise the questions is significant.

One might imagine that today's barrier-free filmmaking would render the bravery of non-theatrical filmmakers as outdated. Actually, the opposite appears to be the case. Corporate-sponsored films have a greater challenge in getting their message across in a succinct and cogent manner to viewers who are savvy to standard-issue marketing ploys. Educational films have also seen the need to adapt to very different social circumstances. It is not cynical to state that both adults and children have shorter attention spans today versus previous generations, so the need to get messages across can easily tax the creativity of the non-theatrical filmmaker

Yet the use of film to relay and reinforce messages is no different than the historic use of any communication media to get a point across. What is unique, however, is that we are cognizant that the most popular entertainment medium is also being used to offer more than a mere short distraction.

And, yes, these films can be very effective.

Corporate-sponsored films (a historical perspective)

Starting at the dawn of the 20th century, corporations and nonprofit organizations have actively pursued the production of films. Many of these films were pure marketing vehicles, although some were fairly subtle in disguising the products, services or concepts being promoted.

In several cases, these films made no attempt to promote a specific product, service or concept. These films, instead, were present under the umbrella of social responsibility and awareness – and, of course, there were plenty of PR points to be gained as being the sponsoring entity of such an endeavor. (For the sake of unity, we will refer to this genre as "corporate sponsored," even if the production source was a nonprofit organization, a medical center or a university.)

While the vast majority of corporate-sponsored films remain obscure, there are some that have moved beyond the realm of the non-theatrical into the wider cultural mainstream. These films, either due to their content or their back stories, have earned classic status within this genre. In many ways, they represent a cinematic timeline of 20th-Century America, detailing changing attitudes and priorities regarding industry, commerce, social sciences, health and the awareness of global interconnectivity.

In chronological order, here is a presentation of what could arguably be considered as the 25 most important corporate-sponsored films of all time:

The Stockyard Series (1901). Armour & Co. commissioned a series of 60 shorts that were filmed at the Union Stock Yards in Chicago. This decision, one of the earliest for corporate-sponsored filmmaking, proved to be prescient: the 1906 publication of Upton Sinclair's *The Jungle* was countered by Armour's re-release of the film to show the sanitary and safe working environment it ran.

The Yanks Are Coming (1918). The Dayton-Wright Airplane Co. produced this feature-length film about its de Haviland DH-4 aircraft, which was used by the U.S. Army Air Service in World War I. Remarkably, the film was pulled from general circulation by the Committee on Public Information, a federal agency set up to coordinate the nation's propaganda efforts during wartime. The agency felt this film was too commercial and ordered its removal from theaters, marking the first time the federal government tried to get a film banned.

The Wizardry of Wireless (1923). General Electric produced this two-reel film, which mixed animation and live action to illustrate mankind's attempts at long distance communication. The efforts conclude with the introduction of the radio, with a brief tour of the company's WGY station. What is curious about this production is that it was a silent film; not exactly the most obvious medium for outlining sound technology.

The World Struggle for Oil (1923). While the film's title may suggest a contemporary view of the ongoing energy crisis, this feature film from the Sinclair Consolidated Oil Corp. offered evidence of the then-growing American addiction to oil. This feature-length film may have been forgotten had Sinclair not arranged for it to be distributed non-theatrically through the U.S. Bureau of Mines. That decision was cited against the company in the wake of the Teapot Dome Scandal that paralyzed the country amid charges of political and corporate corruption.

The Forgotten Frontier (1931). This hour-long silent documentary on the Frontier Nursing Service Inc., a private enterprise that brought medical care to isolated rural communities in Kentucky, is noteworthy in that it was produced and directed by Mary Marvin Breckenridge, who originally worked for the company. Few women directed corporate-sponsored films, and Breckenridge's time behind the camera created a film that was rich in drama (not to mention dramatic reenactments): a nurse giving shots, assisting in childbirths, and physically transporting a shooting victim to medical care in a larger community. The film was selected to the Library of Congress' National Film Registry.

Love, Honor and Obey (The Law) (1935). B.F. Goodrich sponsored this two-reeler, which enjoyed theatrical release thanks to the presence of Harry Langdon in the starring role as an inebriated playboy whose pending marriage to a police chief's daughter hinges on his ability not to get any traffic tickets. The film enjoyed a gimmicky promotion that rewarded winning moviegoers who could recall how many traffic violations took place during the course of the film. The presence of Langdon in this film was significant. Although he was far below the star status he enjoyed during the silent movie era, he still possessed enough clout to warrant starring roles in lower-budget features and shorts.

Master Hands (1936). One of the most artistically striking corporate-sponsored films ever made was this half-hour production from Chevrolet Motor Co. Using almost no dialogue and backed with a sweeping score by Samuel Benavie that was performed with gusto by the Detroit Philharmonic Orchestra, the film presents the manufacturing operations of Chevrolet's Flint, Michigan, plant with boldly framed shots and breathless montage editing that calls to mind 1920s-era Soviet filmmaking. The film had several lives: for sales and marketing training, to promote the company's World War II-era efforts (new footage was added to show military vehicles being produced), and as a vocational education training film in the postwar years. The film was named to the Library of Congress' National Film Registry.

Television: An RCA Presentation (1939). As the first promotional film to highlight the medium that would later challenge the motion picture industry, this RCA-produced one-reeler provided glimpses of early TV broadcasts from the New York World's Fair and the RCA studios at Rockefeller Center.

Art in the Negro Schools (1940). Prior to the passage of the 1960s civil rights legislation, African Americans were virtually unseen in corporate-sponsored films. A few exceptions were made, such as this silent two-reeler celebrating the performing and fine arts curriculum at the nation's leading historically black colleges and universities. The film was part of a series called *Negro Education for American Living* that was produced by the Harmon Foundation, a nonprofit philanthropy that advocated racial tolerance and equality.

Goodbye, Mr. Germ (1940). The National Tuberculosis Association produced this two-reeler that mixed animation and actors in a fanciful tale of a doctor who cures a child of TB. The film is recalled today solely because it was directed by Edgar G. Ulmer, the prolific and peripatetic filmmaker whose career pinballed between the Hollywood studios and the low-budget fringe world of independent productions.

The Green Hand (1940). Based on a novel by Paul W. Chapman, an agriculture professor at the University of Georgia, the film depicted how a potential juvenile delinquent was cured of his miscreant tenden-

cies by joining the Future Farmers of America. Sears-Roebuck & Co.,
for whatever reason, opted to produce a film based on the book. The
production was shot in Athens, Georgia, using a mix of local townspeo-
ple and University of Georgia faculty as the cast. The film, which ran a
half-hour, had a theatrical premiere in Athens on January 12, 1940, that
attracted Georgia's governor (who, one month earlier, was in Atlanta
for the premiere of *Gone with the Wind*).

A Place to Live (1941). The Philadelphia Housing Association sponsored this two-reeler on the lack of affordable housing in the City of
Brotherly Love. Somewhat surprisingly, the film's central focus (a boy
living in a slum) does not wind up living happily ever after in a lovely
home. More surprising was the film's nomination for the Academy
Award as Best Documentary Short Subject – no mean feat, considering
it was a non-studio production and it really wasn't a documentary (the
film used actors to dramatize its points).

Hemp for Victory (1942). The U.S. Department of Agriculture
(USDA) created the 16-minute film *Hemp for Victory* to show farmers
how to successfully cultivate cannibas plants for use in the manufacture
of wartime cordage. The film offers an examination of everything you
ever wanted to know about growing hemp. The film was only shown
during 1942 – it literally disappeared after the war, when the federal
ban on growing hemp took effect again. For years, the USDA insisted
that no such movie ever existed. But in May 1989, a trio of tenacious
advocates for legalizing marijuana – Jack Herer, Maria Farrow and Carl
Packard – combed the Library of Congress' motion picture and film-
strips records in Washington and the USDA library at Bettsville, Maryland, to locate evidence the film existed. They later found a print and
donated it to the Library of Congress.

The Story of Menstruation (1946). This may seem like bizarre trivia,
but the first on-screen use of the word "vagina" took place in a Walt
Disney cartoon. No, Minnie Mouse and Daisy Duck were not involved.
Instead, it turned up in this 10-minute educational film, created on com-
mission by Disney for the International Cellu-Cotton Products Com-

pany (the creators of Kotex feminine products). The film was a staple of health education classes for more than two decades, providing an explanation of the menstrual cycle while offering tips on how to maintain a healthy body and spirit during periods. The film was presented with an accompanying booklet called *Very Personally Yours*, which was *not* created by Disney.

Louisiana Story (1948). Arguably the greatest sponsored film ever made, this feature was directed by Robert Flaherty, who pioneered documentary filmmaking with *Nanook of the North* (1922). What many people don't realize is that *Louisiana Story* was produced by Standard Oil to play up the pro-development aspects of oil exploration in the Louisiana Bayou. While Standard Oil's name is never mentioned in the film, its pro-oil drilling message is difficult to ignore. However, most people were more enchanted with the film's artistic composition than its commercialism. *Louisiana Story*, which enjoyed a theatrical release via Lopert Films, was nominated for the Academy Award for Best Original Story, Virgil Thomson's score won the Pulitzer Prize for Music (the only film score to receive that honor), and is part of the Library of Congress' National Film Registry.

Technicolor for Industrial Films (1949). This unique production is a corporate-sponsored film designed to be seen by the makers of other corporate-sponsored films. The Technicolor Corp. provides a cogent explanation of why its color film process is the best choice for those who want to make industrial and educational films outside of the confines of black and white (and not to mention away from the cheaper color film processes that were encroaching on Technicolor's market).

Breast Self-Examination (1950). Breast cancer was not a subject that was widely discussed in the mainstream media during the 1950s. However, this 42-minute film (co-produced by the American Cancer Society, the National Cancer Institute and the U.S. Public Health Service) showed women how to check for the earliest warning signs of possible breast cancer symptoms. Two different truncated versions of the film would be released later in the 1950s.

Benjy (1951). Henry Fonda narrated and Fred Zinnemann (Oscar-winner for *From Here to Eternity* and *A Man for All Seasons*) directed this short film about a boy with scoliosis who is rejected by his parents for being disabled, but who is cured thanks to the tireless support of his orthopedic pediatrician. Paramount Pictures arranged for the crew to work on this film, which was used as a fundraising vehicle for the Los Angeles Orthopedic Hospital. Paramount also released this film in limited theatrical distribution, qualifying it for the Academy Award. Although the film made heavy use of actors to tell its story, as opposed to presenting its tale in the non-fiction format, it nonetheless won the Oscar as Best Documentary Short Subject.

The Home Economics Story (1951). One of the most infamous films of this genre was produced by the Home Economics Division of Iowa State College. The film insists that young women seeking a college degree inevitably need to be educated in the fine art of homemaking. The incongruity of educating women for a lifetime of housework makes the film very difficult to appreciate today, except as a source of unintentional pre-women's lib humor.

Paradise for Buster (1952). During the latter part of his career, Buster Keaton became something of a regular in the industrial film orbit. The one-time silent film icon starred in short corporate-produced films created on behalf of the National Association of Wholesalers (*The Devil to Pay*, 1960), Maremont Exhaust and the Gabriel Shocks Division of the Arvin Corporation (*There's No Business Like No Business*, 1963), Eastman Kodak (*The Triumph of Lester Snapwell*, 1963), U.S. Steel (*The Fall Guy*, 1965) and the Construction Safety Association of Ontario (*The Scribe*, 1966, Keaton's last movie prior to his 1967 death). Keaton's first exposure to this genre came with *Paradise for Buster*, a 39-minute offering financed by the John Deere & Co. What was curious about the film is that it barely made any mention of the company or its products. Instead, it was a near-silent film (Keaton had two words of dialogue: "I quit") about a bookkeeper who quits his dull job after inheriting a substantial fortune. In his new wealth, he moves to an agricultural estate (hence the John Deere connection), where he gets entangled in all sorts of slapstick. Keaton reworked several gags from his classic movies into *Paradise for Buster*, thus adding an expert degree of humor that many industrial films lack.

The Secret of Selling the Negro Market (1954). This production from Johnson Publishing Co., the force behind black-oriented magazines such as *Ebony* and *Jet*, dared to break the Park Avenue taboo regarding the advertising of mainstream consumer products and services in African-American media. Shot in Kodachrome Color and featuring U.S. Commerce Secretary Sinclair Weeks, the film was meant to show that African-American consumers were an economic force that deserved respect. The film was designed to be shown to potential advertisers who, during the pre-Civil Rights era, often refused to promote their products in African-American media. The film had its premiere in July 1954 at the Joseph Schlitz Brewing Co. in Milwaukee. Whether it made any impact on expanding advertising within African-American media is unclear, but it deserves recognition as an important sociological barrier-breaker.

Our Mr. Sun (1957). American Telephone & Telegraph sponsored this hour-long educational film, which was co-directed by Frank Capra and William T. Hurtz. *Our Mr. Sun* was the first in the Bell System Science series that first appeared on television and was later distributed on 16mm to schools around the country. This film mixed animation and live action to examine the many benefits derived from sunlight. Capra (who had not directed a film since *Here Comes the Groom* in 1951) produced and wrote the films, and he teamed with Hurtz in directing three more titles: *Hemo the Magnificent* (1957), *The Strange Case of the Cosmic Rays* (1958) and *The Unchained Goddess* (1958).

Why Braceros? (1959). Along with African Americans, Hispanics were conspicuously absent from sponsored films for many years. This 19-minute film, commissioned by the Council of California Growers in response to public concern over Mexican immigration, highlighted the importance of Mexican "guest workers" to California's agriculture and ranching industries. The "bracero" program was originally created in 1942 to help fill the labor void created by World War II; it officially ended in 1964, but the use of Mexican laborers, of course, continues to this day.

To Be Alive (1964). Few corporate films have ever enjoyed the pedigree of this production, produced by S.C. Johnson & Son. The film did not sell products, but rather offered a multicultural celebration of children from around the world. It was originally presented at the Johnson Wax pavilion at the 1964 World's Fair in an unusual exhibition format consisting of having the film projected on three separate 18-foot screens (each screen was separated by one foot of space). The film made quite an impression and a bit of history: the members of the New York Film Critics Circle trekked out to the World's Fair to see the film and presented it with a special award, the first ever given by that distinguished group to a non-theatrical production. S.C. Johnson & Co. hoped to take the New York Film Critics Circle Award one better, but its attempt to secure an Oscar nomination was halted when the Academy decided that the three-screen approach did not meet the projection requirements of its rules. S.C. Johnson & Co. paid to have the three-screen film reconfigured into a single-screen presentation that could be seen in 70mm. That satisfied the Oscar rules, and *To Be Alive* won the 1965 Academy Award for Best Documentary Short Subject, beating out another sponsored short, *Point of View*, produced by the National Tuberculosis Association. *To Be Alive* is still playing, at SC Johnson headquarters in Racine, Wisconsin. The S.C. Johnson Golden Rondelle Theater presents the film in its original three-screen version.

A Time for Burning (1966). The upheaval of the civil rights era is reflected in this Lutheran Film Associates feature about the minister of a white Omaha church who faces a revolt from his congregation when he attempts to reach out to a neighboring black church. The film was nominated for the Academy Award as Best Documentary and was selected for the Library of Congress' National Film Registry.

Why Man Creates (1968). Saul Bass wrote, directed and produced this short film on behalf of Kaiser Aluminum and Chemical Corp. The film details creativity throughout the history of civilization, from Socrates

through the Wright Brothers, tracing an idea from its hazy mental ori-
gins through the final presentation of the completed work. The film
received the Academy Award as Best Documentary Short Subject, and
it was later included in the Library of Congress' National Film Registry.

Corporate-sponsored films
(a contemporary perspective)

The concept of corporate-sponsored films still exists and thrives. It is
impossible to keep track of how many of these productions are created
annually, as there is no central clearinghouse that monitors the quantity
of productions. (A competition called the Telly Awards seeks to maintain quality standards, but that endeavor is only open to those who
make an effort to enter their competition.)

Many of these films are not particularly memorable; they are mostly
training efforts to bring people up to speed on particular intercompany
requirements. But as with our earlier list, there are still examples of non-
theatrical films making a significant corporate and cultural difference.

Case in point: the Latino Community Credit Union (LCCU), a
50,000-member institution based in Durham, N.C. In the spring of
2007, LCCU received a grant from the U.S. Treasury Department's
Community Development Financial Institutions Fund to create an educational production designed to introduce the concept of homeownership
to Latin American immigrants.

Initially, LCCU planned to create a straightforward educational
video. In reviewing that option, however, it was decided that another
approach might work better. "We thought it would be fun, attractive
and easier to follow in a fiction manner, with actors and some humor
in it," explained Angel Romero, director of marketing and communications at LCCU.

Thus came LCCU's initial contribution to the world of independent
cinema and financial literacy: *Angelica's Dreams* (also marketed as *Los
SueZos de Angélica*). The 90-minute production follows an immigrant
couple seeking permanent residence status in the U.S. The film involves

challenges and sacrifices - some humorous, some serious. The couple must consider if they wish to remain in the U.S. for the rest of their lives.

A North Carolina filmmaker, Rodrigo Dorfman, wrote, produced and directed the film, which took a breathless three months to complete, from screenwriting to the post-production wrap. For Dorfman, the narrative fiction format made more sense from a viewer standpoint.

"When you hear 'educational video,' you cringe," he says. "There's a lot of baggage attached to that. So we decided to make it a feature film in a telenovela style."

The telenovela style is emphasized by having most of the film in Spanish, with English subtitles (a few scenes involving business transactions are in English). In the flow of the film, the couple agrees to pursue homeownership. Being new to the concept of mortgages, this takes them into new territory - and, in a particular plot twist, directly into an LCCU branch.

"The credit union is featured in several important scenes," says Romero. "Some of these scenes involve loan officers, who are played by the credit union's staff."

Angelica's Dreams premiered on October 21, 2007, at the Carolina Theatre in Durham. Romero recalls the audience was caught off-guard by the film's style and approach.

"Many people though this was going to be a financial education documentary," he says. "They were surprised it was a feature film."

Dorfman adds that the film's plot also had a broad appeal beyond the Latino audience. "I know a lot of people who said: 'I'm not an immigrant, I was born here, and I know what they are going through,'" he says.

Angelica's Dreams played again at the University of North Carolina's Latin American Film Festival in November. Although no additional theatrical screenings took place after that, LCCU began work on non-theatrical DVD distribution.

"We are making DVD copies and will be sending them to credit unions and community organizations across the country," says Romero. "We already have requests from California and Wisconsin."

Beyond the big and small screens, LCCU is planning to divide the feature into three episodes that will be shown on big-screen monitors in the credit union's branches. A special manual has been prepared for viewers of both the in-branch presentation and the DVD.

Another unusual but successful use of non-theatrical film is Novo Nordisk's documentary, *Peaks and Poles: The Will Cross Story.* The film focuses on the Pittsburgh mountaineer who became the first person with diabetes to climb the highest mountain on each of the seven continents and trek to the North and South Poles.

Novo Nordisk, a healthcare company that sponsored *Cross,* used this film for promotional and marketing purposes (it is available in DVD format as 20-minute and 47-minute productions). Copies of the DVD have been distributed to diabetes organizations, healthcare professionals, individuals living with diabetes, and members of the company's international sales force.

The Internet has also been tapped for corporate-sponsored film distribution. Consider the four-part serial *Phished,* created by the Night Agency in New York for webcast on Symantec's Safetytown microsite. *Phished* follows the misadventures of an average Joe who discovers that his financial data has been stolen via the Net (or, in cybertalk, "phished"). Rather than sitting around waiting for outsiders to help solve his problems, this crime victim turns crime fighter in trying to hunt down and bring to justice the miscreants who hooked his information.

Although it is sponsored by Symantec, the anti-virus software company, *Phished* is not a commercial for the company or its product line. If anything, it is a stylish and entertaining production that approaches the serious subject of identity theft with uncommon originality. Scott Cohn, a creative director at the Night Agency, wrote and directed *Phished.* (The agency also built the Safetytown website and coordinated an online PR campaign, thus scoring a triple play with this project.)

Another company, the financial services provider ING Direct, tapped into the online video realm in the fall of 2006. The company launched the website www.MoveOutMoveUp.com with a series of comic video clips showing sitcom-worthy hassles involved in renting while playing up the nirvana of homeownership – via the company's subsidiary Orange Mortgage.

From a PR standpoint, ING Direct's use of low comedy is refreshing, particularly the episode *Tea with Grandma*, where the visit of a visiting grandmother is disrupted by the excessively passionate acrobatics of the neighbors on the other side of the thin apartment walls. The company also discovered the joys of viral video distribution, as its clips have turned up on YouTube, Yahoo Video and other online venues.

The audience for corporate-sponsored films continues to grow. Consider the case of Interthinx Inc., an Agoura Hills, Calif.-based provider of risk mitigation and regulatory compliance tools for the financial services industry. In 2006, the company created a DVD called *FSI, Fraud Scheme Investigation*, which parodied the popular *CSI* franchise of crime-solving TV shows as the setting for its fraud-fighting training lessons. It involved mortgage industry folks who came together to help produce this DVD training film. According to the company, the DVD has been seen by the staffs of the FBI, Dept. of Homeland Security, Secret Service, U.S. Department of Justice, numerous local law enforcement agencies and over 2,000 mortgage professionals. It was even screened at the Toronto International Comedy Film Festival in 2007. The company was so inspired by its success that they created a second parody-themed production, *Fraud Angels*, which offers a good-natured spoof of *Charlie's Angels* in its detailing of how to detect foreclosure rescue and investment club scams.

Educational Films

The other sector in the non-theatrical involves educational films. The first person to openly support the notion of educational films was Thomas A. Edison, which was somewhat peculiar since Edison never bothered to produce films that could be considered as educational. Nonetheless, in 1913 Edison made the lofty proclamation: "It is possible to teach every branch of human knowledge with the motion picture." Edison also predicted that films would one day replace books as the main tool of the nation's teachers.

The first attempt to bring educational films into the American classrooms came in the late 1920s. The Eastman Kodak Company, taking advantage of the recently-introduced 16mm projection technology, produced a series of short educational films made specifically for classroom viewing. Approximately one dozen schools were chosen to participate in a pilot program to determine the value of using film within the daily curriculum. However, the pilot program failed to spawn a wide acceptance of this medium within the educational setting.

What went wrong? For starters, very few (if any) educators of that era viewed movies as a progressive tool for impressionable minds. Movies were seen strictly as low-brow entertainment, something that distracted young minds from their studies, and not something that empowered the future leaders to absorb knowledge.

Second, the concept of learning by watching a film was just too radical to embrace. There was no precedent for using entertainment to impart lessons; American education of the era was strictly by-the-book, both literally and figuratively.

Third, there was the question of expense. Film projectors and films were not going to be given out in a philanthropic gesture from the good people at Eastman Kodak. School boards, particularly those in overcrowded urban areas and isolated rural regions, lacked the funds to invest in this strategy. Even if they wanted to bring films into classrooms, they just could not afford it.

The transition from silent to sound films put a temporary hold on the concept, but in the late-1930s and early 1940s a new effort was made by enterprising independent producers to tap into this untested market. Two leading educational publishers, McGraw-Hill and Encyclopedia Britannica, created small divisions designed to produce and distribute educational film. And school boards that could not afford to consider this strategy found themselves receiving free 16mm sound projectors care of the U.S. government (it is not clear which bureaucrat came up with that idea or what issues or lobbyists influenced the decision).

The initial efforts, admittedly, were not very effective. A major problem came in depicting school-age youth in a negative manner that created an adversarial relationship between the viewer and the film. Typical of these endeavors was *Boy in Court* (1940), about a delinquent teenager who gets his misguided priorities corrected with the help of a very friendly parole officer. *Youth in Crisis* (1943) questioned delinquency in parallel to the societal disruptions of World War II. The absence of parental oversight by fathers who were fighting the Axis and mothers who were helping the war effort at home resulted in boys and girls who were turning into miscreants. The heavy-handed nature of these films seem laughable today, and it is easy to assume the kids of the 1940s (particularly the delinquents) could take these morality plays seriously.

Actually, World War II provided an unexpected boost for educational films. The U.S. military made extensive use of so-called training films to help indoctrinate large numbers of new recruits into understanding what was required of their service. The military kept track of the effectiveness of these films, and the results confirmed that people who viewed educational films were able to retain what they saw and use it productively.

Following the end of the war, American society saw a new domestic upheaval. Men who were away for years fighting the Germans and Japanese returned to a domestic environment they barely recognized. Many men had difficulties re-adapting to civilian life, while others suddenly experienced unexpected new opportunities that were financed through government programs like the G.I. Bill: higher education and access to higher quality housing abruptly created a booming new middle class. Women who were an integral part of the workforce during the war years were abruptly forced out of the offices and factories and back into their homes.

Needless to say, the stress created by the enforced return to a state of domestic servitude created significant problems for many. Caught in between were the children who suddenly found themselves in a peacetime America that was clearly anything but peaceful – at least at home. And this is where the educational films finally began to take root.

In the post-war years, the quantity of educational films abruptly began to rise. Production companies designed solely to create and release these films began to pop up. Companies like Centron Corp., Coronet Films and Sid Davis productions took the leadership position as the top-tier producers of this genre. The Hollywood studios were not interested in chasing this market, although in 1946 Walt Disney (who was going through a rocky financial period) agreed to create an animated short on behalf of the International Cellu-Cotton Products Co. The resulting film was the aforementioned 10-minute animated production called *The Story of Menstruation*, which was designed for viewing by girls' health education classes. Yes, the idea of a Disney cartoon about menstruation was a bit much and even Disney acknowledged he went too far; he never made additional educational films after *The Story of Menstruation*.

Actually, *The Story of Menstruation* is an aberration in another way: it actually had a classroom value that fit into the educational curriculum (in this case, health studies). The overwhelming majority of the educational films that came into schools in the post-war years were not focused on enhancing or expanding the actual classroom lessons relating to English, history, mathematics, science and so forth. Instead, they took on a curious "how-to" element in regard to social interaction. These films offered advice on how young people were expected to fit into the American scene; in domestic interactions with parents and siblings, in educational settings with teachers and school administrators, in the wide world with adult figures (including a great many law enforcement officers), and within the distinctive setting of the youth culture.

In many ways, these films (particularly those produced in the first few years after World War II) offered a warning that all was not copasetic on the home front. With titles such as *Friendship Begins at Home* (1949), *Sharing Work at Home* (1949) and *A Date with Your Family* (1950), it would appear a level of domestic turmoil existed that required the intervention of film projector-wielding educators. Even more peculiar were the topics that many of these films covered: personal hygiene, study habits, how to behave while dating, even how to behave in public.

Consider the self-explanatory titles of educational films such as *Good Table Manners* (1951), *Other People's Property* (1951), *Homework:*

Studying on Your Own (1953), *Emotional Maturity* (1957), *Manners in Public* (1958), and *Exchanging Greetings and Introductions* (1960). The obvious question emerges: just what were parents of the era teaching their kids at home? The notion that the schools had to impart these types of lessons was peculiar. But, then again, 1954 saw the release of two educational films whose titles may have summed up what was brewing in the homes: *Getting Along with Parents* and *Parents Are People Too.*

Many of the educational films created in this era addressed two disturbing trends that emerged in the 1950s and 1960s: irresponsible driving by teenagers and drug usage. In both cases, the films that addressed these subjects often went into overkill by presenting the respective worst case scenarios.

The driving-related films have come down through the years as cult favorites among many film lovers, if only because they present a level of violence and gore that rivaled the more extreme Hollywood sci-fi and horror flicks. Obviously, a film dedicated solely to careful and proper driving would be somewhat monotonous – really, who would want to see a film where people obey the speed limit, stop at the red light, present courtesy to pedestrians and follow traffic regulations to the letter?

Instead, the driving-related films that flooded the schools in the 1950s and 1960s placed a heavy emphasis on teaching how not to behave behind the wheel. These films were filled with images of screaming pedestrians being mowed down and irresponsible drivers getting smashed into bloody pulps when their vehicles plowed into crash-induced stops. Many of these films used actual footage of crash victims, which further enforced the harsh lesson of what happens to people who misuse their vehicular authority.

The drug-related films also have a retro-camp value, as they mostly present insanely melodramatic consequences of casual drug usage. *H: The Story of a Teen-Age Drug Addict* (1951) finds a young man who goes from a single marijuana encounter into a life of heroin addiction. Clearly, this type of film is the heir to *Reefer Madness* and similar anti-drug films created in the 1930s. The proliferation of the drug culture in the mid-1960s was met with a proliferation of anti-drug educational films. However, the effectiveness of these productions failed miserably in trying to stop the drug tide. Of course, it didn't help when you had a less-than-convincing Sonny Bono giving the anti-drug pep talk in the 1968 *Marijuana*.

If the educational films were filling in for the lessons that should have been taught at home, they were also filling in for lessons that should have been taught in the school setting. Many of these films made it clear about what was required of students in the course of their daily academic environment. Films carrying titles such as *Manners in School* (1951), *How Quiet Helps at School* (1953), *Manners at School* (1956), *Lunchroom Manners* (1960), *Preparing Your Book Report* (1960) and *Safety Rules for Schools* (1966) used celluloid instructions in lieu of having a teacher or principal lay down the rules and regulations. In retrospect, it appeared that there was something of a disconnect; students were being told to learn about how to behave by actors in a movie, not by the adults standing in front of the classroom.

But this is not to say that the educational films of the bygone era were completely lacking. Efforts were made to impart genuine academic instructions. *Improve Your Spelling* (1949) provided easy-to-recall tips on how to ace a spelling test (courtesy of the off-screen narrator, a young broadcaster named Mike Wallace). The *Why Study?* series from Centron Corp. detailed the value of the various lessons being presented and how they could be of value to the school children when they would become adults.

And there were more than a few films that tipped off children on the dangers presented by many adult strangers who seemed to be a little too interested in becoming chummy. Although no statistics are available to support their value, it is safe to assume that some children took the lessons of these particular films to mind when approached by dubious grown-ups on streets and in playgrounds. (However, the most notorious of those films, the 1961 *Boys Beware*, miserably and deliberately, sought to confuse homosexuality with pedophilia – a slur that, sadly, continues to this day.)

Viewed today, the educational films of the late 1940s through the mid-1960s offered a very rigid notion of what America was like. The subjects in the films were almost all middle-class, suburban, non-ethnic white families. These films did not take place in urban apartments, but in spacious homes filled with tasteful furniture and the latest appliances. By today's standards, which often go to the other extreme by putting too much emphasis on multiculturalism, the overwhelmingly white population of these older films is difficult to ignore.

On occasion, however, there was some attempt to offer lessons in tolerance. *Skipper Learns a Lesson* (1952) provides a rare gathering of children of different races. The lesson on overcoming racism, however, centers on a prejudiced talking dog who finds himself ostracized by other canines when his color is changed after being accidentally doused in paint. *What About Prejudice?* (1959) takes a curious approach by having the subject of white majority scorn off-screen throughout the film. It is never clear whether this person is being isolated due to his race, religion or ethnic heritage. It is not until the white teenage crowd learns that the off-screen outsider was seriously injured in rescuing people from a fire that the meaning of judging others sinks in.

By the late 1960s and going forward, diversity began to pop up in educational films - if only in a token example of putting one black child amid a group of white classmates. But consider what preceded it. But by this era, the effectiveness of the educational films began to wear off. Those born after World War II came into a world where there was always a television set at home. Awareness of entertainment techniques, coupled with a growing awareness of rapidly changing socio-economic considerations, created the proverbial brave new world in the classroom.

For a while, the educational filmmakers tried to maintain their old formulas, though some attempted to show they were in touch with the cultural zeitgeist. *Telezonia* (1974) was perhaps the most outlandish and elaborate effort: a 26-minute AT&T-produced musical educational film on how to use the telephone. Offering set and costume design that was in keeping with the more outlandish escapades of the Sid & Marty Krofft television programs; *Telezonia* provides an androgynous hero named Telly who takes a group of suburban kids (including a token black child) on a journey through a psychedelic vortex similar to the climactic journey of *2001: A Space Odyssey*. But instead of winding up with Keir Dullea in a white dining room, the characters in the film wind up in a pink alternative universe full of telephones and people dressed like letters and punctuation symbols (the most remarkable is a woman with Frida Kahlo eyebrows and a costume featuring a large question mark).

In the late 1970s and early 1980s, VHS became the prevalent format for non-theatrical film distribution. The 16mm projectors and the films that ran through their sprockets were considered obsolete, and schools began throwing them away. Due to preservation efforts of archivists such as Rick Prelinger, Skip Elsheimer and Dennis Nyback, many of these older films were preserved and are presented today via DVD, film society screenings and Internet video sites.

As stated earlier, it is virtually impossible to keep track of how many of these titles exist. Educational films are still being produced, but the guidelines for their creation and distribution are much tighter. Films that are considered to be blatantly commercial or marketing-oriented are not welcomed in classrooms. Impartial and non-political content is also a key requirement. In some ways, this limits the filmmakers who attempt to create new titles for this sector.

"There are no special groups of interest behind financing, except my good will and not really impressive bank account," says Leszek Drozd, a Chicago-based educational film producer and director who runs Story Tellers Productions. "And I am very proud of that. There are no political ads, no self-glorification in my films – just my sincere will to show to audiences the best quality academic information available today."

Drozd self-distributes his educational DVDs via the Internet, with titles ranging from speech and language pathology to career planning. (Disclosure: the author of this book has appeared in one of Drozd's films.) The Net enables the filmmaker to allow potential customers to watch the films online in order to judge their value for DVD exhibition in classrooms. "Anyone who is interested may watch my videos for free, with no logging in or financial commitment required," he says.

Drozd points out that declining educational standards offer a challenge for today's educational filmmakers. "The very brutal truth is that there is not enough good quality education around the world that is accessible to the public," he says. "I have audiences between single mothers as far afield as Texas and Poland thanking me because they found on my website videos to show to their growing children, simply because they experience difficulties to afford quality education for teens. This is the biggest excitement I have ever received."

He adds that educational films may be enjoying a new renaissance in the very near future. "There are many high-end produced films with great educational value that are now on the market," he says. "Thanks to well-intentioned qualified producers and filmmakers as well as high-quality affordable technology I see a golden age on the horizon. In a 21st-century economy, post-secondary education represents one of the fastest growing fields in the public sector. To me as a producer of educational films, it is no ordinary opportunity."

Another contemporary educational filmmaker is John Farrell, who runs Farrellmedia out of Boston. "I basically manage the production of several educational series," he says. "Each semester we have a new batch in business (to cover marketing, management and finance topics) as well as modern languages and psychology."

Farrell endorses film as a medium for getting academic messages across. "It's a great medium for education; especially for business and language," he says. "Reading case studies about companies is one thing. Watching a new profile about a new start-up or a recognized brand company, with interviews of key players, really helps students who want to pursue a career in business to see what the work is like. For languages, I can't tell you how much it helps students to see real people speaking the language in their home environment in tune with the way the language is spoken today, and not some dusty dated film from the 1980s or 1990s."

Farrell, like Drozd, uses the Net to get his films seen. "The further challenge is delivery: Most students nowadays want it on their laptops, and on their cell phones and iPods. There's a huge push to accommodate that demand and of course it poses lots of challenges – from how do you make it as seamless as possible to how do you protect the content and monetize it. We haven't figured this all out yet, but it is fun working on it."

The non-theatrical market shows no signs of deflating. As long as companies and organizations need to get a message out, and as long as students are in need of lessons, this corner of the independent film world will continue to quietly but actively thrive.

The 10 Most Important Independent Films of All Time:
Michael Legge, underground filmmaker (*Loons, The Dungeon of Dr. Dreck*)

Q: If you were to look over the span of the history of U.S. independent cinema, from the silent era to today's output, what would you list as the 10 Most Important Independently-Produced Films of All Time ... and why?

1. *White Zombie* (1933). The Halperin Brothers scraped up money and rented some standing Universal studio sets to put together this somber, slow but eerie zombie flick, the first one that I know of. They even nabbed Lugosi, fresh from *Dracula*, and gave him one of his most sinister and merciless roles as zombie master Murder Legrande. I'm sure the younger crowd will find this a big yawn, considering their genetic ADD and lack of interest in a black-and-white, non-gut-chewing movie like this. But anyone with an appreciation of good photography, creepy atmosphere and an interesting scenario should watch this one. To me, a zombie working in a sugar mill and accidentally falling into the machinery without a sound while his fellow dead-eyed workers don't react is more horrifying than modern zombies

ripping open someone's abdomen. Maybe because I can imagine that happening with real people in the here and now. I see white zombies every day. I'm one.

2. *Carnival of Souls* (1962). Yet another indie film that had to wait to be appreciated. Herk Harvey was into industrial films when he decided to try making a feature film. He chose the horror genre because it tended to be an easier sell. The story was inspired by an existing but deserted pavilion near a lake that he had seen in his travels. There's something about a huge place that used to be filled with people and which is now deserted that gives you the willies. At least it does me. Using local actors for the most part except for the lead, the film required no elaborate special effects or make-up. Just tons of mood and the small shocks you get when somebody suddenly touches you from behind. Again, without recognizable stars the film is enhanced because you don't know what will happen to them. The fact of the lead actress being a church organist made the choice of the soundtrack being all organ music seem, uhhh, organic. Apparently a foreign film fest screened this sleeper and that's what brought it to the attention of the film cultists. I imagine if Hollywood ever got a hold of it and made a remake it would have some flash-in-the-pan starlet in the lead and explain away the ending. Thank God that hasn't happened. Yet.

3. *Night of the Living Dead* (1968). Analyzed to living death, this is a legendary indie film. Romero didn't have studio backing, but he made one of the most influential horror films of our time. I saw this bugger when it first came out on some double-feature bill at the local drive-in. I was still pretty young and impressionable. I'd

never seen anything like it before. From the first scene where the zombie bangs on car windows to get at his lunch inside, I was really spooked, and there hadn't been any guts yet. When that happened, I was truly appalled. I knew I wasn't seeing a Hollywood movie, but I never expected to see what I did see. I can't say I liked it. I was more repulsed than anything else, but it was definitely scary and unnerving because it was black and white, had a documentary feel, and because there were no stars in it, you didn't have that comfortable feeling of disconnect you have when you see a known actor to remind you that it's not real. I subsequently went to see it again at a midnight show a few years later. At that point, now that I knew what was coming, I began to appreciate its crude artistry and resourcefulness. It's still my favorite of Romero's epics, maybe because it was the one that he had to beg, borrow and steal to do. Later, he didn't have to.

4. *Spider Baby* (1968). Jack Hill made this bizarre black comedy, which seems like a living Charles Addams cartoon. There is nothing overtly gross or violent in this movie, but the atmosphere of it gives you the crawls in spite of the fact that it's tongue in cheek. And what a cast: a cameo by the Mantan Moreland, Sid Haig in full moron mood, the lovely Jill Banner, Beverly Washburn (straight out of some demented *Leave It To Beaver* episode), Carol Ohmart, the only time I've ever seen her outside of [*House on Haunted Hill*], and of course, Lon Chaney Jr. Lon went on the wagon to do this role, the sympathetic part of the family chauffeur, and for once, he's dealing with a bunch of Lennies instead of being one. Probably his most cheerful demeanor in a late-in-

life role, he also has a couple of touching moments that remind us of the fine character he was in flicks like *High Noon* and *The Defiant Ones*. This one sat on its hands for a while until it was released, but didn't become the cult item it is until the last decade or so. All these indie films have one thing in common. They are the movies that the major studios would be afraid to make.

5. *Eraserhead* (1977). David Lynch is a mighty strange chap. This is a movie that I don't feel compelled to watch again, but it was compelling to watch the first time. Much like a nightmare you can't wake up from and that you hope you never have again. Funny, disgusting, bewildering, gross, hypnotic; you name it, almost every adjective applies to this dark, cold dream. Although the baby kind of reminds me of ET, Lynch took years to make this and didn't have to worry about continuity because what nightmare does?

6. *Evil Dead* (1981). Sam Raimi made this student film on 16mm and started a trend of over-the-top gore not seen since Romero's groundbreaking zombie flicks. Raimi's style walked that thin line between horror and comedy and succeeds very well. With its likeable protagonist played by Bruce Campbell, I think we could call the genre "comegore." At a certain point excessive gore becomes funny and this was later exploited to the nth degree in Peter Jackson's *Dead Alive*. However, Raimi succeeds much better because we care about Campbell, whereas in *Dead Alive* we knew we were only there to witness the splatter fest. It's the difference between caring about the people riding the roller coaster instead of the roller coaster itself.

7. *Mystery Train* (1989). Jim Jaramusch is one of my favorite modern directors, although you wouldn't know
it from seeing his films that he's a modern director. I
mean, his camera isn't constantly swirling all over the
place, the editing isn't so fast that you can't afford to
blink, and the movies are about ... people I've seen
just about all his films, but this is still my favorite. Most
of his work is episodic rather than a drawn-out narrative, and it works best here. The three stories are
so different from each other it's like you're watching
three separate movies, if you didn't see little flashes
of places or people from the other stories, that is. The
Japanese couple on their trek to Nashville, the Italian woman who meets the ghost of Elvis in her hotel
room, and the last great story with Steve Buscemi as
the lesser loser in a trio of losers, only left me wanting
their stories to continue. Like a good book, *Mystery
Train* is a good movie you don't want to end. And who
else would have Screamin' Jay Hawkins as the hotel
manager? He's puts a spell on me

8. *Metropolitan* (1990). Director/writer Whit Stillman
brings Jane Austen to the 1980s as he cleverly exam-
ines a group of Manhattan preppies during their early
college years, puncturing their ideas, outlooks, and relationships during a Christmas break. Okay, so this is a
lot of shots of people talking, but it's not like a filmed
play, with the dialog hopscotching between various
groups, hearing snippets of witty and sardonic observations, and getting to know these endearing and not-
so-endearing characters. You want to know what happened to them all after that final fade out. Made with
his own money and borrowed cash from family and

friends, Whitman made his first movie truly independent, and he shows how a movie can be entertaining and fascinating just by using well-developed characters that don't have super powers, aren't rogue cops, or aliens. An observation made in this film was that Jane Austen would be bewildered by the way we act now. I can imagine Martians only seeing our *Star Wars* movies and judging us by them. Let's hope they also see this one, to see what real people can act like. Where have you gone, Whit?

9. *Waiting for Guffman* (1996). Christopher Guest's first excursion into social satire is one of his best and one of my favorite indie comedies of recent years. Guest wisely chose seasoned comedians from Second City, including Eugene Levy and Catherine O'Hara, as well as other familiar faces. The fragile egos involved in a community theater production showcasing the town's history rings true in its characterization of the swishy, pretentious director, the bumbling novices, and the home-town stars. The characters are gently poked fun at. It is never mean spirited or condescending, and I'm sure anyone such as I who has spent years in theater recognize these types. Some of the aftermaths are rather touching as they think they have the potential to make it in the bigger world; not realizing that it is mostly luck and timing rather than talent that counts the most. For a more realistic and charming look into local theater, I also suggest the film adaptation of Kurt Vonnegut's short story, *Who Am I This Time?*

10. *Bubba Ho-Tep* (2002). Here's a movie no studio would make. An Elvis horror/comedy. In other words, something too unique, too unsafe. The director of *Phantasm*

and a short story by Joe Lansdale combine to make one of the best movies I've seen in years. Only Bruce Campbell could have pulled off the aging Elvis without seeming like a cartoon. And Ossie Davis does a fine comedic turn as JFK. This is the kind of movie that I get jealous of for not having thought of it myself. I doubt that Joe American would know what to make of a movie that isn't a remake of a dozen others. A movie that is funny, creepy, and heartfelt is something we rarely see today in mainstream movies. A great indie movie.

CHAPTER SIX:

When Real Life Becomes Reel Life

"Reality is merely an illusion, albeit a very persistent one."   – Albert Einstein

The first motion pictures were documentaries – or, by the very least, documents of everyday life in the late 1890s. In France, the Lumiere Brothers captured scenes of steam-driven trains and well-dressed boulevard pedestrians. In America, Thomas Edison brought the celebrities of the day into his New Jersey studio – Annie Oakley displayed her sharpshooting, Eugen Sandow displayed his muscles, and so forth. These little films rarely lasted longer than a minute or two, since the early cameras were unable to accommodate large magazines of film.

But as the film technology advanced, audiences quickly became bored of watching brief scenes of their society. After all, what was the point of paying to see a movie (in this case, one without sound or color) when you could go outside and see the same thing for free (with sound and color)? Thus, the concept of writing a screenplay and directing actors for the camera took root and movies turned into an entertainment medium.

However, the early filmmakers never entirely abandoned non-fiction films. Cameras began going far afield to capture the more unusual and dramatic aspects of real life. Cameramen began showing up at newsworthy events, documenting the presence of various dignitaries and celebrities as they engaged in speeches, meet-and-greets and other photo opportunities. Theodore Roosevelt, who became president in 1901, was a ubiquitous figure for the newsreels (as this genre became known). Even without a sound recording or color film, Roosevelt's animated body language and larger-than-life enthusiasm for pontificating made him a natural for the camera.

From its beginnings, however, non-fiction film was being used to show a distinctive agenda: reality could easily be manipulated and audiences would not be the wiser.

The first known manipulation of the genre came in 1903, when Thomas Edison used the planned euthanasia of Topsy, a violence-prone circus elephant, as a means to promote the DC electric current. Edison schemed with the owners of the elephant to have the animal electrocuted with AC current electricity, which was being promoted by Edison's rival Nicola Tesla. The thought behind this notion was fairly devious: by showing how dangerous AC current electricity was, it would scare people into using the perceived safety of DC current (and, in the process, scare profits to Edison and away from Tesla).

The fact that Topsy was a severely abused elephant who only lashed out at brutish trainers (including one who tried to force her to consume a burning cigarette) was never mentioned in Edison's brief film, which was released under the title *Electrocuting an Elephant*. Instead, Topsy is shown being led to an area in an open field where her legs are imprisoned in chains and wires. Her human handlers quickly disperse, and within seconds smoke begins to rise from the ground. Topsy collapses into a dead faint amidst a rising cloud of electrified smoke.

Whether *Electrocuting an Elephant* was specifically responsible for the later decline of Tesla's fortunes is not clear (it clearly didn't help). But what Edison achieved, perhaps accidentally, was the blurring of real life with reel life. The audiences in 1903 had no clue about the circumstances behind the production of *Electrocuting an Elephant*. They assumed they were watching a newsreel; it wasn't until many years later that the truth

of the film's production emerged. However, the concept of a manipulated non-fiction film became locked into the filmmaking bag of tricks.

In a way, this was actually not a bad thing. Documentary filmmaking
would not have emerged beyond newsreel glimpses of history makers
and travelogue shots of scenic locations had filmmakers not attempted to
slice and dice reality to fit their particular vision. Two filmmakers, both
working (somewhat ironically) among the indigenous peoples of North
America, laid the foundation for modern documentary productions – if
only by creating their own distinctive concept of what life should be like.

The first filmmaker was Edward S. Curtis, who gained famed in the
late 19th and early 20th centuries for his photographic portraits and
phonographic recordings of the American Indian tribes in the United
States and Canada. In 1914, Curtis set out to create a film focusing on
the culture and customs of the Kwakiutl tribe in British Columbia. But
Curtis did not attempt to create a filmed record of Kwakiutl life. Instead,
he created a somewhat hoary tale of love and revenge in a period before white society intruded on tribal life. Interspersed throughout the
film were shots of tribal dances and traditional warrior costumes.

Despite the provocative title *In the Land of the Head Hunters*, Curtis'
film was a fairly tame affair. Perhaps it was a little too tame for 1914
audiences, who had little enthusiasm for the appreciation of American
Indian cultures. Curtis spent $20,000 of his own money to make the
film, but it was a commercial flop. Ten years later, he sold the negative
and master print of his production to New York's American Museum of
Natural History for a mere $1,500.

Curtis has no role of further significance to independent film – or
to the film industry as a whole, for that matter. His last connection with
the big screen came in 1923 as an uncredited assistant cameraman to
Cecil B. DeMille on *The Ten Commandments*. His one motion picture, *In
the Land of the Head Hunters*, was forgotten for many years. However,
it was rediscovered in 1972, 20 years after Curtis' death, and was re-
stored and retitled with the less scintillating title *In the Land of the War
Canoes*. Today, it is considered a classic of ethnographic film studies.

Eight years after Curtis' *In the Land of the Head Hunters* premiered, another feature-length portrait of North America's indigenous people came to the screen. Unlike the Curtis production, this film had a significant impact on both the motion picture industry and the audiences that supported it. The production was *Nanook of the North*, made by a novice filmmaker named Robert Flaherty, and it is often regarded as the first documentary feature ever produced.

Nanook of the North is the story on an Inuit hunter in the Canadian Arctic (at the time, the Inuit people were referred to as Eskimos – we'll use the word "Inuit" to describe this film). Nanook supports his family as a walrus hunter, and he is adept at fishing, building igloos and surviving in the harsh extreme weather of the frozen north. In the course of the film, Flaherty follows Nanook as he uses spears to hunt his prey. In the film's exciting climax, Nanook and his family work furiously to build an igloo in the face of an approaching storm.

It was all quite compelling to watch back in 1922, when most Americans had little knowledge of Inuit customs and practices. Even today, *Nanook of the North* is an invigorating cinematic experience, particularly the stunning climax in the race against the elements.

There was just one problem: it was all a fake. There was no Nanook – the Inuit subject was actually named Allakariallak. "Nanook" comes from the Inuit mythology meaning "master of the bears." The woman who was allegedly Mrs. Nanook wasn't the hunter's wife, she was a local Inuit woman recruited by Flaherty for the film. Nanook's use of spears for hunting walrus was a practice that vanished in the 19th century; the real Inuit hunters used guns, but Flaherty asked them to dust off the old spears for his camera. Nanook's igloo was also a fake. Flaherty's camera could not get adequate lighting in a real igloo, so a phony half-igloo was built to provide an understanding of the interior design for that icy residence.

Even the climactic race to build an igloo was phony. Flaherty shot the sequence well within distance of Inuit encampments, so the subjects of his film could've easily found shelter from the storm without having to build an igloo.

Of course, no one watching *Nanook of the North* back in 1922 was aware of this chicanery. Indeed, the film's unusual approach to capturing the daily struggle of a distant culture caught everyone by surprise, particularly the booker at New York's celebrated Roxy Theatre, which gave the movie its premiere by putting it on a double bill with Harold Lloyd's popular comedy *Grandma's Boy*. Flaherty was initially unable to secure a distributor and self-booked his film. Apparently, it was booked at the Roxy by default; no dramatic film was available and it was considered a bad idea to buttress the Lloyd hit on the double bill with another comedy.

For Flaherty, *Nanook of the North* was a personal vindication; he had lived in the Arctic for nearly a decade and twice attempted to create a film about the Inuit people. On both occasions, his footage was destroyed in accidents, requiring that he start work from scratch. For *Nanook of the North*, Flaherty had money – he was financed with a $50,000 budget by the French fur company Revillon Freres – and time on his side; the film was shot from August 1920 through August 1921. But despite these conditions, Flaherty insisted it was necessary to reenact and reinvent situations to dramatize Inuit life. Apparently, a genuine filmed record of daily Inuit life might be as monotonous as a genuine filmed record of daily Western life.

Nanook of the North was a monster hit. Pathé Exchange picked up the worldwide distribution after its New York success and the film was heralded around the world. Sadly, Allakariallak never shared in the film's glory. Months after the filming was completed, a genuine tragedy struck: Allakariallak was stranded in the Arctic during a hunt and starved to death in his chilly isolation.

However, lightning never truly struck twice with Flaherty. His career lasted another two decades, but his output was spotty and his grasp on the non-fiction genre grew increasingly shakier with each new film. His follow-up to *Nanook of the North* was the Paramount Pictures-commissioned *Moana*, which was shot in Samoa in 1923 and 1924. But the production was riddled with disasters from start to finish. Flaherty arrived in Samoa without a story and took months to find an angle that would appeal to the notion of documenting exotic indigenous people for Western audiences. But the delays in production agitated Paramount Pictures, which kept wiring Flaherty demanding to see footage. Flaherty repeatedly had to explain that missionaries had Westernized the Samoan people to the point that many of the customs that people associated with the island had vanished (a tattoo ceremony featured in the film, for example, had to be reconstructed from historic texts since it had not been performed in many years).

Even more distressing was an experimental color film camera that Flaherty was given for the Samoan location photography. It malfunctioned and none of the footage could be salvaged. However, Flaherty's use of panchromatic film stock created a deeply beautiful black-and-white experience, as opposed to the flat orthochromatic stock which was standard for the era.

As with *Nanook of the North*, audiences watching *Moana* were unaware that Flaherty was staging scenes for the camera. Even the usually astute Mordaunt Hall, film critic for the *New York Times*, noted: "Not only is Mr. Flaherty to be congratulated on what he has put into this film, but he deserves a great deal of praise for having kept it free from sham."

Unfortunately for Flaherty, *Moana* was as much of a bust as *Nanook of the North* was a success. The film is remembered today only because it inspired writer-turned-filmmaker John Grierson to create the word "documentary" to identify the non-fiction genre.

For Flaherty, *Moana* was the beginning *and* the end of his Hollywood career. He was signed for two additional South Pacific-based features, MGM's *White Shadows in the South Seas* and the F.W. Murnau production of *Tabu*, which he was supposed to co-direct, but he severed his relations with both films prior to the start of production. Other studio-based projects never materialized, and by the early 1930s Flaherty was unable to secure work in America. He went overseas, where he created the memorable features *Man of Aran* in 1934 and *Elephant Boy* in 1937. *Man of Aran*, although presented as a documentary on Irish fishermen, also included blatantly staged sequences (although it was also beautifully photographed). *Elephant Boy*, co-directed with Zoltan Korda, didn't pretend to be a documentary. It was a fanciful adaptation of Rudyard Kipling's *Toomai, of the Elephants* and offered a refreshingly engaging performance by the young Indian actor Sabu.

Flaherty wouldn't make another U.S. film until 1941, when the Department of Agriculture commissioned him to create the documentary *The Land*. The film highlighted the ecological and economic damage created by the overproduction of cotton in what was known as the Dust Bowl. In many ways, it was the closest film Flaherty ever made to a genuine documentary. But the U.S. entry into World War II doomed the project; by the time *The Land* was ready for release in 1942, it was barely distributed out of fear it would be disruptive to wartime morale.

Flaherty's final original project, *Louisiana Story* (1948) was offered as a documentary and is still viewed by many film scholars as such, but it was actually an industrial film using nonprofessional actors and a screenplay. It will be discussed at greater depth in the chapter of this book relating to that genre.

Flaherty has been credited as both director and co-director of the 1950 documentary *The Titan: Story of Michelangelo*, which won the Academy Award as Best Documentary. However, this was actually a 1940 film made by German director Curt Oertel. Flaherty re-edited Oertel's footage and scripted an English-language narration for an American release of the film, but he played no role in its creation and did not truly deserve directing credit.

Flaherty's contribution to non-fiction cinema is problematic. Yes, *Nanook of the North* showed that documentary feature films could be accessible to mainstream audiences and commercially viable for producers and distributors. As a pioneer in putting documentaries on equal footing with narrative features, he deserves credit.

Yet Flaherty's output is spotty and troubling. He made relatively few films, and except for *The Land* he seemed incapable of keeping fiction out of non-fiction filmmaking. Flaherty set a dangerous precedent that still permeates the genre – ignoring real life in favor of a glamorized and exotic reel life. Audiences are still being bamboozled by this artifice. Let's backtrack to the 1920s and the aftermath of *Nanook of the North*. Flaherty was not alone in believing there would be an interest in non-fiction filmmaking. In other parts of the world, American filmmakers were lugging their cameras in search of a great story.

The most dramatic of these productions came from the combined talents of the adventurers Merian C. Cooper and Ernest Schoedsack, who were in Ethiopia at the time Flaherty was finishing up work on his film. Cooper and Schoedsack shot footage of the imperial court of Haile Selassie, but the footage was destroyed in a fire before it was developed. Despite that loss, Cooper and Schoedsack set a new direction to Persia (today's Iran) to document the migration of the nomadic Bakhtiari people. They linked up with journalist and former World War I spy Marguerite Harrison, who financed their expedition on the condition that she share directing credit and appear on camera. The team shot 40,000 feet of footage that was edited into a two-hour film known as *Grass*.

As with Flaherty's landmark, *Grass* found its audience by accident – in this case, Cooper was screening it on the professional lecture circuit when Paramount chief Jesse L. Lasky made an unexpected offer to distribute the film theatrically. *Grass* opened in New York in February 1925 to critical acclaim and modest commercial success.

But unlike *Nanook of the North*, *Grass* did not recreate entire incidents strictly for the camera. Cooper, Schoedsack and Harrison were part of the 50,000-person Bakhtiari odyssey across the Karun River and up Zard Kuh, the highest peak in the Zagros Mountains. Although the film's pacing may seem sluggish by contemporary standards, it nonetheless serves as an invaluable record of Middle Eastern culture.

Lasky was buoyed by the commercial reaction to *Grass* to finance Cooper and Schoedsack's next film (Harrison had no further partnership with the duo). Unfortunately, the follow-up film, *Chang* (1927), was not a non-fiction film but rather a Flaherty-style docudrama that mixed aspects of an exotic culture (in this case, the farmers of rural

Siam, today's Thailand) into a patently staged story regarding the threat of tigers and elephants to a farming village.

But unlike *Nanook of the North* or *Moana*, there was no attempt to pretend this was a documentary. The promotional material for the film defined it as "a melodrama with man, the jungle, and wild animals as its cast."

After *Chang*, Cooper and Schoedsack stayed away from non-fiction filmmaking. Documentary filmmaking's loss was Hollywood's gain; the duo went on to create the 1933 masterpiece *King Kong*.

During the 1920s, Kansas-born adventurers Martin and Osa Johnson were also shooting films in far corners of the globe. The Johnsons were actually ahead of Flaherty in regard to releasing their Pacific-based features *Jungle Adventures* (1921) and *Headhunters of the South Seas* (1922), but the films were viewed as travelogues and not as artistically challenging true-life narratives. In 1923, the Johnsons offered *Trailing Wild African Animals* (1923), a record of their 1921-22 African expedition.

During the 1920s and the 1930s, the Johnsons produced several feature-length films detailing their African trips. By 1930, these silent films were compiled into *Across the World with Mr. and Mrs. Johnson*, which included a narration by Martin Johnson. Genuine sound recording in the Johnsons' films didn't take place until 1932's *Congorilla*, which was noteworthy for taking sound technology on location to Africa.

Time has not been kind to the Johnsons' films, which are barely recalled today. Their self-promoting tendencies, coupled with their badly dated view of African cultures and the continent's ecosystem, make their films painful to watch. In their time, however, the films enjoyed a mild popularity and their footage was often recycled by low-budget films set in the so-called "dark continent."

By the 1930s, audiences began to tire of documentaries of distant exotic cultures. Some filmmakers tried to keep the genre alive, most notably the Marquis Henry de la Falaise de la Coudraye, an aristocrat whose Hollywood star wife Constance Bennett provided financial backing for his Borneo-based documentaries *Legong* (1935) and the Vietnamese-based *Kiliou, The Killer* (1937). These films were unusual since they were shot in two-strip Technicolor, but that novelty wore off when the superior three-strip Technicolor process took dominance in the late 1930s (*Kiliou, The Killer* only survives as a black-and-white print). However, due to the difficulty of lugging sound recording equipment abroad, both films were shot as silents and released with synchronized musical scores – an anachronism for the mid-1930s.

Separate and apart from this travelogue approach were Margaret Mead and Gregory Bateson, who took an anthropological approach to filming the lives and culture of the Balinese people. Mead and Bateson spent the mid-to-late 1930s working in Bali, but their footage was not seen until the early 1950s when they released a series of six short documentaries, most notably *Karba's First Years, Bathing Babies in Three Cultures* (which included footage shot in New Guinea) and *Trance and Dance in Bali*. These films are primarily known to most moviegoers by reputation, not by easily accessible screenings.

Politicizing the Process

But changing tastes and changing times warranted a new outlook. As the Great Depression reshaped America, audiences were less than enchanted with tantalizing glimpses of far-away lands. Problems at home demanded attention, and a new wave of documentary filmmakers fixed their cameras on American socio-economic issues.

Part of the new impetus for U.S. documentary production came from President Franklin D. Roosevelt's administration. Roosevelt and his advisers were clearly aware of the impact that film had on shaping perceptions and opinions. The Soviet Union had successfully defended its existence through the groundbreaking cinema of Sergei Eisenstein and his peers, while the Nazi regime in Germany was using film to propagandize the rise of the Third Reich.

For Roosevelt, however, the controversial nature of his New Deal policies required persuasive selling to both a public impatient for an end to the Great Depression and to a Washington establishment that viewed the president's policies as borderline socialism. This cinematic effort got off to a thunderous start with Pare Lorentz's 1936 *The Plow That Broke the Plains*, a documentary short on the Dust Bowl conditions that plagued the American farmers and the efforts of the U.S. government to correct the situation. Other films followed: *The River* (1937), *The Fight for Life* (1939), *The Power and the Land* (1940) and the aforementioned Robert Flaherty *The Land* (1941) were all produced under the aegis of the U.S. government, which operated a department called the U.S. Film Service from 1938 to 1940. In the 1940s, the U.S. government expanded its filmmaking capacity by churning out documentaries highlighting the roots of the American war effort and the challenges facing the military in the European and Asian battlegrounds.

On the periphery of this, however, was a small but tenacious group that sought to create its own politically-tinged documentaries. Created in 1931 as the New York Film and Photo League, it morphed into Frontier Films in 1937. Its short documentaries touched on both U.S. crises (*People of the Cumberland*, 1937) and foreign conflicts (the Asian *China Strikes Back*, 1937, and the Spanish-based *Return to Life*, 1938). Frontier Films' most ambitious film was its 1942 feature *Native Land*, which looked within the U.S. to promote its message of corporations engaged in anti-union tactics during the 1930s, and much of its content was from testimony delivered before the Senate Civil Liberties Committee in 1938. The film, directed by Leo Hurwitz and Paul Strand, provided a mix of archival news footage and staged reenactments (featuring unknown actors, including Howard Da Silva and Robert Strauss) that indicted goons on the corporate payroll, corrupt law enforcement and even the Ku Klux Klan as wrecking the American right to organized labor. Paul Robeson provided the narration to the film and performed a song written by Marc Blitzstein, who also wrote the film's music score.

Bosley Crowther of *The New York Times* called the film "one of the most powerful and disturbing documentary films ever made, and certainly it will provoke much thought and controversy." Well, he was half-right: the film provoked a lot of controversy, as it hit theaters after

Pearl Harbor. At a time when the nation was trying to come together as a united front, the harsh criticism of Native Land (while well-intended) seemed terribly out of step with the rapidly shifting times. The film barely played in theaters during its initial run, and the postwar years found it impossible to arrange for any screenings when the reign of the McCarthyism Red Scare put many of the people associated with its creation on the Hollywood Blacklist.

Then there was the case of Rey Scott, a St. Louis native who covered China for London's Daily Telegraph. Scott sought to alert Americans to the dangerous situation facing the Chinese people who were attempting to repel Japanese aggression. Although he had no experience as a filmmaker, Scott took it upon himself to create a documentary to highlight the Chinese struggle.

The problem, however, was that most Americans had a negative (if downright hostile) view of Asia in general and China in particular. Scott needed to create a film that would win the hearts and minds of Americans over to the Chinese side.

In 1940, Scott arrived in Hong Kong with a 16mm camera and rolls of Technicolor film. Working as his own cinematographer, he set out on a journey through war-torn China. He stopped in Chongqing, the wartime capital (Beijing was under Japanese occupation), then he took the Burma Road to Lanzhou. From there, he went further east to Tibet, and then he circled back to Chongqing. As luck would have it, Scott was in Chongqing during the August 19-20, 1940 aerial attack by Japanese bombers. An estimated 200 tons of explosives were dropped on the defenseless city. Scott, standing on the roof of the U.S. Embassy, captured the footage in color.

Scott returned to the U.S. and pieced together his footage into Kukan. Remarkably, he was able to get the film into theaters – no mean feat for a film of rather limited commercial viability by an unknown and untrained filmmaker. Carrying the subtitle "The Battle Cry of China" and narrated by Scott, the film offered an extraordinarily progressive view of the Chinese culture. Actually, make that Chinese "cultures," as

Scott went to great lengths to explain how China was not a vast homogenous land, but was a multi-ethnic and multi-religious melting pot. In the film, he included segments relating to the Miao people from the mountains of Guizhou, the Islamic faithful of Lanzhou, Tibet's Buddhist lamas, the nomadic tribes that roamed the Gobi Desert, and the people of Han and Manchu heritage. This was the first U.S. film to clearly identify these distinctive populations.

But what moved most viewers was the film's final 20 minutes, when Chongqing was blasted into smithereens. Bosley Crowther, in his review for the *New York Times*, called the sequence "one of the most awesome bits of motion picture yet seen in this day of frightful news events." Cognizant of the attention being given to the wartime bombings across the Atlantic, Crowther looked to *Kukan* and added that "this wanton violence appears even more horrible than the scenes we have witnessed of London's destruction."

Time Magazine's review, which did not carry a critic's byline, was even more succinct, praising the footage as offering "the most awesome bombing sequence yet filmed of World War II."

Kukan received a great deal of attention. Even President Franklin D. Roosevelt was interested, and Scott arranged a private White House screening. Hollywood paid attention, too, and Scott received an Honorary Academy Award for *Kukan*. Although Scott received a certificate rather than the official Oscar statuette, his efforts were duly noted with glowing praise: "For his extraordinary achievement in producing 'Kukan,' the film record of China's struggle, including its photography with a 16mm camera under the most difficult and dangerous conditions." *Kukan* was one of two non-fiction features from the distant wartime fronts that the Academy honored; the other was the British Ministry of Information's *Target for Tonight.*

One would like to think that Scott and *Kukan* would be more celebrated today. Alas, the filmmaker and his production barely rate footnote status in today's film history. Scott never made another film – his only other known cinematic endeavor was working as an uncredited camera operator on the 1943 documentary *Report from the Aleutians.*

As for *Kukan*, no print of the film is known to exist. The Oscar-honored film that rallied the American people to the Chinese cause has slipped away and is considered to be lost. Independent documentary production virtually halted during World War II. In the postwar world, the focus of non-fiction films took a decidedly animalistic shift.

Nature Calling

In the 1950s, documentary filmmakers discovered the possibilities of aiming their cameras at nature. The person responsible for this was Walt Disney, of all people, and the result of his efforts had a profound effect on film distribution.

In 1948, Disney produced a two-reel documentary called *Seal Island* as part of a new series he envisioned called *True-Life Adventures*. At this time, Disney's films were being released by RKO, but the studio balked at putting this title into theaters. The problem, according to the studio, was the film's lack of perceived commercial viability – who wanted to see a movie about a bunch of Alaskan seals? This marked the first time the studio refused to release a Disney title.

Disney then four-walled a theater in Pasadena for *Seal Island* to have a one-week run, which would qualify it for the Academy Award. The film was well-received and the strategy paid off with Disney snagging the Oscar for Best Two-Reel Short Subject. RKO reluctantly agreed that Disney was right and gave the film a wide theatrical release.

Buoyed by the success of *Seal Island*, Disney sought to create a feature-length documentary focusing on wildlife. Three years in the making, the 1953 production *The Living Desert* offered a unique glimpse at the flora and fauna of the American Southwest, with particular attention paid to the battles between various animals: hawk and rattlesnake, kangaroo rat and sidewinder, wasp and tarantula.

Incredibly, RKO balked again at releasing *The Living Desert*. This was very strange, considering the studio successfully released another feature-length nature documentary, Irwin Allen's adaptation of Rachel Carson's marine biology classic *The Sea Around Us*, and that film won the Oscar.

Fed up with his dealings with the studio, Disney took the uncommon step of creating his own distribution company, Buena Vista Releasing. This marked the first time that an independent producer was also his own distributor. *The Living Desert* created a sensation with audiences and won the Best Documentary Oscar. Due to the success of *The Living Desert*, Disney ascended from independent producer to full-blown studio mogul.

The *True-Life Adventures* have provoked great controversy over the years. Many film critics and zoologists complained that Disney trivialized its presentation of nature through selective editing, inappropriate sound effects and artificially staged sequences. The most egregious example here involved the 1958 documentary *White Wilderness*, which presented the notion that lemmings were suicidal. Nothing was further from the truth, but in making the film the Disney camera crew purchased captive lemmings in Manitoba and brought them to Alberta, where the poor animals were herded in a "migration" sequence that has no equivalent in reality (lemmings don't live in Alberta and they don't migrate in herds). The suicidal plunge by the lemmings was actually created by the camera crew forcing the captive animals to the edge of a cliff; their deaths were not an act of free will, by any definition. The film also won an Oscar and gave rise to the continued misperception of a lemming as being an emotionally unstable animal.

But in fairness, the *True-Life Adventures* introduced a generation of moviegoers to an appreciation of wildlife; many of today's nature documentary creators were clearly inspired by these films. Unlike documentaries from earlier decades that viewed wildlife strictly as strange and savage, Disney tried to present its subject in a manner that would appeal to basic human emotions. The films detailed the animals' struggle for survival in hostile environments, the deep maternal bonds between mother and children in the animal kingdom, and the indefatigable spirit that ensured nature's resiliency despite the unpredictable forces of nature or man-made intrusions.

And Disney can claim some credit for planting the seeds of ecological awareness in the national mindframe: the 1954 documentary

The Vanishing Prairie (also an Oscar winner) was prescient in addressing issues of environmental protection during an age of obnoxious over-consumption.

Furthermore, the Disney *True-Life Adventures* were beautifully filmed. Technicolor documentaries were not common during this time, and seeing nature in its fullest vibrancy was a wonder for 1950s-era moviegoers. In many ways, the films are at a disadvantage when seen on the small screen, since they were clearly meant to be viewed and appreciated on the big screen.

Disney was clearly the leader in cinematic nature documentaries, but by the 1960s his studio's focus was shifting elsewhere and the *True-Life Adventures* series was retired. However, the films continued to be shown on Disney's TV shows in the 1960s and 1970s, and have since been presented on DVD.

In Disney's absence, few American producers were willing to invest in theatrical releases celebrating wildlife. But the big screen's loss was the small screen's gain, as television producers took up the challenge. While most made-for-television nature documentaries run considerably shorter than the average theatrical feature, their appeal has never diminished and they have been a staple of TV viewing for decades. More recently, the genre made a comeback, of sorts, via the theatrical release of the 2005 French-made *March of the Penguins* and Al Gore's 2006 global warming treatise *An Inconvenient Truth* – back-to-back Oscar winners and box-office hits.

Not-So-Real life

But beyond the Disney nature documentaries, the cause of non-fiction filmmaking suffered a setback in the years following World War II. The pre-war travelogue documentaries seemed badly dated to post-war audiences. And few filmmakers (either in Hollywood or within the independent filmmaking world) saw the commercial viability in documenting real life.

During the post-war period, the concept of the filmmaking took a radically different approach following the import of Italian films such as

Open City (1945), *Paisan* (1946) and *Shoeshine* (1947). Falling into a new category that was dubbed "neo-realism," these films had a gritty and earthy tone that was radically different from the polished product coming from Hollywood. The Italian films were shot on the streets and often featured non-professional actors who were cast in rough, raw dramatic stories that emphasized the harsh side of the human condition.

Of course, the neo-realist films were not documentaries. They were carefully scripted and meticulously directed by artists who were breaking new style ground. But to many independent filmmakers in the U.S., the neo-realist approach suggested documentary productions. In the late 1940s and throughout the 1950s, many narrative feature films were created and promoted under the banner of being documentaries.

Ironically, the films were, on the whole, quite good. They explored racial, social and economic subject matter that the Hollywood system was uncomfortable in pursuing. Even by contemporary standards, they still present the viewer with a jolt from their unapologetic and non-sentimental approach. But, nonetheless, they are not documentaries.

The first of these genre-blurring efforts was Robert Flaherty's *Louisiana Story* (1948). The film was sponsored by Standard Oil as a vehicle for promoting the concept of drilling in the Louisiana bayou (to its credit, the company did not insist on being identified in the film). Flaherty, who was no stranger to staging scenes for his earlier work, created a genuine work of fiction with *Louisiana Story* – non-professional actors were cast in an invented story that was shot on location across the bayou. Incredibly, the film was successfully marketed as a documentary. Even today, many film scholars mistake *Louisiana Story* for non-fiction filmmaking.

The Quiet One (1949), directed by Sidney Meyers, followed the same path. The story of an emotionally unstable, maladjusted boy, the film was shot on location in New York's Harlem neighborhood. In many ways, *The Quiet One* outdid the Italian imports for driving home the power of neo-realist filmmaking. Even the Academy Award voters were impressed; *The Quiet One* received an Oscar nomination as Best Documentary, even though it was a work of fiction.

The commercial and critical success earned by *The Quiet One* help bring more socially relevant quasi-documentaries to the screen. Jack Arnold's *With These Hands* (1951) recreated the tragic 1915 fire at New York's Triangle Shirt Factory with a cast that included Sam Levene, Joseph Wiseman and Arlene Francis. The film received a Best Documentary Oscar nomination. Norman Foster's *Navajo* (1952) focused on an American Indian boy who flees into the Arizona wilderness after an unsuccessful attempt to take him off the reservation and into a predominantly white school. That film also received an Oscar nomination for Best Documentary.

Lionel Rogosin's *On the Bowery* (1956) used the residents of New York's skid-row district to play themselves in an examination of destitute men who lived on the streets. Not only did that film get an Oscar nomination for Best Documentary, but one of the destitute men in the production, Ray Sayler, was offered a Hollywood contract (he declined it, preferring to be left alone in his alcohol-fueled poverty).

Not every acclaimed docudrama was pegged by the Academy voters. Fred Pressburger's *Crowded Paradise* (1956) used a mix of professional players (Hume Cronyn and Nancy Kelly) and non-professionals to tell its story of the prejudice and struggle facing Puerto Rican residents of New York City. Rogosin's *Come Back, Africa* (1959), which detailed the rigid cruelty of apartheid, was shot secretly when it was obvious the Pretoria government would not allow an independent American filmmaker to create a film about that nation's racist policies. But not only did Rogosin use non-professionals actors in scripted scenes to get his story across, but he also created a club scene that allowed him to bring in the popular South African singer Miriam Makeba to perform two songs in the middle of the film. (The popularity of the film helped launch Makeba's career outside of her country.)

The Savage Eye (1959), with three directors (Ben Maddow, Joseph Meyers, Sidney Strick), took an acidic view of a divorced woman's trajectory. Kent Mackenzie recruited American Indians living in Los Angeles to dramatize their life stories for *The Exiles* (1961).

Curiously, the Hollywood studios chose not to emulate this independent film trend. Outside of Warner Bros.'s red-baiting *I Was a Communist for the FBI* (1951, which also received an Oscar nomination as Best Documentary), the studios saw no need to create docudramas – or genuine documentaries, for that matter.

Nonetheless, a few genuine non-fiction films managed to get produced during this period. *Helen Keller in Her Story* (1955) provided a moving and inspiring celebration of its eponymous icon's life and accomplishments. Elwood Price's *Mau Mau* (1955) attempted to document the violent uprising in British colonial Kenya; however, the original concept of the film was hijacked by the insertion of patently fake exploitation sequences shot in a Los Angeles studio.

If genuine non-fiction filmmaking was somewhat spotty in the U.S. during the postwar years, it flourished in Europe. Ironically, many wonderful documentaries were imported to the U.S. and released theatrically, albeit with new English-language narrative soundtracks. Some of these offerings won the Academy Award for Best Documentary: *Kon-Tiki* (1951, released by RKO), the Jacques-Yves Cousteau and Louis Malle collaboration *The Silent World* (1956), *Albert Schweitzer* (1957), *Serengeti Shall Not Die* (1959), *The Horse with the Flying Tail* (1960), *The Sky Above, The Mud Below* (1961) and another Cousteau-lensed non-fiction feature called *World Without Sun* (1964). These films were prestige productions that enjoyed supportive reviews and did a nice bit of business in art house release.

But one imported documentary literally rewrote the rules of documentary distribution: the 1962 Italian production *Mondo Cane*. For starters, the film broke a significant taboo by keeping its original non-English title for U.S. release (perhaps *A Dog's World* wasn't considered commercial enough?). It then went further by ignoring the concept of documentaries as a tool for educational advancement. *Mondo Cane* was pure no-holds-barred exploitation that juxtaposed the wildest excesses of the so-called civilized and primitive cultures of the world. In Europe, the film was nominated for the Golden Palm at the Cannes Film Festival.

In the U.S., a small art house distributor called Times Film Corp. dubbed *Mondo Cane* into English and put it into mainstream release.

Thanks largely to aggressive marketing that played up the shock values of its contents and the good fortune of having the lovely ballad "More" as its theme music (that snagged an Oscar nomination for Best Song), *Mondo Cane* was a phenomenal box-office success. A sequel was quickly cranked out, but that offering found itself competing for screen space with a new flurry of so-called "mondo" movies (today called "shockumentaries") coming out of Europe and the U.S. In retrospect, none of these films were particularly jolting and all of them seem terribly tame by contemporary standards. Nonetheless, the promise of non-fiction filmmaking that rivaled Hollywood for audacity and imagination recast the genre into a very different perspective.

This approach to documentary filmmaking petered out by the late 1960s, degenerating into silliness along the lines of *The Wild, Wild World of Jayne Mansfield* (a hodgepodge of film clips and irrelevant sequences linked by a breathy narration by an actress pretending to be the late starlet). In the early 1970s, however, it all began anew when enterprising distributors began to heavily advertise their supposedly non-fiction films on television. These documentaries tapped into that decade's growing obsession with subjects of cryptozoology, extra-terrestrials and conspiracy theories. The result was a wild skein of bizarre and outrageous documentaries that pushed the genre to a new limit.

The fun ramped up 1974 when a small distribution company picked up the rights to a 1970 German documentary that was nominated for the Oscar but was not previously available in the U.S. market. The film offered a strange theory that ancient civilizations were visited by aliens from outer space, and that these visitors from another galaxy gave man the knowledge and tools needed to become an advanced species. Sun International dubbed the film into English and changed the original title from *Memories of the Future* into *Chariots of the Gods?*; the original book that inspired the film, created by a hitherto-obscure Swiss writer named Erich von Däniken, was issued in the U.S. in conjunction with the film's release. Overkill television advertising pushed the message endlessly, but it paid off; *Chariots of the Gods?* was a major box-office hit.

Inspired by this happening, a Utah-based operation called Sunn Classics came into being with the mission of creating theatrical documentary releases that questioned a variety of unusual issues. Sunn Classics didn't necessarily offer the best documentaries, but their films were certainly the noisiest: *The Outer Space Connection* (1975), *The Mysterious Monsters* (1976), *In Search of Noah's Ark* (1976), *The Amazing World of Psychic Phenomena* (1976), *The Lincoln Conspiracy* (1977), *Beyond and Back* (1978), *Encounter with Disaster* (1979), *The Bermuda Triangle* (1979), *In Search of Historic Jesus* (1979) and *Beyond Death's Door* (1979).

The Sunn Classic offerings were variations on a similar theme: the daring attempt to reveal long-hidden secrets that disrupted some sort of status quo. Cheesy dramatizations to bolster the non-fiction elements were par for the course. The most memorable examples included *The Lincoln Conspiracy*, which insisted John Wilkes Booth escaped capture and that a man with a similar appearance was actually killed and presented as the president's murderer, and *In Search of Historic Jesus*, where the mystery of the Shroud of Turin is wrapped around a low-rent Passion Play starring a hirsute John Rubinstein as Jesus.

Sunn Classics's reign came to an end in 1980 when it jettisoned the non-fiction format in favor of a straight narrative feature film called *Hangar 18*. The film was meant to unmask the secrecy surrounding the U.S. military base that supposedly had direct communications with other worlds. But the film was a flop and the company switched its focus to television production.

Oddly, Sunn Classics did not pick up the rights to what may have been the most entertaining offering of this decade's speculative documentary genre: the 1979 production, *The Late, Great Planet Earth*. Featuring no less a figure than Orson Welles as its on-screen narrator, the film tapped into a hodgepodge of alleged Biblical predictions that foretold the upcoming annihilation of the world. The film insisted the Cold War arms race was the starting block for apocalyptic doom, while the anti-Christ may have been either Henry Kissinger or Jimmy Carter. There was also the warning of the so-called harmonic convergence in 1982, when all of the planets lined up in a row that was going to spell the end of the Earth.

American Cinema Releasing, an indie distributor that specialized in low-budget action flicks, grabbed this title and enjoyed significant box-office returns. But if one looks at it today, it is hard not to realize that the film was a bit off in regard to its accuracy. Even worse, today's filmmaking styles makes the doom-and-gloom of *The Late, Great Planet Earth* painfully antiquated. Chuck Dowling, reviewing the film's DVD debut in 1999 for the *Jacksonville Film Journal,* noted the less-than-thrilling denouement to this production: "There's ten minutes of stock footage at the end of the film meant to give us an idea of what the Battle for Armageddon might be like. If it's anything like it's depicted as here then it's going to be incredibly boring."

The shockumentary took on a new life in the early 1980s with *Faces of Death,* a crude hodgepodge of footage depicting gruesome and violent ways for life to be snuffed out. Made in 1978, the film quietly began to circulate theatrically in 1981. Despite oft-repeated reports that much of the footage was blatantly faked, the film proved popular in theatrical release and became a cult favorite on home video. Needless to say, in a repeat of what transpired with *Mondo Cane,* sequels and rip-offs followed.

Flies on the Wall

While the Mondo-style tomfoolery was reigning, another form of non-fiction filmmaking was quietly taking root. It began at the start of the 1960s when filmmaker Robert Drew, working with Richard Leacock, Albert Maysles and D. A. Pennebaker, began creating a series of documentaries for Time-Life called the *Living Camera* series. These films were quite unusual in that they eschewed the normal trappings of documentary filmmaking (most notably, off-screen narration) and created a fly-on-the-wall style of storytelling where the action unfolds on its own. Dubbed cinema verité by critics who prefer non-English expressions, these films offered an unusual sense of intimacy that was previously absent from the genre.

The most notably film in this series was *Primary* (1960), a one-hour production that was originally shown on ABC-TV. The film offered an in-depth close-up of Democratic presidential candidates John F. Kennedy and Hubert Humphrey during that year's Wisconsin Primary. The film offered, for the first time, an insider's view of the political machines in action. Working with lightweight camera and sound equipment, the filmmakers were able to engage their subjects at very, very close range.

The raw power of cinema verité truly resonated in 1967 when first-time filmmaker Frederick Wiseman presented *Titicut Follies*. Wiseman was a professor at Boston University's law school when he decided to try his hand at documentary filmmaking. His subject was the Bridgewater State Hospital in Bridgewater, Massachusetts. Despite its name, it was not a traditional medical facility. Rather, it was part of the Massachusetts Department of Corrections and it was used to confine prisoners deemed criminally insane. Rather than offer the traditional hospital setting of beds and rooms, the prisoners were kept in barren cells without furniture and plumbing; a mattress on the floor and a bucket were used instead.

In viewing the film there is no denying Bridgewater was home to plenty of insanity. Many of the inmates seen on camera appear to be in their own world: men standing around yelling in gibberish, cursing into the air, even breaking into song without provocation (unless they felt they needed to be entertaining for the camera aimed at them). But the criminal backstory behind these men's confinement is largely ignored. Except for one man, who acknowledges his imprisonment for pedophilia, no one in the film ever gets to explain how they wound up as prisoners.

And that is where *Titicut Follies* triumphs and fails. There is no story-line, per se, but only a series of everyday occurrences as the anonymous inmates and the Bridgewater staff interact freely. Yet at the same time, a significant chunk of the story is absent: just who are these people? Not just the inmates, but also the staff (particularly the correctional officers, who appear to have more contact with the inmates than the medical personnel and who clearly had to be affected by the depth of their work).

There are a few clues about some of the people here. A Russian man named Vladimir complains he was transferred from a penitentiary to Bridgewater over a year-and-a-half earlier for observation and he repeatedly requests being transferred back. He states the medication he is being given at Bridgewater is making him ill and the facility is wrecking his emotional health. The doctors he pleads with, however, state he is paranoid and prescribe stronger tranquilizers to calm his visible agitation.

But what is not shown is this: who is Vladimir? Why was he sent to jail? And why was he sent from jail to Bridgewater? And was he really sane, or were the medical experts (who come across as condescending and detached in the film) genuinely knowledgeable about his condition? It is impossible to determine if this is reality or harkening back to the silent era, manipulative filmmaking in the guise of non-fiction filmmaking.

Likewise, another inmate is the focus of a lengthy sequence where two correctional guards take him from his cell to the Bridgewater barber for a shave. The inmate is naked (as many of the inmates are) and he seems totally incapable of communicating. He speaks in weird, loud growls and snarls, and he clearly abhors eye contact. Some critics have faulted the correctional officers for treating the man in a patronizing manner by the way they speak to him (the guards are a bit loud and repeat the man's name in each sentence when addressing him). But I can't see abuse there; if anything, the guards are guilty of trying to communicate with a man who seems beyond the normal range of conversation. At the end of the sequence, there is a brief breakthrough: the inmate acknowledges he was educated to be a teacher. But what happened between his education and his incarceration? The viewer never knows.

However, the film's most dramatic moment is also its quietest. A diminutive inmate, surrounded by three large and lumpy guards, is told to remove his clothing. The inmate obliges and is quickly naked. He is then escorted by the guards up a staircase and through a labyrinth of hallways until he arrives at an open cell which has no furniture or signs of a toilet and sink. Without requiring instruction, the inmate enters the cell. A guard closes the cell's heavy door and bolts it shut. The camera peers through a small window in the cell and finds the inmate looking out the cell's barred window to the outside world. The inmate is in silhouette – as if he no longer existed and became just a living shadow.

Titicut Follies created a sensation when Wiseman debuted it at the 1967 New York Film Festival. It was immediately hailed as a shocking expose of human rights abuse of the mentally ill (though, ironically, no inmate in the film ever complains to the camera of being physically injured and none bear any marks of violent treatment). But Elliot Richardson, the Attorney General for Massachusetts, was horrified with the film and took an extraordinary step of seeking the court-ordered banning of the film. Richardson argued the inmates' right to privacy was violated by Wiseman.

The filmmaker, though, cited he had consensual waivers from the inmates who were coherent and he had a waiver from the Bridgewater superintendent on behalf of the inmates who were not (the superintendent, who actually hoped the film would work to raise funding for his facility, was the legal guardian for his mentally incompetent inmates). The Massachusetts Supreme Court ruled against Wiseman and *Titicut Follies* was ordered removed from exhibition, with the sole exception being small non-theatrical screenings for selected legal, educational and medical professionals.

The ban on *Titicut Follies* marked the first time an American movie was prevented from being shown for reasons other than obscenity or national security. The ban stayed in effect until 1992, and the legal conflict cost Wiseman a great deal of money before he could present his film again. In 1993, Wiseman allowed *Titicut Follies* to be broadcast on PBS, which was the first and (to date) only time it reached a national audience.

So where is *Titicut Follies* today? Wiseman has yet to allow the film to be seen in commercial presentations. It is only legally available for rental through Wiseman's Zipporah Films for non-theatrical screenings in a 16mm or videocassette format. Wiseman will sell a video of *Titicut Follies* to non-theatrical venues – for $500.

Wiseman would continue to create cinema verité documentaries for the next four decades, including *High School* (1968), *Juvenile Court* (1973), *Welfare* (1975), *Belfast, Maine* (1999) and *Domestic Violence* (2001). However, many average moviegoers are not familiar with his work, which is not in commercial DVD release and can only be seen in non-theatrical or retrospective settings.

More cinema verité was offered by the siblings Albert and David Maysles, whose 1968 *Salesman* was an off-beat and unexpected theatrical hit. The filmmakers followed a quartet of Bible salesmen as they make their weary trek from door-to-door in search of customers. The Maysles Brothers, joined by Muffie Meyer and Ellen Hovde, created another cinema verité sensation in 1975 with *Grey Gardens*, an astonishing visit to the world of 82-year-old Edith Bouvier Beale and her 58-year-old daughter Edie, who live in a crumbling mansion on Long Island. The deteriorating structure and its overgrown grounds mirror the deteriorating lives and overgrown self-value of the two women, whose chief claim to fame existed in their being cousins to Jacqueline Bouvier Kennedy Onassis.

Another prominent proponent of cinema verité was Barbara Kopple, whose 1976 *Harlan County U.S.A.* covered a Kentucky miners' strike, providing a rare, raw view of working-class America in a tumultuous upheaval. The film's unsentimental view of the miners' working lives, coupled with its obvious pro-union sentiment, offered a strong dose of genuine reality. It was not surprising that *Harlan County U.S.A.* received a standing ovation at its 1976 New York Film Festival premiere, before going on to enjoy a successful commercial release and winning an Academy Award for Best Documentary.

Pop goes the culture

Also going on during this period was a new focus on creating documentaries that celebrated different aspects, individuals and trends in popular culture.

This began with *Jazz on a Summer's Day* (1960), Bert Stern's record of the 1958 Newport Jazz Festival. In 1967, two arresting, filmed records of provocative entertainers were released: John Magnuson's *The Lenny Bruce Performance Film*, which kept its camera on the controversial comic during one of his final stage performances, and *Don't Look Back*, D.A. Pennebaker's coverage of Bob Dylan's 1965 England tour. The films provided polarizing entertainers at different parts of their lives: Bruce was broken by censorship and legal problems and clearly at the end of his life, while Dylan was at the first heady peak of his ground-breaking career.

Pennebaker kept his camera focused on music with *Monterey Pop*, a concert film of the 1967 Monterey Pop Festival. Featuring performances by Jimi Hendrix, Janis Joplin and The Who, the film was self-released in 1968 and created an invaluable time capsule of the psychedelic era. The following year saw Michael Wadleigh's *Woodstock* (independently produced by the filmmaker and released by Warner Bros.) and the Maysles Brothers' *Gimme Shelter* (released by Cinema 5) generated controversy in graphically showing the beating death of a gun-toting man by Hell's Angels members who were hired to work as security guards during a 1969 Rolling Stones concert at Altamont Speedway outside of San Francisco.

Concert films continued throughout the 1970s and into the 1980s, when the rise of MTV cancelled the desire for moviegoers to see the genre on a big screen. Whether concert films could be considered as documentaries remain to be seen. In 1983, Jonathan Demme's *Stop Making Sense*, a filmed record of the Talking Heads in concert, was disqualified from consideration in the New York Film Critics Circle Awards, as it was determined the film was not a documentary. But the National Society of Film Critics, which included a large number of members from the New York Film Critics Circle, voted the film its Best Documentary Award. Occasional attempts were made to revive the concert film, but they rarely connected with audiences. And in the case of *We Sold Our Souls for Rock 'n Roll*, the 2001 Ozzfest documentary directed by Penelope Spheeris (who elevated the L.A. punk scene to cinematic art via *The Decline of Western Civilization* in 1981), problems with music clearance rights prevented the film from being theatrically released.

But concert films were not the only aspect of popular culture to reach the screen. Documentaries on classic films and the artists who created them began to appear, sparked in large part by Peter Bogdanovich's 1971 *Directed by John Ford*. (Trying to get a full list of non-fiction films about filmmakers and movie stars would fill a book by itself.) Many documentaries recycled old footage to recount bygone eras and issues. *The Atomic Café* (1982) had fun with U.S. government-produced propaganda films from the 1940s and 1950s that offered contradictory and often blatantly incorrect information about safety concerns in the event of nuclear attack.

Sports-related documentaries also percolated, sometimes taking fringe sports into the spotlight. Lee H. Katzin's *Le Mans* (1971) created an apotheosis for both auto racing and its rugged celebrity hero, Steve Mc-Queen. The George Butler-Robert Fiore 1977 bodybuilding celebration *Pumping Iron* create a sensation with its cinema verité presentation of the professional gym rats (most notably a charismatic Austrian named Arnold Schwarzenegger), and it helped redirect Americans back into the habit of lifting weights to build muscle and good health. Steve James' *Hoop Dreams* (1994) focused on two high-school basketball players facing challenges in their quest to become professional players. The film was at the center of a major controversy when it failed to receive a nomination for the Best Documentary Oscar (it received a nomination for Best Editing).

The New Manipulators

Beginning in the 1980s, a new breed of documentary filmmaker began to emerge. They eschewed straightforward non-fiction filmmaking in favor of a highly personalized styled. In some cases, the filmmakers incorporated themselves into their work, thus making their films a from-the-heart statement designed to sell a specific brand of emotional and/or political persuasion.

Ross McElwee hit a nerve with his 1986 *Sherman's March*. Originally designed as a film that traced the route of the Union Army's destructive sweep across the Civil War-era Southern states, the film somehow turned into a deeply personal meditation on the women in his life. The offbeat nature of the film created a sensation with critics. However, McElwee's subsequent attempts to merge non-fiction filmmaking with personalized cinematic essays, including *Time Indefinite* (1993) and *Bright Leaves* (2003), never quite duplicated the on-screen effect or critical enthusiasm.

Errol Morris had directed two somewhat straightforward documentaries, *Gates of Heaven* (1978) and *Vernon, Florida* (1981), before presenting *The Thin Blue Line* (1988). The film argued the case of Randall Adams, who was convicted in the 1976 murder of a Dallas police officer. Morris made jolting use of dramatic reenactments, with a vigorous Philip Glass music score to heighten the film's case that Adams was framed.

Morris' unique approach was immediately recognized. Janet Maslin, writing in the *New York Times*, noted that Morris "has fashioned a brilliant work of pulp fiction around this crime and that re-invents its story even as it re-examines it. Mr. Morris's graceful camera isolates witnesses and evidence against dark backgrounds, glides eerily through re-enactments of certain episodes, and selects and enlarges particular images (huge kernels of popcorn accompany a discussion of whether the drive-in's refreshment stand was really open as late as Mr. Harris said it was; in fact it closed early). In this deliberately artificial context, justice begins to feel as remote for the viewer as it undoubtedly feels to Mr. Adams."

Adams was later exonerated through the courts, although the Morris film was not permitted to be presented as evidence. The film was also disqualified for Academy Award consideration, with the Oscar planners nitpicking that it was a work of non-fiction and not a documentary.

Although Morris followed up *The Thin Blue Line* with the forgettable dramatic narrative *The Dark Wind* (1991), he would continue a highly successful career in non-fiction filmmaking, even scoring the Oscar for the 2003 film *The Fog of War*.

The year after *The Thin Blue Line* was released, another non-fiction filmmaker emerged – and he never left the spotlight. Michael Moore, adopting the on-screen persona of the rumpled everyman, used his 1989 *Roger & Me* as a broad swipe against the economic devastation brought to Flint, Michigan, by the closing of a General Motors manufacturing plant. The title's "Roger" is General Motors' chairman Roger Smith, whom Moore repeatedly attempts to secure for an on-camera interview.

But the film's real star was the other title character of "Me" – Moore was even featured in the poster art, which was unprecedented for the promotion of a non-fiction film. By putting himself front and center in the film in such a bold and political manner, he took the role of the documentary filmmaker from being an objective and unseen observer to a subjective and highly visible commentator. McElwee, in comparison, was more of an essayist; Moore was an unapologetic rabble rouser.

Not everyone appreciated Moore's tactics. Pauline Kael, writing in *The New Yorker*, questioned Moore's presentation of facts and complained the film was "shallow and facetious, a piece of gonzo demagoguery." But the film created enough of a stir to enable Moore to continue to present his political agenda and oversized personality in productions such as the Oscar-winning *Bowling for Columbine* (2002), *Fahrenheit 9/11* (2005) and *Sicko* (2007). Moore was, himself, the subject of the critical documentary feature *Manufacturing Dissent* (2007), which openly questioned his tactics and political agenda.

Other non-fiction filmmakers followed Moore's example and made themselves an integral part of their output. Caveh Zahedi served up his distinctive neuroses and family problems with films such as *I Don't Hate Las Vegas Anymore* (1994). Jonathan Caouette exposed his family's convoluted emotional history in *Tarnation* (2003). Morgan Spurlock made himself the subject of a McDonald's-only diet in *Super Size Me* (2004) and the search for the world's most notorious terrorist in *Where in the World is Osama bin Laden?* (2008).

The 10 Most Important Independent Films of All Time:

Christopher Null, editor, FilmCritic.com

Q: If you were to look over the span of the history of U.S. independent cinema, from the silent era to today's output, what would you list as the 10 Most Important Independently-Produced Films of All Time ... and why?

1. *THX-138* (1971). George Lucas's start. Got sci-fi going.

2. *Eraserhead* (1977). Not a triumph of storytelling, but a touchstone for the avant-garde.

3. *Halloween* (1978). Launched modern horror as we know it.

4. *Roger & Me* (1989). The shockumentary is born.

5. *sex, lies, and videotape* (1989). That really got indie film in the U.S., as we know it, going strong.

6. *Slacker* (1991). Richard Linklater's greatest work. Proved that ambience could win out over plot.

7. *El Mariachi* (1992). Obvious choice – low-budget film-making at its finest.

8. *Pulp Fiction* (1994). Maybe the biggest pseudo-indie ... inspired a whole genre.

9. *The Blair Witch Project* (1999). Legitimized digital video as a medium.

10. *The Passion of the Christ* (2004). Proved the power of the religious right.

CHAPTER SEVEN:

The Rise and Rise of Digital Cinema

*"Any sufficiently advanced technology is indistinguish-
able from magic."* — Arthur C. Clarke

In 1955, the entertainment industry trade newspaper *Daily Variety* published an edition with the headline "Film is Dead." This intriguing obituary was meant to signal the arrival of the Ampex video recording system, which replaced the use of film with magnetic tape.

The video technology was aimed for the television industry, which lacked a satisfactory method of preserving live broadcasts. Prior to the arrival of videotape, television shows that were broadcast live were preserved by a kinescope, which was basically a 16mm film of the broadcast images taken from a television monitor. The picture tended to be blurry and slightly distorted, which is not surprising given that a kinescope is basically a picture of a picture.

In the 1950s, videotape did not present any practical usage for motion picture production. In fact, the traditional film technology actually had a practical usage for television production: the ugliness of the kinescope resulted in many major shows, such as *The Abbott and Costello Show*, *Amos 'n' Andy*, the original *Dragnet* and *I Love Lucy*, being shot on

35mm film to ensure the visual quality of the programs were pristine. The 35mm productions also guaranteed these programs could enjoy an afterlife in American TV syndication and in foreign sales. *Dragnet* and *I Love Lucy* were the first U.S. programs to be shown on British television thanks to their being shot on the universal 35mm film.

Programs saved on kinescope, however, did not get syndicated due in large part to their poor visual quality. These kinescopes disappeared for many years – some would be discovered by archivists many decades later, but too many others were lost due to neglect or improper storage. And, of course, programs that were broadcast but never copied on kinescope were literally lost as soon as they went off the air.

Cinema and video existed in separate worlds up until 1964, when a curious notion was hatched. An independent production company called Theatrofilm decided it would be quicker and cheaper to shoot a feature film on video, and then create a 35mm print of the video for release in theaters. In retrospect, it was a thoroughly bizarre and illogical notion at every imaginable level: it was plagued with the extra costs of the video-to-film transfer, the visual degradation that would accompany that transfer, and the primitive nature of the Theatrofilm technology that restricted the cinematography to black and white. The latter was particularly bothersome, given that the quantity and appeal of monochromatic movies were declining rapidly at this point in time.

However, the Theatrofilm team had rather deep pockets, so deep that they could fish in and come up with enough funds to attract one of the world's biggest stars for their initial endeavor. In that case, it was Richard Burton, who was at the height of both his popularity and notoriety following his romantic entanglement with Elizabeth Taylor. Burton was coming off a highly successful Broadway production of *Hamlet* when the Theatrofilm team made the suggestion of recording the stage show and releasing it to movie theaters. Burton's marquee value, it was determined, would guarantee a quick and easy profit, even though the production would basically be a black-and-white videotaped record of a colorful stage show.

Incredibly, this scheme worked. On June 30 and July 1 of 1964, three separate performances of *Hamlet* were recorded in Theatrofilm's video process, which was dubbed Electronovision. There was no attempt to bring a cinematic style to the proceedings; this *Hamlet* was basically shot in the multi-camera set-up that was typical for assembly-line TV productions. However, neither of the film's credited directors, John Gielgud (who helmed the direction of the stage production) or Bill Colleran (a TV variety show veteran making his first and only foray into cinema), were able to adapt the stage show into a visually interesting film. The result was an aesthetically monotonous production, where Burton and his bravura ensemble (including Hume Cronyn, Alfred Drake and Eileen Herlie) were either too far, too near or off-center from the Electronovision cameras to have any true dramatic impact.

Ultimately, it didn't matter. Warner Bros. snagged the distribution rights to *Hamlet* and Burton was brought in to shoot a lengthy commercial promoting both the film and the Electronovision process (the commercial is unintentionally funny, as a groggy-looking Burton clumsily reads his lines from cue cards).

Two months after *Hamlet* was shot, Warner Bros. distributed it to approximately 1,000 theaters for a unique weekend release, on September 23 and 24 of 1964. The result was a $4,000,000 box-office gross, and Electronovision was hailed as a success.

But it was not a success that would be duplicated. Indeed, *Hamlet* vanished after its very brief theatrical presentation. For no clear reason, the prints of *Hamlet* were destroyed after it played in theaters. The film was considered lost for many years, but a print was located in the possession of Richard Burton's estate and was subsequently made available for restoration and DVD release.

In 1965, Theatrofilm tried to expand on its success with three productions. One was a concert movie featuring the top rock and R&B acts of the day. *The T.A.M.I. Show* (the acronym stands for Teenage Awards Music International) was a hodgepodge variety revue featuring performances from the Rolling Stones, the Supremes, James Brown, Chuck

Berry, the Beach Boys, Leslie Gore, Smokey Robinson and the Miracles, Gerry and the Pacemakers, the Barbarians, and Billy J. Kramer and the Dakotas; Jan and Dean served as hosts of the event. Despite the stellar line-up, many of the performances were curiously lethargic. American International Pictures gave the film a quick theatrical release, but it later fell out of circulation due to music clearance issues.

Theatrofilm's second Electronovision production for 1965 was *Harlow*, a tacky quickie that was solely designed to steal attention and audiences from Paramount Pictures' heavily hyped big-budget biopic on the 1930s movie icon Jean Harlow. The Paramount production was also called *Harlow*, which added to the confusion.

This time, Theatrofilm overplayed its hand. No major distributor would touch their film, so they put the film out through Magna, a tiny company specializing in foreign films. Reviews were awful and audiences, who were ready for the Paramount production, smelled the fraud and stayed away. *Harlow* was a bomb.

Another Electronovision film came out in 1966. This time, American International used the technology to create *The Big TNT Show*, which was meant to duplicate *The T.A.M.I. Show* with an all-star line-up: Ray Charles, Ike and Tina Turner, the Ronettes, the Byrds, Bo Diddley, the Lovin' Spoonful, Petula Clark, Donovan, Joan Baez and Roger Miller hit the stage and were preserved in Electronovision black and white. But after that release, Theatrofilm soon went out of business. No one sought to pick up the Electronovision technology, leaving Theatrofilm's titles as a trio of curios.

At this point, video filmmaking seemed like a solution without a problem. No one bothered to consider the possibilities of using video technology until 1971, when filmmaker Victor Stoloff attempted to create a feature called *Why?* that would be shot on video and transferred to 35mm film. While the film had an intriguing concept – a group therapy session concerning a number of highly verbose, tightly-wound individuals – and included such unlikely casting as folk singer Tim Buckley and football star O.J. Simpson, *Why?* was neither completed nor released.

In 1975, video filmmaking managed to make a breakthrough with the independent production *Give 'em Hell, Harry!* The film captured (with nine video cameras) Samuel Gallu's one-man stage play starring James Whitmore as President Harry S Truman. The video-to-film transfer was perfectly fine, and the production enjoyed a significant cred when Whitmore's performance received an Academy Award nomination for Best Actor. (The nomination sparked a minor controversy, with some detractors arguing that Whitmore's performance was simply a record of a stage show and was not tailored for the screen.) This marked the first time that Oscar voters nominated a video film for their coveted prize.

But *Give 'em Hell, Harry!* did not spark a new interest in video filmmaking. It seemed impractical to shoot a movie on video and then put it on film – why not shoot it directly on film? Cost-effectiveness and the time savings in guerrilla-style filmmaking seemed to be a good argument. Emile de Antonio used video to shoot his 1982 courtroom docudrama *In the King of Prussia* in two-and-a-half days, but no one was eager to follow his example. In fact, few people were even aware of it; this independently-produced endeavor was barely released.

While video did not seem to have a place in cinemas, it did find a niche in the art gallery scene. Sony introduced its Portapak in the mid-1960s, which allowed for mobile videography. Artists such as Nam June Paik and Peter Campus and underground filmmaker Shirley Clarke were among the earlier experimental leaders in this format. Psychologist Philip Zimbardo used videotape to document his controversial 1971 mock-prison study that became known as the Stanford Prison Experiment. The 1974 documentary *Lord of the Universe*, which was shot on half-inch videotape, was broadcast on PBS and won several awards.

Into the late 1970s and early 1980s, the concept of home video began to take root. Video cassette recorders (VCRs) offered consumers the ability to tape programs from their televisions and to watch pre-recorded films. Since video filmmaking had no niche on the big screen, it appeared that it could find a home on the small screen.

Initially, the earliest video filmmakers were in the pornography industry. The lower-cost video technology offered time and financial savings for filmmakers – and, besides, audiences for these films didn't really care if they were shot on 16mm, Super 8 or videotape. The proliferation of adult videos opened new doors to the skin-flick industry while closing doors on the theaters that exclusively offered such smutty diversions.

Yet serious filmmakers were also starting to dip into the digital realm. A 1988 Italian-based production called *Julia and Julia*, starring Kathleen Turner and Sting, was shot on an early version of high-definition video tape. It played theatrically, albeit in a 35mm transfer, but the results were impressive. Vincent Canby, the chief film critic for the *New York Times*, opined that the high-definition videography looked "as good as anything shot on film to start with."

In the late 1980s and early 1990s, independent filmmakers working on shoestring budgets took advantage of new low-cost video technology for their film productions. Sometimes, the shoestrings were extremely thin. For Boston-area bodybuilding champion Paul DeSimone, his desire to create a documentary on his extensive training regimen brought him to a neighborhood electronics store in 2001. "We didn't have much money, so we shot *The Underground Lifting Video*, our first title, on a high-grade consumer video camera," he recalls. "The camera cost $1,000, but I talked the guy at the store down to $850."

Also in 2001, California-based filmmaker Young Man Kang used video technology to shoot his feature-length comedy *Cupid's Mistake* for a mere $980. The achievement was recognized by the *Guinness Book of World Records* as the lowest-budgeted film to receive a theatrical release. (Jonathan Caouette's 2003 *Tarnation* seemingly broke that record when it was announced it was shot on video for $218.32 by using free iMovie software on a Macintosh computer. However, the theatrical print, which was transferred to 35mm, saw a total budget of roughly $400,000 due to the need to polish the footage's visual and sound elements and to clear the classic rock music desired for the soundtrack.)

But whereas the 35mm technology remained standardized, the changes in video technology development were often quite rapid. Bos-

ton-based John Farrell learned that when he shot his modern-dress adaptation of Shakespeare's *Richard the Second* in 1987 using a broadcast 1
format, with the idea of transferring the video to 35mm. "We shot with
an Ikekami camera and used Sony reel-to-reel," he recalled. "I even did a
test trailer in the edit suite which we sent to a place in Los Angeles called
Image Transform, which sent us back the trailer on 35mm; this was when
laser transfer was the new thing for video to film (no scan lines)."

However, Farrell's film ran out of funds after principal shooting concluded. By the time he returned to the film in the late 1990s, the video
system he originally used was considered antiquated. However, the introduction of MPEG technology enabled Farrell to transfer the film to a
purely digital format.

Falling into the Net

Simultaneous to these low-cost, high-tech advances was another significant development. As digital video reshaped how independent films
were produced, the Internet reshaped how independent films were
seen. The Internet's influence on independent cinema has been profound at many levels. However, the relationship has been mutual: without independent cinema, the Internet's development as a source for
entertainment would have been severely limited.

The union of motion pictures and the online environment was con-
summated on May 22, 1993. At the time, the Internet was primarily a
text-driven network used by academicians, government agencies and
research labs for the sharing of information and data. Consumer usage
of the Net was nil. Most people with home computers focused their
energies on word processing and games. Online communication was
limited, and the early pioneers in driving consumers into cyberspace
(America Online, CompuServe and Prodigy) were just barely beginning
to make inroads with the marketing of their services.

However, that fateful day in 1993 was significant for the first-ever
broadcast of a film across the Internet. It was a daring idea, but also a
foolish one. Cyberspace in 1993 was significantly slower than today's

edition, and the primitive parameters of that technology would not allow for a smooth, broadcast-quality transmission.

For no very clear reason, the film chosen to make that initial journey into the digital ether was a 1992 avant-garde feature called *Wax: Or the Discovery of Television Among the Bees*. The film, created by David Blair, offered a surreal mix of comedy and experimental visuals to relay the tale of a weapons designer and amateur beekeeper that fall victim to the mind-control tactics of his buzzing yellow-and-black insects. Writer Williams Burrough and Clyde Tombaugh, the astronomer who discovered Pluto, turned up in the course of the movie.

The decision to transmit the 85-minute *Wax: Or the Discovery of Television Among the Bees* created problems that were never adequately solved. Although the film was shot in color, its Net broadcast had to be presented in black and white. Even worse, the projection speed was slowed to an excruciating two frames per second, a far distance from the 24-frames-per-second speed of the standard film projection. The slower running speed also played havoc with the film's soundtrack, thus assuring the visual and audio elements would remain out of synchronization for the length of the broadcast.

Ultimately, it didn't matter because the film was hard to locate online during its Net debut. Engineers at Sun Microsystems, who were among the few people waiting for this event, missed the first half of the broadcast because they were unable to locate the film's transmission within their company's Internet data stream. By the time they found the film, it was virtually unwatchable and completely incoherent.

Nonetheless, it was a start. Net technology began to improve over the 1990s, and by the tail end of the decade the situation was somewhat better. Net transmission speeds were still fairly slow (dial-up connections were the norm and a 56k modem was considered the fast track to the information superhighway). But even under those circumstances, one could be able to sit back at the computer monitor and watch a movie online.

Except for one problem: there were barely any films online. The Hollywood studios were wary and apprehensive of cyberspace, particularly in regard to the threat of online piracy, so mainstream films were kept offline. The few films that were shown on the early webcasting sites were either amateur shorts or old public-domain movies that could be presented thanks to their expired copyrights.

In March 1998, the Net's potential as a film distribution channel took a huge leap forward with the debut of the first contemporary feature film that could be viewed in real-time in cyberspace. The film was *Walls of Sand*, a 1994 independently-produced drama from San Francisco filmmaker Erica Jordan. Running 110 minutes, the film was presented on The Sync, a webcasting network based in Laurel, Maryland.

In many ways, *Walls of Sand* was the right film at the right time. It was a black-and-white, conversation-driven production, which made it ideal for a 1998 webcast (the technology of the time could not accommodate a *Lawrence of Arabia*-style visual extravaganza). The film also lacked commercial distribution; it already wore out the festival circuit and was not in circulation when The Sync put it online. Erica Jordan was not concerned about piracy of her film. If anything, the Internet gave her a chance to reach a global market.

Likewise, The Sync needed to spice up its online presentations. The company was run by a young couple, Tom Edwards and Carla Cole, and its initial offerings were fairly weak: audio simulcasts of speeches by Vice President Al Gore, a few short films that looked more like home movies than professional productions, a public-access-style talk show starring Cole and her friends, and two public-domain silent movies, *The Cabinet of Dr. Caligari* and *Nosferatu*.

The arrival of *Walls of Sand* created a media sensation. The film and The Sync were profiled in the *New York Times* Arts & Leisure section, the first time a Net-based entertainment story appeared in that newspaper. Additional press coverage followed, with The Sync enjoying attention from the *Wall Street Journal*, the *Washington Post* and *Entertainment Weekly*.

To keep the momentum flowing, more independently-produced feature films were added. The Sync partnered with two small distribution companies, Moore Video of Richmond, Virginia, and Sub Rosa Studios of Syracuse, New York, and acquired the online rights to several of their films. But whereas *Walls of Sand* was a sensitive art film, the next round of features on The Sync placed an emphasis on horror and camp: the 1972 vampire flick *Lemora*, no-budget contemporary horror romps *5 Lost Souls* and *Zombie vs. Mardi Gras*, and a documentary on the septuagenarian punk rocker Dika Newlin called *Dika: Murder City*. A couple of older classics were also added: *Reefer Madness* and, incongruously, Pasolini's *The Gospel According to Saint Matthew*.

However, digital lightning did not strike twice. The Sync quickly discovered that Net surfers were not seeking out feature-length movies. The media attention for the new features was less intensive – after all, the novelty appeal had evaporated and the presence of online features was starting to feel commonplace.

If the site's web traffic for its features was limited, other areas of The Sync devoted to shorter programming drew more attention. An online film festival that enabled viewers to vote for the short films on the site became popular, and a partnership with the distribution company Microcinema helped bring a wave of entertaining shorts to The Sync. Edwards and Cole also concentrated on producing original made-for-the-Net programs, including a forerunner of reality TV called *The Jenni Show* that starred Jennifer Ringley of the racy JenniCam website.

As for *Walls of Sand*, it was removed from the site in 1999 following a disagreement between Erica Jordan and Edwards and Cole. Its absence was never rued by The Sync's audience. The film managed to snag a brief VHS video release following its online exposure, but it was never released on DVD and remains out of circulation.

Sadly, The Sync fell victim to the dot-com bubble's burst. In 2000, the site ceased all original productions. For the next few years, Edwards and Cole slowly dismantled The Sync's pages, removing its films and programs while turning the site into a webcam and blog. Eventually, it disappeared into the digital ether and its pioneering efforts in the linkage of independent film and the Internet were quickly forgotten as the Net evolved into the 21st century.

But while The Sync faded off the Net, other aspiring online artists were starting to make a name for themselves. One of the leading figures at this time was Nathan Bramble, who worked from his home studio in Bensalem, Pennsylvania (just north of Philadelphia) as a documentary filmmaker. His productions *Centralia, PA–Modern Day Ghost Town* and *2001 Inauguration: Voice from the Street* (both from 2001) offered a haunting and rueful examination of dreams that were deferred to the point of ruin: the former film examined the remains of a mining village whose residents were forced to flee thanks to an underground fire which has burned out of control for over two decades while the latter presented a montage of protestors and counter-protestors who populated the fringes of George W. Bush's inauguration, kept out of sight and ear from the main events by a fat blue line of police and an overwhelming sense of being shut out of the democratic process.

Bramble came to documentaries in a roundabout way. His art school education focused on computer and film animation, but the realities of daily existence and the price tags that come attached dictated the pursuit of a financially lucrative job. Bramble put filmmaking aside and took a job as a webmaster for a software company; he currently holds a full-time position as a quality assurance engineer for a software firm in Princeton, N.J. However, Bramble's filmmaking ambition never truly disappeared and a new inspiration came in the form of outsider-inspired documentaries such as *Crumb*.

Cashing in stock options, Bramble purchased a DV camera and a high-speed computer to enable editing and post-production work. Combining his techie skills with a natural eye for cinematic journalism, he began to create films and also present them online via his Digital Video Documentaries website. Bramble's site is the rare online exhibitor to offer both low-quality, high-quality and download-ready versions of his streamed films, plus links to related sites that focus on his films' subjects and stills from the productions. Other web distributors, including iFilm, have also shared Bramble's work with the Net audience.

Bramble created his own website to premiere *Centralia, PA* online in early 2001; the site cost $120 to set up and $18 a month to maintain. "When I first put the film up on my website, I was surprised at the almost immediate response I got," he recalled. "I was receiving e-mail with positive feedback from people the same day I uploaded it. Since putting it up on the web I've received comments from people running Centralia websites, from students doing a geological report on Centralia, and from someone who runs a multimedia production company in Kansas encouraging me to keep making documentaries. The most interesting reaction to the film was from a government official in Wyoming who was trying to get more federal funding to help put out several mine fires burning in his state. He wanted to use my film as an example of what could happen if they were left to burn."

However, some enterprising filmmakers discovered that the Internet could be used for more than mere exhibition. In 1999, a strange buzz began to circulate around an offbeat website connected to a new film. Websites connected to movies were not new at the time, but this one was a bit different: it focused on a new feature about three would-be filmmakers who disappeared in the Maryland woods while trying to create a documentary about something called the Blair Witch.

Many people who came to the website for *The Blair Witch Project* were under the impression that this new production was a documentary. While the film's visual style – a mix of Hi8 camcorder and black-and-white 16mm film shot by the actors – gave the impression of a glorified home movie, the film's website was intentionally vague on whether or not this was a non-fiction film. Directors Daniel Myrick and Eduardo Sanchez also sought out online-exclusive critics to review and talk up their film – at the time, this was a relatively new strategy.

Dustin Putman, editor of The Movie Boy film review site, was among the first critics to review *The Blair Witch Project* and he considered the Net strategy was an act of genius that could never be duplicated. "Had it not been for the film's and the director's official websites and the early Internet reviews, it would have come and gone in theaters in a flash," he says. "The key to the marketing – and it was a genius idea that hasn't been done nearly as successfully before or since – was that it captured the audience's imagination. So many people were convinced that it was a real documentary (even after they had seen it), and the summer the movie was released I was inundated with e-mails insisting it was non-fiction."

The potential of the Internet as a marketing tool to drive interest in films was picked up by other indie productions. Palm Pictures, which acquired the rights to Lance Mungia's *Six-String Samurai*, and filmmaker Sarah Jacobson, who self-distributed her film *Mary Jane is Not a Virgin Anymore*, were among the first to use e-mail marketing to spread the word on their respective releases. And the Net wasn't just limited to building interest in well-considered films. A skein of harsh reviews by online critics for the 1999 horror-comedy *Zombie vs. Mardi Gras* (including the proclamation by Rob Firsching's Amazing World of Cult Movies site that this was the worst cult movie of the 20th century) helped propel that previously obscure release into an Ed Wood-worthy cult following among fans of so-bad-they're-good films.

On the big screen

While the computer screens were busy, the big screens were curiously absent of video productions. Some non-theatrical venues, most notably the Pacific Film Archive in Berkeley, California, offered the ability to screen video productions, first-run cinemas stuck to their 35mm projectors. Even art house theaters that offered 16mm projection were slow to embrace video exhibition.

This was curious, since on many levels there were significant breakthroughs on the digital front. In the mid-1990s, Sony's DCR-VX1000 ushered in the age of the digital MiniDV format, which could edited on personal computers. This opened the doors of filmmaking to a wider number of people. Panasonic, Sharp and JVC also offered their own digital video products.

In 1996, the British adventure *Rainbow*, directed by and starring Bob Hoskins, was shot entirely with Sony's first Solid State Electronic Cinematography cameras. However, *Rainbow* needed to be transferred to 35mm for theatrical distribution – and the film's breakthrough remained barely known in the U.S., as it never received an American release.

In 1997, there was something of a breakthrough: a video feature that was commercially released on video, not in a film transfer. Fred Parnes' documentary *Spread the Word: The Persuasions Sing Acapella* had a brief commercial run at the Walter Reade Theatre at New York's Lincoln Center. The venue installed a video projection system that enabled the production to be shown in its original format; a 35mm transfer was not required. But other venues around the U.S. did not rush to follow suit and the film's theatrical run ended shortly after it began (it later found wider audiences via a PBS broadcast).

Slowly, however, major art house venues began to bring in video projection to accommodate independent films that were not produced on film. One filmmaker who helped speed this process along was Ted Bonnitt, whose 2001 documentary *Mau Mau Sex Sex* celebrated the glory days of exploitation cinema. Bonnitt shot his film in digital video and he initially faced slim prospects in seeing the film on the big screen. "We did not see getting back the 40-plus thousand dollars it would have cost to make a 35mm transfer and prints," he recalled in a 2002 interview on *Film Threat*. "I also did not want to degrade the final digital image on film."

Bonnitt was also working as his own distributor for *Mau Mau Sex Sex*, which could have presented him with even weaker leverage. However, he realized at the time that a growing number of art house venues were beginning to show films in the digital video format. "We called theaters around the country and found that sufficient video projection venues existed to play in the cities that we targeted," he said. "This is an independent art house movie, and those venues tend to have more diverse projection equipment and put more effort into promoting your run. However, these being the early days of DV, many theaters did not have video projection equipment, and the cost to rent the projector and playback machine were prohibitive. So, we had theaters wanting to book the movie, but unable to do so."

And this is where history is made: Bonnitt not only offered theaters his film, but also a new type of projector. As luck would have it, during this time a major electronics company was eager to test its latest equipment. Bonnitt found an unlikely but practical answer to his distribution dilemma. "Our solution came from Sharp Electronics, which introduced a high quality portable LCD projector (P-20) that we were able to ship overnight to theaters," he continued. "We tested it with a DVD player, and the image was remarkably good, considering the compression on the DVD. Sharp provided the projector in order to introduce their new product to the theatrical marketplace, and we suggested that theater owners bring their DVD player from home and plug it in."

Despite the unlikely manner that Bonnitt offered in having his film projected, he did not face any negative concerns from exhibitors when he informed them how *Mau Mau Sex Sex* was going to be screened. "The typical response was: 'Huh? Really? Wow. Okay. We'll do it,'" he said. "Exhibitors are refreshingly down to earth. They'll try anything if they think that it will sell tickets. So, the fact that 'Mau Mau Sex Sex' was the first movie to be distributed theatrically on DVD was no problem for a great majority of them, just a cost-effective solution."

The DVD projector technology was literally too easy to be believed. "All that was needed was a connection to the theater's sound system, and usually with a simple RCA plug," added Bonnitt. "We included an easy three-page step-by-step instruction manual on how to plug in the DVD player to the projector and point it toward the screen. Everything else was automatic."

Even better: no one watching the film (either critics or audiences) realized they were viewing *Mau Mau Sex Sex* off a DVD (the film's theatrical press push made no mention of the DVD angle). "We never had a complaint from a customer, and we received big press reviews in every city we played without any mention of how we showed it," he said. "It was a successful road show sleight-of-hand trick. And the theaters were even willing to pay for the projector's $100 shipping cost, because after all, their take of the box office sales is in part to cover the cost of their facilities, which we were in part providing to them with projection capability."

Mau Mau Sex Sex played in DVD-based theatrical release in approximately 20 U.S. cities, including major markets like New York, Los Angeles, San Francisco, Chicago, Boston, Philadelphia and Seattle. The film enjoyed strong press coverage, which later helped fuel the home entertainment DVD sales for the title.

"It was a win-win solution for everyone involved, including the audience, who otherwise would never have seen 'Mau Mau Sex Sex,'" said Bonnitt.

Oh, there was also another winner in this tale: Sharp Electronics, the company that provided its projector to Bonnitt for the *Mau Mau Sex Sex* release. "As a result of our film, theaters started buying the Sharp projector, because it costs less than a 35mm projector, which represented a breakthrough for them," added Bonnitt.

For Bonnitt, the digital technology pried open the distribution door and helped usher in a new era for aspiring independent filmmakers. "New digital video, design and management tools are an exciting remedy for much more common dead-end distribution deals," states Bonnitt. "New digital cinema exhibition circuits will emerge that will provide these critical services for moviemakers who want to stick to making movies. New, accessible technologies are democratizing independent production, making it easier for movies to reach the big screen, and without filmmakers having to give away their rights to do it. As one distributor kidded me: 'It's bastards like you who are going to put us out of business.' That may not be accurate, but the business is taking notice. It represents an exciting, new opportunity to restore the true meaning of 'independent' to the term 'independent moviemaking.'"

More breakthroughs began to occur on the high-tech front, but there was still resistance in getting theaters to play the new wave of video-based films. The 2001 French film *Viodcq* was the first to be shown using a Sony HDW-F900 camera that offered a 24-frames-per-second high-definition digital video; the film was not shown in the U.S.

until 2007 and remains barely known to most Americans. George Lucas shot his 2002 release Star *Wars Episode II: Attack of the Clones* with the Sony HDW-F900 camera, and it was estimated Lucas spent $16,000 for 220 hours of digital tape (the same amount of 35mm film would have cost $1.8 million). But relatively few theaters were willing to present it in a high-definition video projection; the film had to be transferred to 35mm in order for it to enjoy a wide theatrical release.

Today, both Hollywood blockbusters and independent productions are being filmed in digital video, yet the major Cineplex chains have not installed the projection equipment to enable the presentation of these works in their digital format. Outside of the art house circuit (which balances all possible projection formats), these films can only reach wide audiences via 35mm prints.

Whether theater chains are willing to invest in digital video projectors remains to be seen; it would appear the expense of the installation and the lack of audience demand for the change would argue against such an investment. Even the industry seems to balking at a total digital switchover: the Academy of Motion Pictures Arts and Sciences will not consider any film for its Oscars unless it was presented in 35mm or 70mm; no digital formats are currently allowed for Academy Award consideration.

The 10 Most Important Independent Films of All Time:

Antero Alli, filmmaker *(The Drivetime, Crux, The Greater Circulation)*

Q: If you were to look over the span of the history of U.S. independent cinema, from the silent era to today's output, what would you list as the 10 Most Important Independently-Produced Films of All Time ... and why?

All these films, in one way or another, demonstrate serious courage and boldness in their depiction of outsiders, social misfits and marginalized men and women and often times, through reinventing and/or recontextualization of pre-existing cinematic conventions. These films are all branded by their own maverick seal of zero compromise and an innate disdain for external approval.

1. *Shadows* (1960). Directed John Cassavetes. For its daring cinema verité driven by a forceful personal vision of racial bigotry.

2. *Mean Streets* (1973). Directed by Martin Scorsese. For its ruthless pursuit of street-level reality and for characters as real as were never seen before onscreen.

3. *Dead Man* (1995). Directed by Jim Jarmusch. For the sly way it destroys the annoying stereotypes of wild west cowboy culture with wit and panache.

4. *The Thin Blue Line* (1988). Directed by Errol Morris. For its audacity to confront audience assumptions about the truth of what they are viewing.

5. *Anchoress* (1993). Directed by Chris Newby. For its revolutionary attack on religious themes and personal redemption through forced isolation.

6. *Julien Donkey-Boy* (1999). Directed by Harmony Korine. For its reinvention of cinema as a vehicle for the experience of mental illness.

7. *Decasia* (2002). Directed by Bill Morrison. For its sensitive assemblage of rare silent film footage into a montage masterpiece of cinematic history.

8. *Inland Empire* (2006). Directed by David Lynch. For its liberating and outrageous subversion of audience expectations.

9. *Brand Upon the Brain* (2006). Directed by Guy Mad-

din. For the highly imaginative way this feature-length super-8 film creates its own idiosyncratic genre of storytelling.

10. *The Diving Bell and the Butterfly* (2007). Directed by Julian Schnabel. For its deliriously poetic delivery of an otherwise unbearable and tragic reality.

EPILOGUE:

And Where Do We Go From Here?

*"The best thing about the future is that it comes only
one day at a time"*   – Abraham Lincoln

History has never been stagnant, and today's events and develop-
ments will be reviewed in the not-so-distant future as a history lesson. The question, however, becomes complex: what will tomorrow's
students of independent film history gather from the contemporary
happenings within this environment?

For starters, it will be impossible to overlook the depth and scope
of independent films (both features and shorts, narratives and non-fiction productions) that are now being produced. The low-budget, high-
quality digital video technology has enabled an unprecedented number
of filmmakers to grab a camera and begin shooting. This situation has
been buoyed by the seemingly endless hype involving the fortunate soul
who gets selected from the cinematic slush pile to become part of the industry elite. An extraordinary number of would-be Quentin Tarantinos
and Kevin Smiths are literally waiting in the wings for their lucky break.

The wait may be longer than these filmmakers are anticipating, for
no shortage of reasons.

For starters, the quantity of independent films being made today has created a glut of almost biblical proportions. There is no official statistic keeping track of independent films in production across the United States, but an empirical guess could easily put the number in the tens of thousands (factoring in student films would drive the number even higher).

Quantity, of course, is not synonymous with quality, and there would be no accusation of cruelty leveled at the charge that many of today's independent productions are not at a level that would warrant professional exhibition and distribution. Part of this situation is typical for this genre, or for any genre where the artist wears the multiple hats of creative force and business supervisor (a casual overview of self-published books, for example, would confirm the folly of writing books without having an impartial outside editor examining the text prior to the actual printing of the work).

Today's independent filmmakers, for the most part, are functioning as both producer and director. Those with self-discipline and genuine artistic talent will be able to maneuver through the complexity of their multiple roles and create worthy movies. Those who confuse self-indulgence with artistic expression, however, will create works that are less fortunate – particularly for the poor audiences subjected to such follies.

But that would assume there are audiences for these films. They might exist, but connecting to them is increasingly difficult in today's film business schematics. Theatrical distribution remains a costly endeavor in today's movie world; one could be bold enough to call it a gamble, given the unpredictable nature of trying to predict what audiences will reject and embrace. It is easy to forget that many of the classics of the independent film genre were not box-office bonanzas when they were first presented, but only achieved legendary status over time thanks to changes in critical and popular tastes and their ubiquity on home video and television broadcasts.

Show business is, of course, a business, and film distributors are in business to make as much money as possible from the titles they put into release. But today's distributors specializing in independent films face their own obstacles: a shrinking number of venues that will give screen time to indie titles, the rising costs of marketing films, and the competition from both the multiplex and the home entertainment sectors.

Not surprisingly, today's distributors are highly selective of the films they will acquire. Occasionally, a quirky little movie with an unknown director and a no-star cast can snag a distribution deal based solely on the merits of its contents (*Napoleon Dynamite* is among the most notable examples in recent years). But for the most part, distributors will be looking for easily identifiable factors that can be parlayed into successful release: Today's independent filmmakers often overlook one key consideration: most audiences do not seek out a film because it was produced outside of the studio system. The average moviegoer wants to be entertained, whether through amusement, provocation, cheap thrills, casual distraction, or whatever. If the entertainment originated in a $100,000 film or a $100,000,000 film is, increasingly, irrelevant; both genres have their share of hits and flops. But if the film is marketed with persistence and imagination, it can find an audience.

Yes, there are a few cable television channels and DVD labels that cater exclusively to independent film. And most major American cities have at least one art house theater that puts independent films on its screen. But this represents a niche market, not a mainstream market. Limitations in promotion and (truth be told) content ensure their core audiences are small (although they are also very devoted).

Of course, a small audience is better than no audience. A history of independent cinema can only focus on films that actually found their way in front of viewers. The films cited in this book's previous chapters all share the common bond of having made it into release. One might think that is an obvious achievement, but it is only obvious if one considers the number of films that never get released. And this is not the domain of the unknown filmmaker, either: Orson Welles' *The Other Side of the Wind* and Jerry Lewis' *The Day the Clown Cried* were both shot in 1972 but remain, as of this writing, in legal limbo and have never been screened for the public.

One might think the film festival circuit would be the answer, but that domain is also facing problems of excess quantity matched against problems with quantity. There are an estimated 2,500 festivals being held around the world annually, and the number is growing thanks to the increasing volume of independent films. Yet relatively few of these festivals offer the genuine ability for an independent filmmaker to enjoy immediate access to fame and fortune. For every Steven Soderbergh who got tapped at Sundance, there are countless others with films in somewhat more obscure events.

Also, it is crucial to realize that film festivals do not exist for the purpose of making the motion picture industry a happier place. "A filmmaker has to realize that film festivals have to make money, too," says Ryan Dacko, an independent filmmaker based in Syracuse, N.Y., and the director of *And I Lived* (2003) and *Plan 9 from Syracuse* (2008). "That's how they afford the theater time, staff, and all that goes into the festival circuit. So I do not blame them for taking a more controversial film that may not be that great, but will bring in the media attention and audience numbers. I still don't blame them for accepting a million-dollar feature film from Hollywood under the guise of independent cinema, because having a major Hollywood star show up at your festival is great for numbers in audience and future marketing of the festival. Filmmaking is a business and so is the festival circuit. This needs to be realized and told to those younger filmmakers who can find themselves spending hundreds upon hundreds of dollars to enter their movie into a major festival, and in reality, they don't stand a chance of getting into the festival or even being fairly screened."

Dacko's films have received awards in festivals: *And I Lived* won Best Supporting Actor and Best Musical Score honors at the B-Movie Film Festival and *Plan 9 from Syracuse* won Best Picture and Best Director at the New Haven Underground Film Festival. "In my experience, I had found there are three tiers of film festivals," he says. "The upper, middle, and lower tiers. It was in the lower tiers where I found a home, as do thousands of other filmmakers who can't afford the million-dollar budget. I have noticed a more open attitude to incoming films – no matter what the packaging, or storyline – your movie is given a fair viewing and your chances of obtaining a screening are greater. In the middle tier, your chances are reduced some, but still good. However, in the upper tier, unless you have a representing agent or a good budget to 'push' your film to the judges, you have no chance at all. There are hundreds of examples of movies that were made in the early 1990s that were festival darlings across the screens of Sundance, Toronto, and Berlin. Many of today's independent films made with similar budgets dwarf those early 1990s films in terms of technical and artistic proficiency, but unfortunately, they'll never see acceptance by the big boys. With my first film, *And I Lived*, I was denied festival entry all over the world. And it took an entire year until it was accepted to its first film festival. The movie was not incompetent or abstract; it just didn't have the backing to push through the ranks. How many feature films made on $23,000 budget ever do? I quickly learned this lesson and still use it today when viewing festivals and deciding which ones to submit to."

Another independent filmmaker, Connecticut-based Thomas Edward Seymour, whose films include *Land of College Prophets* (2005) and *London Betty* (2009), has found many festivals to be less than satisfactory for independent filmmakers. "I've easily attended a dozen festivals and found that many of the people there are just like me, meaning there's very little connections to be made," he says. "They are almost all fun, so don't get me wrong; I love talking to my fellow struggling filmmakers, but it ain't gonna get my movie sold! Some festivals are rackets designed to make money, you can tell if the fees are really high and the venue sucks. Then some are run by film lovers who only want to be a part of the filmmaking process. So if they are run poorly or the attendance is low, how can you possibly blame them?"

Nonetheless, Seymour is not giving up on this environment. "To run my films in the festival circuit is very important to me," he continues. "I always have a great time at the festivals. I gather some wins or official selections and move on to try to sell the film. The only two festivals I was directly approached by a 'buyer' were the Bare Bones and the B-Movie Film Festival. I didn't end up going with either of those buyers, though, again, I made some good friends."

Of course, exhibition is no longer limited to a theater. "Independent cinema has become more independent due to the Internet," observes Eric Phelps, former development director with the Atlanta International Film Festival. "A professional or amateur filmmaker no longer has to rely on the traditional distribution methods in order to find their audience. Avenues like YouTube have brought back an audience for short films, independent documentaries and very creative short features and comedic pieces."

Phelps adds this digital outlet has its pluses and minuses. "Obviously, you might not make money from these screenings," he says. "And depending on the production costs, this may not be viable. But the viral effect of e-mail means that you can have a huge audience and independent feedback for your project. It also helps new and younger filmmakers make some of their projects very cheaply before they spend lots of money working with more expensive [media]."

Indeed, the quantity of films being offered on YouTube, MySpace, Google Video and other websites defies all attempts at inventory – more films are added each day. Whether any can achieve genuine breakthrough popularity remains to be seen.

Independent film is also serving a significant social purpose by targeting demographics that are often overlooked or badly handled by the Hollywood studios. Strangely, there is often surprise when these supposedly niche films reap a substantial commercial harvest.

African American cinema, as cited earlier, has historically relied on independent productions to provide a non-stereotypical portrait of black communities. In recent years, under the radar indie efforts such as *Woman, Thou Art Loosed* (2004), based on the book by television evangelist T.D. Jakes, who co-starred in the film, and *Diary of a Mad Black Woman* (2005), based on the work of playwright/actor Tyler Perry, created seismic reactions when their box-office tallies hit the top ten lists.

Also operated under the radar, for the most part, has been the so-called queer cinema, which focuses on subject matter relating to gays and lesbians. The independently-produced 1970 film version of Matt Crowley's off-Broadway play *The Boys in the Band* can be considered the launchpad of the genre. Yet indifference (if not downright hostility) from non-homosexuals have kept these films in something of a commercial ghetto; urban markets with sizeable gay populations and an art house cinema have been open to this genre, both in theatrical presentations and festivals exclusively focused on the subject. But most mainstream venues will not book gay and lesbian films, except if they come from a Hollywood studio or if they feature major stars, such as *Brokeback Mountain* (2005) starring Heath Ledger and Jake Gyllenhaal and *Milk* (2008) starring Sean Penn.

Films made by and for Latinos have also experienced problems in regard to marketing and distribution. The Latino population is not homogenous, and films made about a specific community (such as Puerto Ricans or Mexican-Americans) will not necessarily appeal to all Latinos due to a Spanish-language soundtrack. Not surprisingly, many independent Latino films, such as *Luminarias* (2000) and *Maria Full of Grace* (2004) were marketed as art films for all audiences and were not targeted specifically to the Latino community. The same concern can be traced to Asian-American and American-Indian films, although films made by and for those demographics are usually stuck in festivals and rarely find wide distribution. Christian cinema has also found itself deconstructed among congregations, with relatively little in the way of crossover. The Church of Jesus Christ of Latter-Day Saints has enjoyed its own mini-indie world, with titles such as *The Best Two Years* (2003) and *The Book of Mormon Volume 1: The Journey* (2004). Evangelical Christians helped make *Left Behind: The Movie* (2000) and *Facing the Giants* (2006) into successful films. In all cases, these films were barely acknowledged by the film media and the major U.S. media; most major cities never saw these films in their cinemas.

A few exceptions in crossover Christian cinema have been seen. Billy Graham produced a highly ambitious short film, *Man in the 5th Di-*

mension, which was shot in the 70mm Todd-AO process and presented at the evangelical preacher's pavilion during the 1964-65 New York World's Fair, where it was seen by thousands of people of multiple faiths. In 2004, Mel Gibson's *The Passion of the Christ* became a controversial hit through its overly aggressive marketing to evangelical and Roman Catholic audiences, coupled with provocative charges of anti-Semitic content.

And on more than a few occasions, films made by Hollywood insiders with A-list stars are frequently marketed as independent films, if only to gain a sense of cred-by-association. *My Big Fat Greek Wedding* (2002) and *Sideways* (2004) rode marketing waves as indie films, when in fact they received financing from Home Box Office and Fox Searchlight Pictures, respectively.

In many ways, tomorrow's independent cinema will be no different from the century that preceded it. If past experience is any guide, independent cinema will continue to break new ground in regard to content, style, technology and attitude. The enemy will always be the cultural status quo, and it is impossible not to imagine that enemy will be toppled yet again.

Mark Bell, the former editor of *Film Threat*, sums it up best: "As much as I preach knowledge of cinema history, I truly think it's a case-by-case basis on what one can learn from the past. I think it's important, in many cases, to realize that others came before and may've made mistakes that, thanks to their experiences you as a filmmaker don't have to make. In that respect, I think watching bad movies is as educational as watching the classics or masterpieces. Filmmakers don't have to reinvent the wheel every time out of the gate, just try to improve on it."

Indeed, independent filmmakers have been improving on cinema since the medium took shape. Stay tuned, for there will be more provocative breakthroughs to come!

ABOUT THE AUTHOR

Phil Hall is the author of the books *The Encyclopedia of Underground Cinema* (2004), *Independent Film Distribution* (2005) and *The New PR* (2007). He is a contributing editor for the online magazine Film Threat and a member of the Governing Committee of the Online Film Critics Society. His film journalism has been published in the *New York Times*, *New York Daily News*, *Hartford Courant*, *Wired Magazine* and *American Movie Classics Magazine*.

Printed in the United States
216463BV00002B/1/P

9 781593 933357